Slurs and Expressivity

Philosophy of Language: Connections and Perspectives

Series Editors: *Margaret Cameron, Lenny Clapp, and Robert Stainton*

Advisory Board: Axel Barceló (Instituto de Investigaciones Filosóficas), Chen Bo (Peking University), Robyn Carston (University College London), Leo Cheung (Chinese University of Hong Kong), Eduardo García (Instituto de Investigaciones Filosóficas), Sandy Goldberg (Northwestern University), Robin Jeshion (University of Southern California), Ernie Lepore (Rutgers University), Catrina Dutilh Novaes (Vrije University Amsterdam), Eleonora Orlando (University of Buenos Aires), Claude Panaccio (University of Quebec at Montreal), Bernhard Weiss (University of Cape Town), and Jack Zupko (University of Alberta)

Philosophy of Language: Connections and Perspectives comprises monographs and edited collections that explore connections between the philosophy of language and other academic disciplines, or that approach the core topics of philosophy of language in the Anglo-American analytic tradition from alternative perspectives. The philosophy of language, particularly as practiced in the Anglo-American tradition of analytic philosophy, has established itself as a thriving academic discipline. Because of the centrality of language to the human experience, there are myriad connections between the core topics addressed by philosophers of language and other academic disciplines. The number of researchers who are exploring these connections is growing, but there has not been a corresponding increase in the venues for publication of this research. The central purpose and motivation for this series is to address this shortcoming.

Titles in the series
Slurs and Expressivity: Semantics and Beyond, edited by Eleonora Orlando and Andrés Saab
Slurs and Thick Terms: When Language Encodes Values, by Bianca Cepollaro
Rationalist Pragmatism: A Framework for Moral Objectivism, by Mitchell Silver
Reference and Identity in Jewish, Christian, and Muslim Scriptures: The Same God?, by D. E. Buckner

Slurs and Expressivity

Semantics and Beyond

Edited by
Eleonora Orlando and Andrés Saab

LEXINGTON BOOKS
Lanham • Boulder • New York • London

Published by Lexington Books
An imprint of The Rowman & Littlefield Publishing Group, Inc.
4501 Forbes Boulevard, Suite 200, Lanham, Maryland 20706
www.rowman.com

6 Tinworth Street, London SE11 5AL, United Kingdom

Copyright © 2021 The Rowman & Littlefield Publishing Group, Inc.

All rights reserved. No part of this book may be reproduced in any form or by any electronic or mechanical means, including information storage and retrieval systems, without written permission from the publisher, except by a reviewer who may quote passages in a review.

British Library Cataloguing in Publication Information Available

Library of Congress Cataloging-in-Publication Data

Library of Congress Control Number: 2020944998

ISBN 978-1-7936-1436-0 (cloth)
ISBN 978-1-7936-1438-4 (pbk)
ISBN 978-1-7936-1437-7 (electronic)

For Lucio, Valentina, and Julián

Contents

List of Tables and Figures		ix
Preface		xi
1	Dualism and Monism in the Study of Slurs and Beyond *Eleonora Orlando and Andrés Saab*	1
2	On the Locus of Expressivity: Deriving Parallel Meaning Dimensions from Architectural Considerations *Andrés Saab*	17
3	The Discursive Dimension of Slurs *Nicolás Lo Guercio*	45
4	A Bidimensional Account of Slurs *Ramiro Caso*	67
5	Expressives and the Theory of Bias *Ludovic Soutif and Carlos Márquez*	95
6	Taboo: The Case of Slurs *Stefano Predelli*	117
7	Slurs: The Amoralist and the Expression of Hate *Justina Díaz Legaspe*	135
8	On the Moral Import of Using Slurs *Eleonora Orlando*	159
9	*Sudaca*: Slurs and Typifying *Alfonso Losada*	187
Index		209
About the Contributors		213

List of Tables and Figures

TABLE

Table 1.1   Dualism and Monism in the Study of Expressivity   8

FIGURES

Figure 2.1   Meaning Dimensions and Grammatical Architecture   19
Figure 2.2   Architecture of the Grammar   21
Figure 2.3   Bias for "*laburar*"   23
Figure 2.4   Lexical-Syntactic Identity   32
Figure 2.5   Derivation of a "*Vesre*" Word at PF   34
Figure 4.1   Unidimensional semantic parsetree for (7), "Mary sings"   72
Figure 4.2   Unidimensional Functional Application (FA)   73
Figure 4.3   Multidimensional semantic parsetree for (7), "Mary sings"   74
Figure 4.4   Ordinary Functional Application (OFA) and Expressive Functional Application (EFA)   74
Figure 4.5   Multidimensional semantic parsetree for (8), "Juan is Hispanic"   75
Figure 4.6   Multidimensional semantic parsetree for (9), "Juan is a spic"   76

Figure 4.7	Multidimensional semantic parsetree for (10), "That damn Juan is Hispanic"	76
Figure 4.8	Multidimensional semantic parsetree for (4), "Juan is not a spic"	78
Figure 4.9	Multidimensional semantic parsetree for "that spic"	78
Figure 4.10	Multidimensional semantic parsetree for (5), "If Susan marries that spic, Peter will be shocked"	79
Figure 4.11	Multidimensional semantic parsetree for (6), "Peter thinks that Juan is a spic"	79
Figure 4.12	Syntactic tree for (19), "Who danced?/who danced"	84
Figure 4.13	Unidimensional semantic parsetree for (19), "Who danced?/who danced"	84
Figure 4.14	Unidimensional semantic parsetree for (20), "Juan dijo cuáles estudiantes vinieron a la fiesta"	85
Figure 4.15	Multidimensional semantic parsetree for (16), "Juan dijo cuántos bolitas vinieron a la fiesta"	86

Preface

The project of preparing this volume started while we were in the process of writing a book on expressive meaning in Spanish—which we hope to finish in the near future. We have been working on the issue of expressivity and slurs in the framework of the interdisciplinary research group that we jointly coordinate at SADAF (the BA-LingPhil group) for the last five years. Most of the ideas present in the essays contributed to this volume, written by the members of that group, have been discussed in our periodical meetings, and in several workshops and conferences in Brazil, Uruguay, and Argentina.

We want to thank Margaret Cameron, Lenny Clapp, and Robert Stainton, editors of the *Philosophy of Language: Connections and Perspectives* series for Lexington Books, for their trust, as well as Jana Hodges-Kluck and Nicolette Amstutz, for their kind help throughout the process. We also want to thank the members of the BA-LingPhil for the discussions that made this volume possible in the conceptual sense: in particular, Ramiro Caso, Justina Díaz Legaspe, Nicolás Lo Guercio, and Alfonso Losada, who made insightful contributions. Moreover, we are equally grateful to the other participants, Carlos Márquez, Stefano Predelli, and Ludovic Soutif, for their immediate and enthusiastic disposition to collaborate by sending us original essays. Stefano Predelli's participation and support have been particularly significant to our project.

Besides, we want to acknowledge the help provided by the University of Buenos Aires, under the form of the research project UBACyT 20020170100649BA, and the National Agency for Scientific and Technological Promotion, with the grant PICT 2016-0438. We are thankful to these institutions as well as to the National Research Council for Scientific and Technical Research (CONICET), and especially our dear workplace, the Institute of Philosophical Investigations of the Argentinian Society of Philosophical Analysis (IIF-SADAF).

Finally, we dedicate this book to our children, Lucio, and Valentina and Julián, respectively, with the hope that they can live their adult lives in a world free of hate and injustice.

Eleonora Orlando and Andrés Saab
Buenos Aires, June 4, 2020

Chapter 1

Dualism and Monism in the Study of Slurs and Beyond

Eleonora Orlando and Andrés Saab

1. INTRODUCTION

This book is mainly focused on the analysis of the expressive aspects of slur-words, namely, those words prima facie related to the conveyance of contemptuous or derogatory feelings for the members of a certain group of people identified in terms of their ethnicity ("spic"), sexual orientation ("faggot"), religion ("kike"), political ideology ("fascist"), and other personal qualities.[1] In as far as they are systematically used to express emotional attitudes of some sort slurs can be considered a kind of expressive words. As is clear, not all words are expressive in this sense, namely, in the sense of having, in some way to be further characterized, an emotional load: many of them are expressively neutral. Consider, for instance, the loaded "bureaucrat" in contrast with the neutral "public employee," and the loaded "rat" as opposed to the neutral "informer." Now, in as far as traditional semantics considered natural language to be mainly a vehicle for knowledge, it focused on the representational properties of language that are responsible for its informative role, to the point of putting forward a replacement of natural language with a logical or a properly regimented one. For Frege, a paradigmatic representative of the traditional approach, expressive aspects were not part of the *thought* (i.e., the proposition) semantically expressed by a sentence; they determined a separate, non-semantic dimension, its *color*. Consider, for instance, the following, well-known paragraph:

> It is useful to the poet to have at his disposal a number of different words that can be substituted for one another without altering the thought, but which can act in different ways on the feelings and imagination of the hearer. We may think, e.g., of the words "walk," "stroll," "saunter." These means are also used

to the same end in everyday language. If we compare the sentences "This dog howled the whole night" and "This cur howled the whole night," we find that the thought is the same. The first sentence tells us neither more nor less than does the second. But whilst the word "dog" is neutral as between having pleasant or unpleasant associations, the word "cur" certainly has unpleasant rather than pleasant associations and puts us rather in mind of a dog with a somehow unkempt appearance. Even if it is grossly unfair to the dog to think of it in this way, we cannot say that this makes the second sentence false. True, anyone who utters this sentence speaks pejoratively, but this is not part of the thought expressed. What distinguishes the second sentence from the first is of the nature of an interjection. (Frege 1897: 140)

Expressive components of words, namely, those having an effect on "the feelings and the imagination" are not related to the representation of features of the world, and hence they play no role in determining the truth-conditions and truth-value of the sentences in which they occur. In a nutshell, expressive components are not representational. Consequently, in as far as traditional semantics was only concerned with representational properties like reference and truth, the expressive components of natural language words were not considered to be part of their meanings, and hence were thrown out of the semantic reflection.

The first attempts to theoretically acknowledge the fact that some words are associated with emotions took place in the realm of metaethics, mostly within the framework of the different non-cognitivist approaches (Ogden and Richards 1923; Barnes 1933). For instance, for traditional emotivists (Barnes 1933; Stevenson 1944), thin moral terms such as "right"/"good" and "wrong"/"bad" semantically expressed, respectively, attitudes of approval or preference and disapproval or rejection. Moral Expressivism (Blackburn 1993; Gibbard 1990) has been their natural heir: according to it, sentences containing moral terms are vehicles of different sorts of non-cognitive attitudes and mental states, different from the paradigmatically cognitive beliefs, and, hence, they are not apt for being true or false.[2]

Nowadays, when the study of all aspects of natural language use has moved to central stage, the study of expressivity has crossed the borders of the reflection on moral language.[3] Kaplan (1999) is one of the philosophers who paved the way for the formal study of those aspects of words that are not related to the properties being represented and contributed to the truth-conditions of the sentences in which they occur. His idea is that expressivity in general is related to a restriction on the contexts of use: a sentence containing an expressive word will be expressively correct if it is uttered in those contexts in which the agent is properly related to an emotional attitude associated with the word at stake. This idea can be clearly identified in the following quote:

> Now here is the new idea: we can get an equally useful measure of the expressive information that is in a sentence—or, in the case of exclamatories like "ouch" and "oops," in an expressive standing alone—*by looking at all the contexts at which it, the sentence containing the expressive or the expressive standing alone, is expressively correct.* [...] I claim that "ouch" is an expressive that is used to express the fact that the agent is in pain. What is the semantic information in the word "ouch" on this analysis? The semantic information in the word "ouch" is—more accurately, is represented by—the set of those contexts at which the word "ouch" is expressively correct (since it contains no descriptive information), namely, *the set of those contexts at which the agent is in pain.* That set of contexts represents the semantic information contained in the word "ouch." (Kaplan 1999: 15–16, our emphasis)

Among the kind of words to be considered, there are, for instance, pure interjections or Kaplan's "exclamatories" (such as "ouch" and "oops"), words with an intuitive emotive load (like the previous "bureaucrat," "rat," and "cur"), the so-called baby talk (encompassing expressions like "bunny," "kitty," etc.), honorifics (such as the Spanish "*usted*" and the Italian "*Lei*"), and pejoratives, including, among other terms, adjectives like "stupid" and what will be our main focus of interest, namely, group slurs like "spic" in our initial list.[4]

As far as exclamatories are concerned, what can be characterized as a purely expressivist account can do the job, since they seem to lack any representational dimension. However, the other members of the list, crucially including the slurs, have an expressive as much as a representational dimension, and hence seem to call for a hybrid or dualistic semantics. In this connection, it is worth pointing out that even some of the early emotivists, like Stevenson, suggested that words for general moral evaluation, like the abovementioned thin moral terms, have not only what they called an "emotive" or "non-cognitive" meaning but also a cognitive or, in our terms, a representational one—an idea that has been developed by contemporary hybrid expressivists, like Barker (2000). Therefore, directly inspired by Kaplan (1999), some theories have encompassed the existence of two meaning dimensions for different kinds of expressives: a representational or truth-conditional dimension, determinant of the *at-issue* content of sentences, and an independent expressive or non-truth-conditional one, constitutive of their expressive content (Potts 2003, 2005, 2007; McCready 2010; Predelli 2013; and Gutzman 2015, among others). Consequently, those sentences containing that kind of expressions turn out to be not only representationally true or false but also expressively correct or incorrect, which depends not on the world-conditions they represent but on the contexts in which they are used.

Considerations along the previous lines gave thus rise to different versions of Dualism about some pejoratives, in particular, those that are our main topic of concern, namely, slurs. Note that slurs, like most expressively charged expressions, have a neutral counterpart, namely, they form pairs with neutral ones ("spic" / "Latin American," "cur" / "dog," "bunny" / "rabbit," the Spanish personal pronouns "*tú*" "you$_{informal}$" / "*usted*" "you$_{formal}$," etc.). Based on this idea, those approaches have endorsed the Identity Thesis, according to which the representational dimension of a slur-word is equivalent to the representational dimension of its neutral counterpart. In terms of the previous example, the representational meaning of "spic," the property of having a Latin American origin (or the set of people with a Latin American origin), is identical to the representational meaning of its neutral counterpart, "Latin American"; then, all instances of

(1) Diego is a spic.

and

(2) Diego is Latin American.

have the same truth-condition or *at-issue* content, namely,

(3) "Diego is a spic" is true = "Diego is Latin American" is true iff Diego has a Latin American origin.

But, unlike "Latin American," "spic" has also an expressive meaning—it is not an expressively neutral word. Accordingly, the sentences uttered in using (1) and (2) will not be *expressively* equivalent.

Moreover, the Identity Thesis presupposes that the two dimensions are independent from each other. This independence has been mostly grounded on a feature that is characteristic of slurs, their Non-Displaceability or Hyper-Projectability. According to it, the expressive dimension of slurs projects out of the scope, or "scopes out," of the usual sentential operators affecting truth-conditions, such as negation, conditionals, non-factive attitude verbs, modals, and so on. In terms of an example, setting aside the possibility of a metalinguistic interpretation,

(4) Diego is not a spic.

appears to be as derogatory as its affirmative counterpart.[5] Likewise,

(5) If those spics move into our neighborhood, I will try to sell my house.

seems to express an unconditional derogatory attitude toward Latin Americans: the conditionalization introduced by the antecedent does not affect the expressive charge of the slur. Moreover, in uttering

(6) Peter thinks that Diego is a spic.

the speaker conveys a derogatory attitude toward Latin Americans, independently of the content of Peter's belief and whatever emotional attitude he may hold toward them. The last example also serves to make it manifest the Agent-Centered feature of slurs, namely, the fact that, barring some exceptional scenarios, they have a strong tendency not to be separable from the speaker's attitude.[6] So, it is concluded that there must be an aspect of the meaning of a slur related to the negative emotional components in question, which is non-truth-conditional, in as far as it is independent of its contribution to the truth-conditional content of the sentences in which it occurs. These results are thus compatible with different conceptions of that independent dimension and its specific relation to the truth-conditional one.

Therefore, Dualism encompasses different proposals concerning the nature of the expressive meaning at stake: it has been alternatively conceived of as a conventionally implicated propositional content (Potts 2003, 2005, 2007; Williamson 2009; McCready 2010; Whiting 2013), a bias understood as a set of contexts of use (Predelli 2013), an encoded contemptuous attitude constitutive of a rule of use (Jeshion 2013a,b), a use-conditional proposition (Gutzmann 2015), a list of register features (Díaz Legaspe, Liu and Stainton 2020), an associated stereotype (Tirrell 1999; Camp 2013; Orlando and Saab 2020a,b), among other possible options. It is worth taking into account that the expressive meaning need not be identified, as in the pioneer ethical theories, with an encoded non-cognitive attitude; more specifically, the relation between a slur-word and the emotion of contempt or derogation can be more indirect—for instance, on a stereotype account, the slur is semantically associated with a stereotype of the target group constituted by a set of concepts with a general negative valence, which involves that its use will be paradigmatically, but not always, accompanied by an emotion of contempt on the speaker's part. Accordingly, being expressive or having an expressive charge does not amount to being just the vehicle of an emotion—but to encoding some conventional aspects, which might include descriptive components, that are systematically, though not unconditionally, related to the expression of an emotion.[7] Moreover, it must be taken into account that the emotion of contempt can be considered to be a complex mental state, encompassing not only an affective component (or a feeling) but also a cognitive as well as an evaluative one.

To present a paradigmatic example of what we classify as a dualistic theory, McCready (2010), modifying Potts's (2005) logic for conventional implicatures, has put forward a semantic system in which it is possible to derive two different, parallel (hence, not interacting) propositions in association with any use of (1), repeated below,

(1) Diego is a spic.

p: Diego is Latin American • q: The speaker despises Latin Americans / Latin Americans are bad.
(the symbol "•" being the meta-logical operator introduced by Potts (2005) to separate the two dimensions of meaning)

Here, whereas p constitutes the truth-conditional or *at-issue* content of the statement, q is its expressive one, determined just by the expressive contribution made by "spic."

This kind of approach can then be considered to be a form of Propositional Dualism. There are also non-propositional versions of Dualism: Potts (2007) provides us with a clear instance of this alternative strategy, according to which the expressive meaning is not modeled as a proposition but as a simple expressive index. Our previous example would then be rendered as follows:

p: Diego is Latin American • i_e

The point of introducing expressive indexes is offering an instrument to denote purely affective states on the speaker's part. This second kind of Dualism can be thus characterized as Expressivist Dualism. Jeshion (2013a,b) provides a different variant of the same kind of approach.[8]

On the other hand, other authors have resisted any form of Dualism about slurs by embracing a position that can be characterized as Lexical Monism, that is, a monistic approach according to which those terms have an expressively charged representational meaning, more specifically, they take them to represent properties that are not purely factual or descriptive but *constitutively normative* in the sense that they embody a derogatory conception of the corresponding target group (Hom 2008, 2010, 2012; Hom and May 2013, 2018).

From this perspective, "spic" and "Latin American," far from being truth-conditionally equivalent, have two different denotations:

Lexical Monism
a. $[\![$Diego is *Latin American*$]\!]$ = L_1(Diego), where $[\![L_1]\!]$ = $\lambda x.$ x is Latin American
b. $[\![$Diego is a *spic*$]\!]$ = S_2(Diego), where $[\![S_2]\!]$ = $\lambda x.$ x is despicable for being Latin American

The lexical entry in (b) corresponds to an empty term since of course nobody is despicable on account of his/her origin. A different version of Lexical Monism, on which slurs are correlated with prototypical concepts representing sets of properties with different degrees of saliency, has been defended by Croom (for instance, Croom 2011, 2013, 2014, 2015). We also refer the reader to Richard (2008) for a particular monistic approach, according to which, even though slur-sentences are representational, they are not truth-apt.

The so-called presuppositional accounts can be considered to be another variant of Monism: on this view, there is only one meaning, the representational one, which is not expressively charged, while expressivity is accounted for at the presuppositional level, namely, as an aspect of slur-words contributing to the presuppositional content of the sentences in which they occur (Macià 2002; Sauerland 2007; Schlenker 2007; Cepollaro 2015; Marques and García-Carpintero 2020). Our example would turn out to be analyzed along the following lines:

Presuppositional Monism

p : Diego is Latin American. (proposition expressed)
q: Latin Americans are despicable.
The speaker believes that Latin Americans are despicable. (proposition presupposed)

Finally, there are other monistic approaches on which the expressive components of slur-words are considered to be not part of what is conventionally transmitted by the sentences containing them but part of *what those sentences pragmatically communicate*. More specifically, on some views, expressive components are thought to give rise to conversational implicatures (Nunberg 2018). Since what is at stake is a conversational implicature, each time a slur is used there is an additional proposition that is conversationally implicated by means of a Gricean mechanism (involving, from Nunberg 2018's perspective, a violation of the Maxim of Manner). This kind of view can be regarded as a monistic alternative, which, as opposed to

Table 1.1 Dualism and Monism in the Study of Expressivity

Approaches	Dualism	Monism
Propositional	Yes	No
Expressivist	Yes	No
Lexical	No	Yes
Presuppositional	No	Yes
Pragmatic	No	Yes

Credit: Eleonora Orlando and Andrés Saab.

Lexical Monism, conceives of slurs as purely factual or descriptive words at the representational level.

Pragmatic Monism
p: Diego is Latin American.   (proposition semantically expressed)
q: The speaker despises Latin Americans.   (proposition pragmatically communicated)

Moreover, other pragmatic approaches do not appeal to Gricean implicatures: for instance, the use of slurs has been conceived of in terms of impolite behavior, namely, a kind of behavior that signals an endorsement of certain associations with the power of causing warranted offense (Bolinger 2017; see also Hess 2018).[9]

The main different approaches to the semantics of slurs that have been sketched are schematically represented in table 1.1. (The position described in footnote 9 would be an Expressivist Monism but we have not included it in the chart due to its implausibility.)

Independently of the approach one favors, it is undeniable that the use of words with expressive aspects has important social, political, and moral effects. So, expressivity links the semantics and pragmatics of words to sociological, political, and ethical considerations. Therefore, there is the issue of exploring the theoretically interesting relations, if there are any, holding between, on the one hand, the abovementioned approaches and, on the other hand, the adoption of a particular political ideology or a certain moral perspective.

2. A BRIEF SUMMARY OF THE BOOK

In this subsection, we will briefly describe the different contributions to this book, and how they connect to the issues introduced in the previous section. The following two chapters develop new insights for dualistic approaches to expressivity, in general, and to slurs, in particular. In chapter 2, "On the Locus of Expressivity: Deriving Parallel Meaning Dimensions from Architectural

Considerations," Andrés Saab proposes a new foundation of Dualism based on architectural considerations related to the interfaces between syntax, phonology, and semantics. In his view, there are certain non-truth-conditional meanings that are exclusively triggered by properties of vocabulary items (in the sense of Halle and Marantz 1993 and subsequent work). In other words, those meanings arise "late" and are not part of the syntactic-semantic derivation. Thus, the notion of a parallel meaning dimension is derived from architectural considerations without the need of any meta-logical operator (e.g., the "•" symbol in Potts 2005 or McCready 2010, among others). This proposal finds some interesting support from certain interactions involving biased words and ellipsis. The basic expressive paradigm involves pairs of words whose contribution to truth-conditional content is equivalent: they can only be differentiated by register (e.g., "*comer*" "to eat" vs. "*morfar*" "to eat$_{informal}$") or by register plus a derogatory dimension (e.g., "boliviano" "Bolivian" vs. "*bolita*" "Bolivian$_{pejorative}$").

In chapter 3, "The Discursive Dimension of Slurs," Nicolás Lo Guercio develops a dualistic account focused on considerations concerning the kind of illocutionary act involved in using slurs. On this approach, slur-words express a standard *at-issue* content along with a conventional implicature; but, in contrast with other extant conventional implicature accounts (McCready 2010), Lo Guercio argues that the *non-at-issue* content of a slur is a property instead of a proposition. Moreover, when complemented with a dynamic pragmatic framework like that of Portner (2004), the view implies that a sentence containing a slur carries two different discursive functions, that is, it updates two different components of the context. On the one hand, the *at-issue* content updates the common ground. On the other hand, the *non-at-issue* content updates the to-do list. It is then showed how the view can provide a general explanation of the way in which uses of slurs are capable of modifying permissibility facts and hence of bringing harm to their targets. Finally, the chapter shows how the proposed account can deal with different conversational moves that slurs make available, such as propaganda, attack, and complicity.

Then, we have included a series of papers concerned with the above-described hyper-projectability of slurs—to the point that sometimes they cannot even be mentioned, namely, they turn out to be taboo expressions. Working within a bidimensional semantic framework derivative of Gutzmann (2015), in chapter 4, "A Bidimensional Account of Slurs," Ramiro Caso focuses on the systematic ambiguity of some slurs ascriptions. He argues that the semantic type of a slur's non-truth-conditional dimension is a particular kind of *de se* use-conditional proposition, which attributes the derogatory attitude to a contextually salient agent. A pragmatic interpretation principle warrants that the default attribution is speaker-oriented. However, conditions are clearly stated under which non-speaker-oriented attributions are licensed.

In chapter 5, "Expressives and the Theory of Bias," Ludovic Soutif and Carlos Márquez review the Theory of Bias proposed in Predelli (2013). They show that the two-tiered account of the meaning of expressives (notably, sentential interjections and pejorative epithets) favored by that framework has the resources to provide a consistent explanation of their semantic behavior in prima facie awkward statements such as "Alas, I am unfavorably disposed toward something" or "That stupid Trump isn't stupid." On the critical side, they argue that the theory has a hard time at explaining the unshiftability of their bias, as opposed to the shiftability of the bias of discourse particles—a further member, according to some authors, of the category of expressives *lato sensu*—and that it fails to pinpoint unpluggability as the crucial test for expressive content.

Within the framework of the dualistic theory advanced in his *Meaning without Truth* (2013), in chapter 6, "Taboo: The Case of Slurs," Stefano Predelli focuses on an additional conventional element for some slurs, their taboo status. After an informal description of the peculiar conversational role of taboo-words, he pauses on their radical non-displaceability, namely, on the ability of some of their effects to resist the otherwise semantically neutralizing outcomes of pure quotation. He continues by comparing slurs that are on a par from the truth-conditional and derogatory viewpoint but that are distinguishable from the viewpoint of taboo. And he concludes with some comments about the relationships between taboo and conventional meaning, and with some tentative remarks about the significance of taboo from the viewpoint of semantic theorizing.

The last group of chapters focuses on the offensive or derogatory nature of the expressive component of slurs, its independence with respect to individual attitudes, the moral import of using slurs, and their relation to cultural stereotypes and group typifications. In chapter 7, "Slurs: The Amoralist and the Expression of Hate," Justina Díaz Legaspe points out that slurs are not, as one may feel inclined to think, type-expressive words, like "asshole" or "jerk"; if anything, they are token-expressive words, more like "fuck" or "shit". They may acquire on occasions an expressive dimension, but for the most part, they are referential terms only appropriate within a given practice. These aspects of slurs and slur usage come to sight when illuminated by the comparison with the figure of the amoralist. The plausibility of the amoralist, a fully competent speaker who uses moral terms without committing herself to the associated actions, is highly contended in debates on hybrid approaches to moral terms. Similarly, the sole idea of a non-expressive slur user seems implausible on the basis of the gut reaction we get when exposed to slur usage, which we ascribe to the rejection of the emotions and attitudes typically associated with their use. However, there is nothing wrong with the figure of non-expressive slur uses, except for the awkwardness of the words used out of context. In contrast, it is the figure of the nondiscriminatory slur user that is implausible, for, due to the role of slurs in discriminatory practices, all uses of slurs constitute discriminatory acts.

In chapter 8, "On the Moral Import of Using Slurs," Eleonora Orlando explores the question of whether there is any theoretically interesting relation between the semantic explanation of slurs and the adoption of a moral stance regarding moral issues such as racism, homophobia, and sexism. In particular, she considers the thesis put forward by Hom and May (2013, 2018), according to which a morally innocent stance on such issues requires subscribing to a particular version of a truth-conditional account of the meaning of slur-words, what we have previously called Lexical Monism, which implies that slurs have a null extension. She argues that (i) subscribing to Hom and May's account neither warrants moral innocence nor precludes moral corruption, and (ii) subscribing to a different, dualistic account is equally compatible with holding a morally innocent stance. From her perspective, moral innocence regarding such crucial moral issues comes in degrees and depends on taking a decision regarding our linguistic heritage, namely, the decision to not endorse certain prejudicial stereotypes.

Finally, in chapter 9, "*Sudaca*: Slurs and Typifying," Alfonso Losada puts forward an original monistic semantic analysis according to which slurs express complex concepts that are the product of a morally condemnable practice of classifying human beings on the grounds of negative stereotypical features. These concepts are structured by, on the one hand, a neutral component, representing the property in terms of which the target group is primarily identified, and, on the other hand, a descriptive component, encompassing those traits thought to belong to its members by those who are convinced that the slur offers a proper representation of them, that is, the bigots. Thus, Losada's analysis denies the Identity Thesis: he defends the stance according to which slurs are empty terms. However, unlike Hom and May (2013), who ground Null Extensionality on moral facts, Losada's approach focuses on the representational error of deploying certain conceptual types of human beings.

NOTES

1. Even if the slur-words that appear in this chapter are never used but always mentioned, we apologize in advance, in case someone finds their very mention offensive. We are conscious that some of them have become taboo.

2. Although restricted to moral discourse, some authors have proposed detailed semantic accounts, in order to show how moral sentences can interact with sentences

that are correlated with cognitive states like beliefs and are hence truth-apt. See, for instance, Gibbard (1990) and Schroeder (2008).

3. Although, see Anderson and Lepore (2013a,b), for a recent restatement and defense of Frege's notion of color.

4. As is clear, expressivity is related to register, namely, the phenomenon of language variation determined by the type of social context involved. For the idea that the register of a word is constitutive of its expressive meaning, see Predelli (2013). See also Díaz Legaspe (this volume) for a different application of the concept of register in accounting for slurs—the thesis that registered words, including slurs, are token-expressives in cross-contextual uses.

5. The same result is achieved by the *Denial* test: according to it, in the following dialogue:

A: Diego is not a spic.
B: That is not true / That is false.

B is questioning not the expressive dimension but just the truth-conditional one, namely, the fact that Diego is Latin American.

6. However, although they are not common, there are some non-speaker-oriented uses, which led some authors to take slurs to be perspective-dependent expressions (Bolinger 2017; Hess 2018). For examples of non-speaker-oriented uses of expressives in general, such as "My father screamed that he would never allow me to marry that bastard Webster," see Amaral et al. (2007) and Harris and Potts (2009).

7. As a consequence, Díaz Legaspe (this volume) is driven to make a distinction between type and token-expressives.

8. Importantly, the theory in Potts (2007) is particularly designed for dealing with other types of expressives (epithets like "bastard" and expressive attributive adjectives like "fucking"). Indeed, the same is true for Potts's (2005) logic, which explicitly excludes hybrid terms like slurs from the set of expressives. In his own words, "all predicates that appear in copular position must necessarily fail to be expressive, because they provide no argument for the copular verb (nor a functor that could apply to it)" (Potts 2007: 194). Slurs, unlike attributive expressives, naturally occur in predicative position (*"The keys are damn." vs. "Juan is a spic."). McCready (2010), as already observed in the main text, extended Potts's (2005) logic to derive slurs as expressives (see also Gutzmann 2015). So, in principle, we see no principled reason to reject the theoretical possibility of an Expressivist Dualism. The same idea about the plausibility of extending Potts's (2007) approach to slurs can be found in Popa-Wyatt (2016) and Popa-Wyatt and Wyatt (2018). In both works, it is suggested that such an extension could be a good way to remedy the expressivist semantic approach in Jeshion (2013b) which, in principle, cannot account for the slur variability in the degree of offensiveness.

9. Some philosophers (Hedger 2012, 2013) have taken slurs to have a *purely expressive* meaning, understood in terms of the presence of an associated emotional attitude. This position would thus amount to a version of what can be called Expressivist Monism. Although the position can be maintained concerning the

abovementioned exclamatories, it seems to be counterintuitive if applied to slurs: by definition, a slur is a term that is paradigmatically used to express a derogatory attitude toward a particular group of people, namely, the one it applies to. Even if we take derogation/insult to be the purpose of the original and most paradigmatic use of a slur, derogating/insulting someone by calling him "faggot" seems to be very different from derogating/insulting someone by calling him "spic": in the former case, we insult him by classifying him into the group of homosexuals, which is the object of a certain negative emotion, whereas in the latter, we insult him by classifying him into the group of Latin Americans, which is another object of a negative emotion. Therefore, the acknowledgment of an expressive component should not be a reason (or the occasion) to deprive words like slurs of a truth-conditional meaning. As emphasized by Croom (2014), the presence of that meaning is revealed by the way different slurs interact with other descriptive general terms, as can be exemplified by the following adaptation of his examples:

(i) Diego is a faggot but I did not say anything about his origin.
(ii) # Diego is a spic but I did not say anything about his origin.

Clearly, there is here a contrast between the intelligible (i) and the problematic (ii).

BIBLIOGRAPHICAL REFERENCES

Amaral, Patricia, Craige Roberts, and E. Allyn Smith. 2007. "The Logic of Conventional Implicatures." *Linguistics and Philosophy* 30: 707–749.
Anderson, Luvell, and Ernie Lepore. 2013a. "Slurring Words." *Noûs* 47(1): 25–48.
Anderson, Luvell, and Ernie Lepore. 2013b. "What did You Call Me? Slurs As Prohibited Words." *Analytic Philosophy* 54(3): 350–363.
Barker, Stephen. 2000. "Is Value Content a Component of Conventional Implicature?" *Analysis* 60: 268–279.
Barnes, Winston H. F. 1933. "A Suggestion About Value." *Analysis* 1: 45–46.
Blackburn, Simon. 1993. *Essays in Quasi-Realism*. New York: Oxford University Press.
Bolinger Jorgensen, Renée. 2017. "The Pragmatics of Slurs." *Noûs* 50(3): 439–462.
Camp, Elisabeth. 2013. "Slurring Perspectives." *Analytic Philosophy* 54(3): 330–349.
Caso, Ramiro, and Nicolás Lo Guercio. 2016. "What Bigots Do Say: A Reply to DiFranco." *Thought: A Journal of Philosophy* 5(4): 265–274.
Cepollaro, Bianca. 2015. "In Defense of a Presuppositional Account of Slurs." *Language Sciences* 52: 36–45.
Croom, Adam M. 2011. "Slurs." *Language Sciences* 33: 343–358.
Croom, Adam M. 2013. "How to Do Things with Slurs: Studies in the Way of Derogatory Words." *Language and Communication* 33: 177–204.
Croom, Adam M. 2014. "The Semantics of Slurs: A Refutation of Pure Expressivism." *Language Sciences* 41: 227–242. http://dx.doi.org/10.1016/j.langsci.2013.07.003.

Croom, Adam M. 2015. "The Semantics of Slurs: A Refutation of Coreferentialism." *Ampersand* 2: 30–38.

Díaz Legaspe, Justina. 2020. "Slurs: The Amoralist and the Expression of Hate." This volume.

Díaz Legaspe, Justina, Chang Liu, and Robert Stainton. 2020. "Slurs and Register: A Case Study in Meaning Pluralism." *Mind and Language* 35(2): 156–182.

Frege, Gottlob. 1897. "Logic." In *Posthumous Writings*, edited by Hand Hermes, Friedrich Kambartel, and Fiedrich Kaulbach, 126–151. Oxford: Basil Blackwell, 1979.

Gibbard, Allan. 1990. *Wise Choices, Apt Feelings*. Cambridge: Harvard University Press.

Gutzmann, Daniel. 2015. *Use-Conditional Meaning: Studies in Multidimensional Semantics*. Oxford: Oxford University Press.

Halle, Morris, and Alec Marantz. 1993. "Distributed Morphology and the Pieces of Inflection." In *The View from Building 20*, edited by Ken Hale and Samuel Keyser, 111–176. Cambridge, MA: MIT Press.

Harris, Jesse A., and Christopher Potts. 2009. "Perspective-Shifting with Appositives and Expressives." *Linguistics and Philosophy* 32: 523–552. https://doi.org/10.1007/s10988-010-9070-5.

Hedger, Joseph. 2012. "The Semantics of Racial Slurs: Using Kaplan's Framework to Provide a Theory of the Meaning of Derogatory Epithets." *Linguistic and Philosophical Investigations* 11: 74–84.

Hedger, Joseph. 2013. "Meaning and Racial Slurs: Derogatory Epithets and the Semantics/Pragmatics Interface." *Language and Communication* 33: 205–213.

Hess, Leopold. 2018. "Perspectival Expressives." *Journal of Pragmatics* 129: 13–33.

Hom, Christopher. 2008. "The Semantics of Racial Epithets." *The Journal of Philosophy* 105: 416–440.

Hom, Christopher. 2010. "Pejoratives." *Philosophy Compass* 5(2): 164–185.

Hom, Christopher. 2012. "A Puzzle About Pejoratives." *Philosophical Studies* 159(3): 383–405.

Hom, Christopher, and Robert May. 2013. "Moral and Semantic Innocence." *Analytic Philosophy* 54(3): 293–313.

Hom, Christopher, and Robert May. 2018. "Pejoratives As Fiction." In *Bad Words. Philosophical Perspectives on Slurs*, edited by David Sosa, 108–131. Oxford: Oxford University Press.

Jeshion, Robin. 2013a. "Slurs and Stereotypes." *Analytic Philosophy* 54: 314–325.

Jeshion, Robin. 2013b. "Expressivism and the Offensiveness of Slurs." *Philosophical Perspectives* 27: 231–259.

Kaplan, David. 1999. "The Meaning of 'Ouch' and 'Oops': Explorations in the Theory of Meaning as Use." Ms., University of California, Los Angeles.

Macià, Josep. 2002. "Presuposición y significado expresivo." *Theoria* 3(45): 499–513.

Marques, Teresa, and Manuel García-Carpintero. 2020. "Really Expressive Presuppositions and How to Block Them." *Grazer Philosophische Studien* 97, special issue on *Non-Derogatory Uses of Slurs*, edited by Bianca Cepollaro and Dan Zeman, 138–158.

McCready, Elin. 2010. "Varieties of Conventional Implicature." *Semantics and Pragmatics* 3(8): 1–57.
Nunberg, Geoffrey. 2018. "The Social Life of Slurs." In *New Work on Speech Acts*, edited by Daniel Harris, Daniel Fogal, and Matt Moss, 237–295. Oxford: Oxford University Press.
Ogden, Charles K., and Ivor A. Richards. 1923. *The Meaning of Meaning*. New York: Harcourt Brace & Jovanovich.
Orlando, Eleonora, and Andrés Saab. 2020a. "Slurs, Stereotypes and Insults." *Acta Analytica*. https://doi.org/10.1007/s12136-020-00424-2.
Orlando, Eleonora, and Andrés Saab. 2020b. "A Stereotype Semantics for Syntactically Ambiguous Slurs." *Analytic Philosophy* 61(2): 101–129. https://doi.org/10.1111/phib.12184.
Popa-Wyatt, Mihaela. 2016. "Not All Slurs Are Equal." *Phenomenology and Mind* 11: 150–156.
Popa-Wyatt, Mihaela, and Jeremy L. Wyatt. 2018. "Slurs, Roles and Power." *Philosophical Studies* 175: 2879–2906.
Potts, Christopher. 2003. "Expressive Content As Conventional Implicature." In *Proceedings of the North East Linguistic Society* 33, edited by Makoto Kadowaki and Shigeto Kawahara, 303–322. Amherst, Mass.: GLSA.
Potts, Christopher. 2005. *The Logic of Conventional Implicatures*. Oxford: Oxford University Press.
Potts, Christopher. 2007. "The Expressive Dimension." *Theoretical Linguistics* 33(2): 255–268.
Predelli, Stefano. 2013. *Meaning Without Truth*. Oxford: Oxford University Press.
Richard, Mark. 2008. *When Truth Gives Out*. Oxford: Oxford University Press.
Sauerland, Uli. 2007. "Beyond Unpluggability." *Theoretical Linguistics* 33(2): 231–236.
Schlenker, Philippe. 2007. "Expressive Presuppositions." *Theoretical Linguistics* 33(2): 237–245.
Schroeder, Mark. 2008, "Expression for Expressivists." *Philosophy and Phenomenological Research* 76(1): 86–116.
Stevenson, Charles L. 1944. *Ethics and Language*. New Haven: Yale University Press.
Tirrell, Lynne. 1999. "Derogatory Terms: Racism, Sexism, and the Inferential Role Theory of Meaning." In *Language and Liberation. Feminism, Philosophy, and Language*, edited by Christina Hendricks and Kelly Oliver, 41–80. Albany: State University of New York Press.
Whiting, Daniel. 2013. "It's Not What You Said, It's the Way You Said It: Slurs and Conventional Implicature." *Analytic Philosophy* 54(3): 364–377.
Williamson, Timothy. 2009. "Reference, Inference, and the Semantics of Pejoratives." In *The Philosophy of David Kaplan*, edited by Joseph Almog and Paolo Leonardi, 137–158. Oxford: Oxford University Press.

Chapter 2

On the Locus of Expressivity

Deriving Parallel Meaning Dimensions from Architectural Considerations

Andrés Saab

1. INTRODUCTION

In this chapter I would like to defend the claim that certain non-truth-conditional meanings are exclusively triggered by properties of vocabulary items (in the sense of Halle and Marantz 1993, and subsequent work). In other words, those meanings arise "late" and are not part of the syntactic-semantic derivation. Thus, I capture the notion of *parallel meaning dimension* from architectural considerations without the need for any metalogic operator (e.g., the symbol • in Potts 2005; McCready 2010, among others) especially designated to separate meaning dimensions. The basic expressive paradigm I am concerned with involves pairs of mixed words in Argentinian Spanish whose contribution to truth-conditional meaning is equivalent. They are only differentiated by register (e.g., "*comer*" "to eat" vs. "*morfar*" "to eat$_{inf}$") or by register plus a derogative dimension (e.g., "*sudamericano*" "South American" vs. "*sudaca*" "South American$_{pejorative}$"). Here are two crucial properties of both informal and slur terms:[1]

(A) In the general case, expressives form doublets:[2] "*sudamericano*"/"*sudaca*" "South American"/"South American (pejorative)," "*comer*"/"*morfar*," "to eat"/"to eat (pejorative)."
(B) One of the members of these pairs contributes to a certain meaning dimension: style, tone or expressivity.

My initial conjecture is that at least some forms of expressivity are the direct result of free (lexical) variation; that is, competition in the paradigmatic space among truth-conditionally identical terms gives rise to expressive meanings, an idea that has its roots in the functionalist tradition initiated by Trubetzkoy (1939) and others. Free variation implies competition in the paradigmatic (and phonetic) space and, at least in some cases, a non-truth-conditional contribution to meaning. The final picture, I claim, results in a theory that integrates Fregean tone into semantics, against Frege's original considerations in this respect.

> It makes no difference to the thought whether I use the word "horse" or "steed" or "cart-horse" or "mare." The assertive force does not extend over that in which these words differ. What is called mood, fragrance, illumination in a poem, what is portrayed by cadence and rhythm, does not belong to the thought. (Frege 1918/1956, 23)

The idea that tone is not involved in the notion of truth in any relevant sense and, consequently, "does not belong to the thought" was revived, although not literally, by Capelen and Lepore (2013a,b) and by Lepore and Stone (2018).

> [T]one, unlike meaning, does not seem to be a feature of language that speakers negotiate among one another and coordinate on. Indeed, tone, unlike meaning, does not seem to be something that speakers generally command in virtue of knowing their language or universally respect in their choices of linguistic behavior. [. . .] In short, Frege was right: tone "is not part of the thought expressed." (Lepore and Stone 2018, 144)

In a few words, Lepore and Stone share Frege's view that tone is not part of the semantic agenda. Once one acknowledges the basic fact that linguistic expressivity is subject to linguistic regularities (i.e., to a set of conventions that governs some sort of semantic competence), that view turns out to be somewhat mistaken. To be competent with the use of an informal term or a slur is to know the rules that make such uses expressively correct (see Kaplan 1999 and, more recently, Predelli 2013, 2020). That the conditions behind expressive correctness don't involve the notion of truth doesn't make expressivity in natural language less "semantic" than those conditions that guarantee truth or falsity. Then, I agree with Kaplan and Predelli in that there is no obvious reason why the limits of semantics should be restricted in the narrow sense Frege suggested. Put differently, expressivity has the right to pertain to the research agenda of the theory of linguistic meaning or, perhaps more properly, I should say to the theory of linguistic *meanings*. Following also original insights in Trubetzkoy (1939), I call this research agenda "stylistic semantics." Stylistic semantics is about a parallel dimension of conventional, non-truth-conditional meaning. In this respect, the theory is (at least) two-dimensional, as in Kaplan (1999), Predelli (2013), Potts (2005), McCready (2010), and Gutzmann (2015), among others. However, as I have already advanced, I contend that expressivity is not represented in the logical form (LF) of a sentence, but it is deduced at phonetic form (PF), through a principle of lexical competition to be discussed in the next section. Assuming the Y-model of grammar, we can get a flavor of the division of labor in semantics in figure 2.1.

Here, the symbol •, used in Potts (2005) and others to separate meaning dimensions, is derived from the division in the Y-model. In this way, we dispense with this operator and propose that the division is given by the architecture of the grammar. The consequence of this is that I also dispense with mixed lexical entries like the following one for words like "*sudaca*," which is the pejorative term for South Americans in Argentinian Spanish:

(1) [[sudaca]] = λx.South American(x) ♦ *Bad*($\cap$South American): $<e,t>^a \times t^s$

This is the lexical representation proposed in McCready (2010) for slur terms. It contains both truth-conditional and non-truth-conditional information. The latter is modeled as a conventional implicature (following Grice 1975 and, in particular, Potts 2005). The symbol ♦ in this representation is changed for the symbol • through a rule that allows interpreting conventional implicatures in the semantic derivation. Putting technical details aside, compare the lexical entry in (1) to the following simplified lexical entry I propose is active in the syntax:

(2) Syntax-semantics: [[sudaca]] = λx.South American(x)

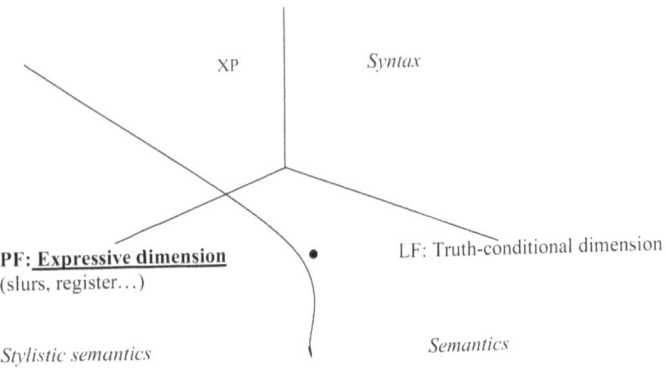

Figure 2.1 **Meaning Dimensions and Grammatical Architecture.** Image Credit: Andrés Saab.

According to (2), the denotation of "*sudaca*" is equivalent to that of "South American"; both denote the set of South Americans. It is only when this word is sent to the PF component of the grammar (i.e., after syntax) that the expressive meaning is added to the phonological matrix of the relevant lexical item. This requires some particular implementation of lexical representation. In particular, it requires taking for granted that the phonetic makeup of lexical items is determined after syntax, concretely, at the PF interface.

The empirical argument in favor of this implementation of stylistic semantics comes from the behavior of expressives in the realm of ellipsis. The observation is that expressivity doesn't survive ellipsis.[3] This was already shown by Potts et al. (2009) for ellipsis sites that take as antecedents predicates containing attributive adjectives like "fucking" in English (< > = ellipsis site):[4]

(3) A: I saw your fucking dog in the park.
B: No, you didn't <see my dog>—you couldn't have <seen my dog>. The poor thing passed away last week.

(Potts et al. 2009, 364, ex. (32))

Here, the two ellipsis sites are modeled without expressives, an analysis justified by the clear intuition that B doesn't endorse A's hostility to the dog at hand. Potts et al.'s conclusion is that ellipsis only requires recovery of descriptive content, an idea in consonance with the approach to ellipsis in Merchant (2001), according to which ellipsis identity boils down to mutual entailment between the antecedent and the ellipsis site. In principle, this seems to be correct when it comes to evaluating the distribution of mixed terms in ellipsis. Consider the following short dialogue:

(4) A: Qué   morfaste?
        what   ate.2SG.INFORMAL
        "What did you eat(informal)?"
    B: Una   pizza <?>, pero   no   tolero   cuando
        a   pizza   but   not   tolerate.1SG   when
        hablás   tan   informalmente. Yo   nunca lo   hago.
        speak.2SG so   informally   I   never it   do
        "A pizza. But I don't tolerate when you speak informally. I never do it."

Here B's answer contains an ellipsis site that, unlike what happens in the antecedent, cannot be interpreted as containing the verb "*morfar*," which is the informal term for the verb "*comer*" "to eat." In principle, we can generalize Potts et al.'s argument and conclude that given that "*morfar*" and "*comer*" can be substituted *salva veritate*, mutual entailment is satisfied and ellipsis applies. If this approach is correct, then ellipsis cannot help us distinguish different theories of expressivity in competition. However, I argue, following previous proposals, that ellipsis requires lexical identity as a necessary condition (Chomsky 1965; Chung 2006; Saab 2008, among many others). If this is correct, then ellipsis can be indeed used as a relevant test, one that seems to favor the approach to expressivity that I sketch in this chapter. I elaborate the argument from ellipsis in section 3 for informal terms and, in section 4, I extend the analysis to slurs. But before entering into the details concerning the behavior of mixed terms under ellipsis, I sketch my analysis for mixed terms. As I have already advanced, my implementation requires two core ingredients: (a) a model of late insertion for phonological information, and (b) a principle of lexical competition that, among other things, accounts for the fact that certain expressive terms require a non-expressive counterpart. These are the themes of the following section.

2. IMPLEMENTATION: EXPRESSIVITY AS A PF PROPERTY

2.1. Background Assumptions

I assume the distributed morphology framework (Halle and Marantz 1993, 1994 and, in particular, Embick 2000, 2007; Embick and Noyer 2001; Arregi and Nevins 2012; Marantz 2013; Harley 2014, among many others). The general architecture is shown in figure 2.2.

A crucial property of this conception of the grammar is form-meaning separation, that is, the fact that meaning-form connections are determined by the syntax in an all-the-way fashion (Halle and Marantz 1994). Syntax manipulates abstract objects (from List 1) that are supplied with a given phonological form after syntax through a set of lexical insertion rules that

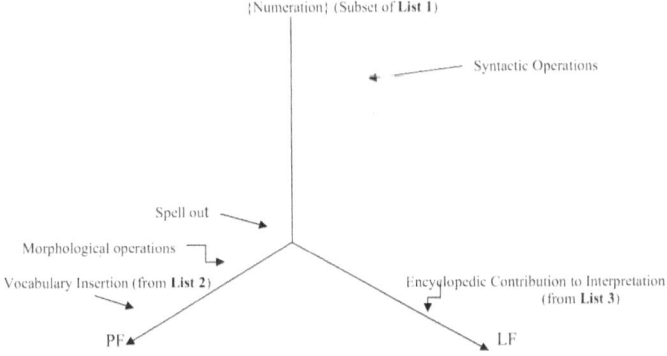

Figure 2.2 Architecture of the Grammar. Image Credit: Andrés Saab.

adds items from List 2. The primitives that syntax manipulates are Roots and abstract morphemes. Abstract morphemes are features drawn from a universal inventory and encode things like [past], [plural], and so on. Roots are represented by an index that is replaced at PF by a phonetic matrix (Chomsky 1995; Embick 2000; Saab 2008; Acquaviva 2008; Harley 2014, among others). Finally, as for the LF side, syntax provides an abstract object built out from Roots and abstract morphemes, which is interpreted on the basis of the information available in List 3. Let me summarize the information contained in each of the lists in (6) (simplified from Harley 2014, 228):

List 1: *Feature bundles*: Syntactic primitives, both interpretable and uninterpretable, functional and contentful.
List 2: *Vocabulary items*: Instructions for pronouncing terminal nodes.
List 3: *Encyclopedia*: Instructions for interpreting terminal nodes.

Thus, the full representation of an abstract morpheme like, say, the imperfect in Spanish ("*-ba/-ía*") requires information taken from the three lists:

List 1: [imperfect past]
List 2: [imperfect past] ↔ /-ía/   / thematic vowel$_{2,3}$ __
         [imperfect past] ↔ /-ba/
List 3: [imperfect past] ↔ ⟦truth-conditional meaning⟧

For a Root like "*gat(o)*" "cat," the relevant information, distributed in each list, can be summarized as follows:

List 1: √13
List 2: √13 ↔ /gát-/
List 3: √13 ↔ ⟦$\lambda x.$ Cat(x)⟧ / ___n

In sum, on a DM conception, there is not a generative lexicon that syntax uses to construct syntactic objects; lexical objects are instead syntactic constructs derived by the same principles that allow us to derive phrasal objects. I contend now that expressivity, at least for the cases I am concerned with, is an exclusive property of vocabulary items, that is, of objects taken from List 2.

2.2. Expressivity as a List 2 Property

With these background assumptions in mind, we can now state the basic hypothesis in the following way:

(5) (At least) some forms of expressivity are exclusively encoded in List 2.

Let's illustrate the theory with the pair *"trabajar"* "to work" vs. *"laburar"* "to work$_{informal}$." The crucial step is adding the informal flavor of *"laburar"* as part of the vocabulary item:

(6) a. *trabajar*
    b. List 1 $\sqrt{122}$
       List 2: $\sqrt{122}$ ↔ /trabaj(ár)/ / ___ v
       List 3: $\sqrt{122}$ ↔ ⟦ λx. Work(x)⟧ / ___ v
(7) a. *laburar*
    b. List 1: $\sqrt{221}$
       List 2: $\sqrt{221}$ ↔ /labur(ár)/$_{BIAS}$ / ___ v
       BIAS: $c \in CU$(laburar) only if, in c, c_a is a participant in register informal
       List 3: $\sqrt{221}$ ↔ ⟦ λx. Work(x)⟧ / ___ v

Let's assume that the expressive meaning of *"laburar"* is a bias on contexts of use (CU), which, in this particular case, characterizes the agent of the context as a participant in an informal register (Predelli 2013). We can illustrate the representation in (7) with the scheme in figure 2.3, assuming that the index for the Root of the informal term *"laburar"* is $\sqrt{35}$ (see figure 2.3).

As I advanced in the introduction, on this theory, the metalogic symbol • is trivial; it is deduced from architectural considerations and a principle of lexical competition. A crucial question is, of course, how lexical competition in the paradigmatic space is determined. I conjecture that the following general principle of lexical competition is active in natural languages:

(8) *Principle of stylistic meaning (PSM):* Given a pair of abstract nodes X and Y, taken from List 1, if X and Y are not semantically distinguishable at LF (List 3), they are "semantically" distinguished at PF (List 2).

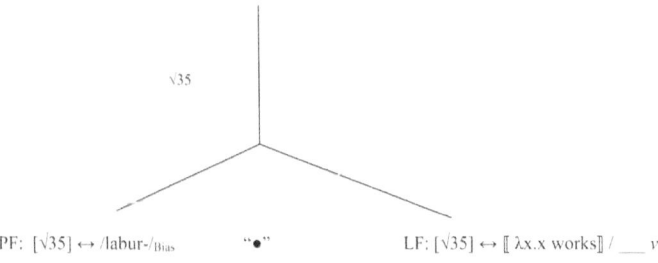

Figure 2.3 Bias for *"laburar."* Image Credit: Andrés Saab.

The notion of *meaning* in this formulation requires some qualifications. If Y is semantically distinguished from X at LF, we say that the meaning contribution of both lexical items is truth-conditionally relevant. If Y is semantically distinguished from X at PF we say that the meaning contribution of both lexical items is stylistic or expressive, that is, non-truth-conditionally relevant. Alternatively, we can characterize as *stylistic* those meanings that arise only at PF by virtue of a principle of lexical competition. In any case, the distinction is semantic in the favored sense of stylistic semantics. PSM is observed for the pairs of Roots "*laburar*" and "*trabajar*." And in this case in particular, we are led to conclude that the difference is purely stylistic. At any rate, note that PSM is not a principle of synonymy blocking: "*trabajar*" and "*laburar*" are still synonymous (truth-conditionally equivalent). I think this is an important result, but I will not explore its consequences here.

The considerations made here must be taken as a general sketch of how a theory of stylistic semantics should look like according to my assumptions. My main aim in this chapter is just to argue that there is preliminary evidence that a radical dissociation between truth-conditional and expressive meaning is needed. If the general sketch turns out to be correct, then an explicit theory of stylistic semantics can be developed on a formal basis. There are, of course, many questions opened by this general approach. A pressing one is how the conceptual-intentional cognitive system accesses the information provided by the computational system of the language faculty. According to Chomsky (1995, 2000, 2001), there are two cognitive systems that use the information provided by the PF and LF interfaces, namely, the sensorimotor, articulatory-perceptual system (S-M) and the conceptual-intentional system (C-I) related to systems of thought. In the classical Y-model, the C-I system only uses information from the LF interface. According to Reinhart (2006), it seems that such a cognitive system relates lexical and syntactic information to a set of disparate interpretation processes, involving, at least, inference, context, and concepts. Reinhart (2006) proposes, then, associating these processes to three distinct cognitive systems, namely, context, concept, and inference. For the purposes of this chapter the context system is the most relevant one and also the hardest to define:

> The hardest to define given our present state of knowledge are the context systems that narrow the information transmitted through the derivation (coded in the relevant representation), and select the information that is useful for the context of use. (Reinhart 2006, 4)

To be competent with a slur, for example, requires knowing the conditions that make it correct in a certain context of use. This supposes manipulation of information other than purely inferential or conceptual. Both are required, yet. A pair of terms opposed in register is constituted as such because the concepts expressed by each member are identical. Yet, they are used in different contexts for different purposes, and this is something that requires linking lexical, and inferential content to particular contexts of use. It is in this sense that I assume here that the context system must have access both to the PF and LF interfaces. I leave these issues open and turn my attention to the empirical argument in favor of the proposed meaning division.

3. THE ARGUMENT FROM ELLIPSIS

3.1. Expressive Mismatches under Ellipsis

For many kinds of ellipses in natural languages, the following generalization seems to be relevant:

Vehicle Change Generalization (Barros and Saab 2016):[5]
(9) Recoverability conditions in ellipsis make reference to content not character.

This observation generalizes over different types of well-known ellipsis mismatches, Vehicle Change and indexical mismatches being two prominent ones:

Classic Vehicle Change (Fiengo and May 1994; Merchant 2001):
(10) a. They arrested the man$_3$, but he$_3$ doesn't know why.
b. They arrested the man$_1$, but he$_1$ doesn't know why <they arrested *the man$_1$/him$_1$>.

Indexical mismatches (Thoms 2013, 2015):
(11) A: Can you help me? [requesting help]
B: Yes, I can <help you>.

This type of mismatches follows if identity in ellipsis is stated in purely semantic terms. Merchant (2001) famously proposed a semantic condition based on the crucial notion of *e*(ellipsis)-GIVENness. Here is Merchant's condition:

Focus condition:
(12) A constituent α can be deleted only if α is *e*-GIVEN.
(13) An expression E counts as *e*-GIVEN iff E has a salient antecedent A and, *modulo* ∃-type shifting,

i. A entails the Focus closure of E (written F-clo(E)), and
  ii. E entails F-clo(A)
(14) F-clo(α) is the result of replacing F-marked parts of α with ∃-bound variables.

Take as an example a simple case of VP-ellipsis in English like (15a) and its associated (and simplified) semantic derivation in (15b):

(15) a.   [$_F$ Ann] loves Peter and [$_F$ Mary] does <love Peter> too.
    b.   F-(clo)(⟦A⟧) = ⟦∃x. x loves Peter⟧
        F-(clo)(⟦E⟧) = ⟦∃y. y loves Peter⟧
        Therefore, ⟦A⟧ entails F-clo(⟦E⟧) and ⟦E⟧ entails F-clo(⟦A⟧).

When it comes to the mismatches in (10) and (11), the crucial point is that descriptive properties of indexicals or R-expressions do not alter the mutual entailment relation under some variable assignment. If this is on the right track, then other mismatches should be allowed beyond indexicals and R-expressions. Consider, for instance, pairs of words opposed to each other only by the bias they express. As I have already noted, in Argentinian Spanish, for instance, the "neutral" verb "*comer*" "to eat" is semantically indistinguishable from the biased verb "*morfar*." This can be demonstrated by well-known substitution tests: any occurrence of the verb "*comer*" can be replaced (*modulo* metalinguistic and sociolinguistic tones) by an occurrence of the verb "*morfar*" and vice versa. The predictions for mutual entailment as formulated in (12) are more or less clear. In principle, register mismatches between A and E should be allowed, in a way such that modeling the following E(llipsis)-sites as indicated should be possible in fragments like the following ones:

(16) A: Qué   comiste?
        what   ate.2SG.NEUTRAL
        "What did you eat?"
    B: Una   pizza   <morfé>.
        a   pizza   ate.1SG.INFORMAL
        "A pizza."
(17) A: Qué   morfaste?
        what   ate.2SG.INFORMAL
    B: Una   pizza   <comí>.
        a   pizza   ate.1SG.NEUTRAL

Of course, without any discursive clue, it would be just impossible to know whether such E-sites are possible or not. Consider in this respect the following discourse:[6]

(18) A: Qué   morfaste?
        what   ate.2SG.INFORMAL
     B: Una   pizza <?>,   pero   no   tolero   cuando
        a   pizza   but   not   tolerate.1SG   when
        hablás   tan   informalmente. Yo   nunca   lo   hago.
        speak.2SG so   informally   I   never   it   do
        "A pizza. But I don't tolerate when you speak informally. I never
        do it."

At first sight, the metalinguistic comment introduced by B allows us to reject an E-site modeled as containing the informal counterpart of the verb "to eat." Note that a non-elliptical version of (19) is infelicitous here:[7]

(19) A: Qué   morfaste?
        what   ate.2SG.INFORMAL
     B: #Una   pizza   morfé,   pero   no   tolero   cuando
        a   pizza   ate.2SG.INFOR   but   not   tolerate.1SG   when
        hablás   tan   informalmente. Yo   nunca   lo   hago.
        speak.2SG so   informally   I   never   it   do
        "#I ate(informal) a pizza. But I don't tolerate when you speak informally. I never do it."

The mutual entailment approach apparently provides the right answer to the problem, as the neutral form "*comer*" could take the informal form "*morfar*" as antecedent and outputs a legitimate E-site.

(20) A: Qué [$_{TP}$ *pro*   morfaste *t*]?
        what   ate.2SG.INFORMAL
     B: Una   pizza <[$_{TP}$ *pro* comí *t*]>,   pero no   tolero
        a   pizza   ate.1SG.NEUTRAL   but   not tolerate.1SG
        cuando   hablás   tan   informalmente.
        when   speak.2SG so   informally

I call this "Bias Vehicle Change," cases where the change between A and E is produced in the particular bias of some lexical expression. For (18), and assuming that short answers are derived as cases of TP-ellipsis (Merchant 2004), mutual entailment between A and E should be permitted under focus closure:[8]

(21) a. F-clo([[A]]) = [[A]] = $\exists x[g(1)$ morfar $x]$ entails [[TP$_E$]] = $\exists y[g(1)$ comer $y]$
     b. F-clo([[E]]) = [[E]] = $\exists y[g(1)$ comer $y]$ entails [[TP$_A$]] = $\exists x[g(1)$ morfar $x]$
     c. [[A]] entails F-clo([[E]]) and [[E]] entails F-clo([[A]]).

On the basis of the grammaticality of (18), we can then state the following generalization:

Generalization 1 (G1):
(22)   Bias Vehicle Change is licensed under TP-ellipsis.

As far as I can tell, examples similar to (18) can be constructed for myriads of pairs of words contrasting only in register. Here is a non-exhaustive list of pairs of verbs from Argentinian Spanish:

(23)

Neutral	*Informal*	
tomar	chupar	"to drink"
sudar/transpirar	chivar	"to sweat"
eyacular	acabar	"to ejaculate/to come"
pagar	garpar	"to pay"
trabajar	laburar	"to work"
escapar	rajar	"to escape"
defecar	cagar	"to defecate/to shit"
delatar	buchonear	"to betray"
molestar	joder	"to bother"
pasarse	sarparse	"to cross the limits"

However, G1 does not hold for every type of ellipsis. Consider in this respect Spanish NP-ellipsis (see Saab 2019 for a detailed discussion on NP-ellipsis). In this language, words like "*culo*" "ass" and "*cola*" "tail" when applied to humans refer to the same body part, the difference being, once again, in the bias dimension of each word. Thus, "*culo*" is coarse language and "*cola*" is the polite form at least in some dialects (Argentinian Spanish, for instance). Interestingly, both nouns differ in gender: "*culo*" is masculine, but "*cola*" is feminine. This allows us to test their behavior in NP-ellipsis contexts. As shown below, bias mismatches are fully ungrammatical in any direction:

(24) a. El   *culo*   de Juan es   más   grande
         the.MASC.SG ass.MASC.SG of J.   is   more big
         que el   <*culo*>   de María.
         that the.MASC.SG ass.MASC.SG   of M.
      b. La   *cola*   de Juan es   más   grande
         the.FEM.SG tail.FEM.SG   of J.   is   more big
         que la   <*cola*>   de María.
         that the.FEM.SG tail.FEM.SG   of M.

c. *El   *culo*   de   Juan   es   más   grande
   the.MASC.SG ass.MASC.SG of   J.   is   more   big
   que   la   <*cola*>   de   María.
   that the.FEM.SG <tail.FEM.SG >   of   M.

d. *La   *cola*   de   Juan   es   más   grande
   the.FEM.SG tail.FEM.SG of   J.   is   more   big
   que   el   <*culo*>   de   María.
   that the.MASC.SG <ass.MASC.SG >   of   M.

Note that, as far as mutual entailment under focus closure is concerned, the fact that "*culo*" and "*cola*" differ in gender is irrelevant, since gender is semantically arbitrary here. We arrive then at our second generalization:

Generalization 2 (G2):[9]
(25) Bias Vehicle Change is not licensed under NP-ellipsis.

Here is the problem: either we have a dissociated identity condition or one of the two generalizations is spurious. The impossibility of Bias Vehicle Change in Spanish NP-ellipsis casts doubts on the alternative of extending mutual entailment (or relatives) to this particular elliptical construction. We can of course dissociate the identity condition in one semantic condition for TP-ellipsis and one lexical-syntactic identity condition for NP-ellipsis, after all we already know that different types of ellipsis are subjected to different conditions beyond identity (e.g., parallelism conditions regulating the correlate/remnant distribution and discourse conditions regulating the legitimacy of some types of ellipsis but not others). This would be compatible with generalizations 1 and 2, but such a solution would be unappealing under uniformity considerations. Alternatively, we can make an attempt to solve semantic identity for ellipses in general by adding some non-truth-conditional conditions to the theory. In what follows, I argue that such an alternative cannot handle the entire set of facts and, then, I show that a uniform identity condition, with lexical identity as a necessary condition, plus my theory of expressivity, accounts for why expressivity doesn't survive ellipsis sites in the TP-ellipsis cases. The NP-ellipsis cases are, in turn, ruled out as a simple failure of lexical identity.

3.2. A Pragmatic Alternative: No Telepathy

Let's assume that the choice of remaining silent (i.e., making use of ellipsis) nullifies the bias of whatever expression the silence is replacing. This would have obvious consequences for any theory of information recoverability in ellipsis involving the communicative force of non-elliptical expressions regarding bias, metalinguistic uses, and register. By remaining silent, such information is unrecoverable, no matter what your favorite theory of identity is (semantic or syntactic). Put differently, we are not telepaths. Let's assume that the phenomenon under discussion falls under some No Telepathy Condition:

No Telepathy (NT):
(26) Information regarding lexical choices is unrecoverable under ellipsis without additional discourse clues.

By "lexical choices" I understand some competition among lexical items in the same semantic space (de Saussure's paradigmatic relations), where the selection of such and such lexical item would depend, among other things, on the speaker's attitude toward the content of the speech act. Such choices, arguably, also convey information regarding the speaker's gender, age and socioeconomic status. NT then prevents us from introducing new lexical material in the E-site that would require some sort of telepathic activity. Crucially, NT correctly rules in standard cases of Vehicle Change like (10), repeated as follows:

(27) They arrested [the man]$_3$, but he$_3$ doesn't know why <they arrested *the man$_3$/him$_3$>.

One reasonable way to approach (27) under NT is just claiming that the use of the pronoun is unavoidable, that is, there is no lexical choice to make, given that one of the possible choices provided by the paradigmatic space introduces a flagrant violation of principle-C of binding theory (although see Johnson 2012). As for (20), the situation is different: we can guess a lexical choice made in the E-site on the basis of the metalinguistic comment made by B. So, NT seems to be sufficiently flexible as to allow some bias change between A and E and sufficiently constrained as to rule out mismatches in lexical choices.

Thus far, it seems that the NT is a good alternative theory that would account for Bias Vehicle Change. The NT condition, however, would have to explain the impossibility of coarse mismatches in NP-ellipsis as illustrated in (24). The question here is why gender information does not suffice to recover the missing information that the speaker has chosen the coarse "*culo*" or the polite "*cola*" in the relevant cases. The answer would be that gender information cannot resolve the issue of how to know whether in (24c) we are talking, for instance, about María's nose ("*nariz*" "nose" is feminine in Spanish). Yet, this problem should be avoided by contextual and discursive factors. So, suppose we are walking behind Juan and María, and pointing out to Juan's relevant body part, I say:

(28) *El   culo   de Juan es grande pero...
     the.MASC.SG ass.MASC.SG of J.   is big   but
     [now pointing out to María's relevant body part]
     la   <cola>   de María es más   grande.
     the.FEM.SG   tail.FEM.SG of M.   is more big

Even when we are no telepaths, we should be able to recover the relevant information in this case, but we cannot. Compare with cases of pragmatic recoverability of empty nouns in general:

(29) a. Yo quiero ese   con   rueditas.
        I   want   this.MASC   with wheels
        "I want that one with wheels."
        [pointing to some toy; the word "toy," "juguete," is masculine in Spanish]
     b. Cuando era   chico, tenía   una   como
        when   was.1P.SG boy   had.1P.SG   one.FEM like
        esa.
        that.FEM
        "When I was a child, I had one like that."
        [pointing to a bike; the word "bike," "bicicleta," is feminine in Spanish]

The contrast between (28) and (29) constitutes a strange state of affairs under the NT condition. It seems that some degree of telepathy should be permitted for (29) but not for (28). In other words, the addressee in (29) is able to guess that the speaker is talking about toys or bikes, but the same guessing capacity is impossible in (28). This is connected to the fact that recoverability conditions are different for surface and deep anaphora in Hankamer and Sag's (1976) terms. As Merchant (2010) has shown, whenever ellipsis (i.e., surface anaphora) and deep anaphora compete, ellipsis is always preferred. This is exactly what seems to be happening in (28), where there is a linguistic antecedent for the E-site that blocks pragmatic recoverability. If this is on the right track, there is some basis to concluding that NT is a suspicious condition at least as a recoverability condition for surface anaphora.

As it stands, the entire paradigm discussed in this section remains as a puzzle for this attempt to formulate a uniform semantic identity condition supplied with a pragmatic constraint. Yet, in the following section I show that generalization 1 is a spurious observation. I argue that lexical/syntactic identity is the right condition for several types of surface anaphora, in particular, for the type of ellipsis I am concerned with.

3.3. A Syntactic Solution

Generalization 1 is spurious. Ellipsis does not allow for the type of mismatches that mutual entailment predicts. A uniform syntactic identity condition applying in narrow syntax plus the theory of expressivity I am defending are enough to make the right predictions. Let's assume that identity in ellipsis applies in narrow syntax and makes reference to the lexical content of both Roots and abstract morphemes, although other structural or semantic recoverability conditions must also apply (see figure 2.4).

If lexical identity (strictly speaking, List 1 identity) is a necessary condition for ellipsis to apply, then the impossibility of Bias Vehicle Change in NP-ellipsis follows without further ado as a general violation of lexical identity. In order to see this, let's reconsider the ungrammatical example in (24c) and assume that $\sqrt{38}$ is the index for "*cola*" and $\sqrt{83}$ for "*culo*":

(30) *El   [$_{NP}$ $\sqrt{83}$ + masculine] de Juan   es más grande
     the.MASC.SG   of J.   is more big
     que la   [$_{NP}$ $\sqrt{38}$ + feminine] de   María.
     that the.FEM.SG   of   M.

As shown in (30), the strong ungrammaticality of (24c) follows now as an extreme violation of the identity condition, where both the abstract morpheme for gender and the Root in the E-site do not match the features of the corresponding phrases in the antecedent. We derive thus generalization 2.

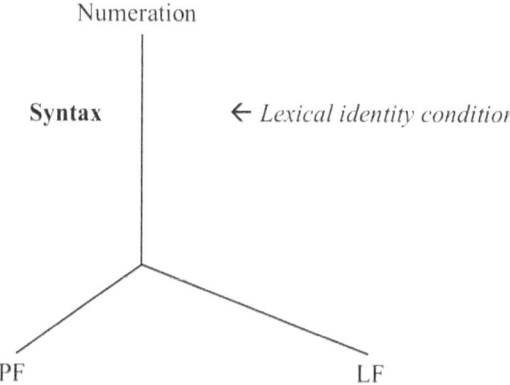

Figure 2.4 **Lexical-Syntactic Identity.** Image Credit: Andrés Saab.

This analysis opens the question of why TP-ellipsis in fragments seems to behave different to NP-ellipsis. Recall the analysis sketched in (20B) and its associated (putative true) empirical observation:

(31) A: Qué [$_{TP}$ pro morfaste t]?
       what   ate.2SG.INFORMAL
    B: Una pizza <[$_{TP}$ pro comí t]>, pero no tolero
       a   pizza   ate.1SG.NEUTRAL but not tolerate.1SG
       cuando hablás tan informalmente.
       when   speak.2SG so informally

Generalization 1:
(32) Bias Vehicle Change is licensed under TP-ellipsis.

It is clear now that taking for granted that the same identity condition is operative in TP and NP-ellipsis, such an analysis should be regarded as impossible, given that "*comer*" and "*morfar*" are the PF realizations of distinct Roots. So, (32) should be regarded as false. Under uniformity considerations, we expect (33) to hold:

Bias Vehicle Change Generalization (Final):
(33) Bias Vehicle Change is licensed neither under TP-ellipsis nor NP-ellipsis.

Fortunately, the theory of expressivity I am defending here gives rise to an alternative analysis for (31) according to which the same Root for "*morfar*," say $\sqrt{102}$, is generated both in the antecedent and the elided TP. Given that all other syntactic features are identical *in the syntax* (agreement information being supplied at PF), we conclude that both TPs are strictly identical:

(34) A: Qué [$_{TP}$ pro $\sqrt{102}$ t]?
     B: Una pizza <[$_{TP}$ pro $\sqrt{102}$ t]> ...

Thus, bias mismatches in TP-ellipsis are just illusory, that is, just the surface reflex of the basic fact that bias is encoded in List 2 at PF. Such information, however, cannot be accessed under ellipsis, whose PF effect is precisely blocking vocabulary insertion, the operation that introduces information from List 2.

Additional evidence comes from related facts. Other cases from the list in (23) point to the conclusion that, at least in some instances, the bias/conventional implicature of a given word is not present at LF. The relevant cases are the so-called "*vesre*" "reverse" words illustrated in the list in (23) with words like "*garpar*" "to pay_informal" and "*sarparse*" "to cross the limits_informal." *Vesre* speech is an informal way to speak that consists of reversing the syllable structure of a given word. Thus, "*pagar*" is converted into a *vesre* word by inverting the two syllables it contains (e.g., *pa—gar* and *gar—par*). *Vesre* speech uses to be productive in informal registers in a way such that even non-lexicalized *vesre* words are subject to the rule (e.g., *mesa—same* "table"). From a DM perspective, *vesre* speech can only be obtained after syntax (see Bohrn 2019). A rough derivation for the verb "*garpar*" is shown in figure 2.5.

If this analysis is on track, a parallel example to (31) containing the verb "*garpar*" in the antecedent should be analyzed as in (35):

(35) A: Qué [_TP *pro* garpaste *t*]?   (*garpar* = $\sqrt{75}$ in the syntax)
          what   payed.2P.SG.INFORMAL
          "What did you pay?"
      B: Una   pizza <[_TP *pro* $\sqrt{75}$ *t*]>, pero no   tolero   cuando
          a   pizza   but   not tolerate. 1P.SG when
          hablás   tan informalmente. Yo nunca lo hago.
          speak.2P.SG   so   informally   I   never it do

Like in the case of "*morfar*," we also have here the same syntactic Root both in the antecedent and in the E-site. It is only after a process of syllabic inversion applying at PF that we obtain informal register for the inverted *phonological* word. Such a process is obviously blocked by ellipsis.

4. SLURS

Paradigmatic slurs are expressions prima facie associated with the expression of a contemptuous attitude concerning a group of people identified in terms of their origin or descent ("spic"), ethnicity ("nigger"), sexual orientation

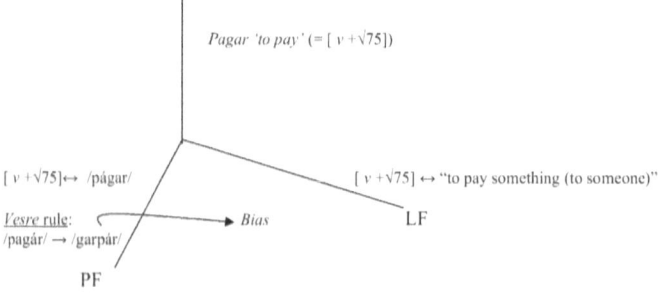

Figure 2.5 Derivation of a "*Vesre*" Word at PF. Image Credit: Andrés Saab.

("faggot"), ethnicity or religion ("kike"), gender ("whore"), and so on. They meet the two criteria I initially proposed to determine the type of expressivity I am concerned with:

(A) In the general case, expressives form doublets: *"sudamericano"*/ *"sudaca"* "South American"/"South American (pejorative)," *"comer"*/*"morfar,"* "to eat"/"to eat (pejorative)."
(B) These doublets contribute to a certain meaning dimension: style, tone, or expressivity.

That the first criterion is satisfied is shared by most extant accounts of slurs. This comes in the form of the so-called Identity Thesis, the idea that the representational dimension of a slur is equivalent to the representational dimension of its neutral counterpart.[10] Thus, according to this conception, the two sentences in (36) are extensionally equivalent:

(36) a. Juan es sudaca.
J. is South American$_{\text{PEJORATIVE}}$
"Juan is South American (pejorative)."
b. Juan es sudamericano.
J. is South American
"Juan is South American."

In several accounts, the additional meaning slurs contribute is conceived of as independent of the *at-issue* content. This content is modeled as a bias on contexts of use (Predelli 2013), a conventional implicature (McCready 2010), or a stereotype (Orlando and Saab 2020a,b), among other options. Regardless of particular implementations, the expressive meaning of slurs projects out of at-issues operators (see McCready 2010):

(37) a. Juan no es sudaca.
Juan not is South American$_{\text{PEJORATIVE}}$
"Juan is not South American (pejorative)."
b. Juan cree que Ana es sudaca.
Juan believes that Ana is South American$_{\text{PEJORATIVE}}$
"Juan believes that Ana is South American (pejorative)."
c. Juan puede ser sudaca.
Juan might be South American$_{\text{PEJORATIVE}}$
"Juan might be South American (pejorative)."
d. ¿Es sudaca Juan?
is South American$_{\text{PEJORATIVE}}$ Juan
"Is Juan South American (pejorative)?"

Part of the debate is whether these projection effects are presuppositional or not.[11] The problem is subtle as it is not easy to construct the relevant tests. Yet, I think that the behavior of slurs under ellipsis favors a non-presuppositional account of slurs as much as it favors the particular approach to stylistic semantics I am pursuing here. In order to see how the argument works, let's consider an example of NP-ellipsis in Spanish for which we have enough evidence that the ellipsis site contains a full-fledged NP structure which is deleted at PF:

(38) A: ¿A cuántos sudacas viste en la fiesta?
to how-many South Americans$_{PEJ}$ saw.2SG in the party
"How many South American$_{PEJ}$ did you see at the party?"
B: Vi a tres <sudacas>, pero podrías evitar
saw.1SG to three South American$_{PEJ}$ but could.2SG avoid
ese modo de hablar de los sudamericanos.
that way of speaking of the South American$_{PEJ}$
Yo nunca hablo así de ellos.
I never speak so of them
"Three, but you could avoid talking that way about South Americans. I never talk that way."

By eliding the noun phrase, the speaker B provides the relevant information asked in A's question and, at the same time, objects A's xenophobic way of speaking. Not eliding the noun, obviously, leads to infelicity, unless air quotations or a similar strategy is employed:

(39) A: ¿A cuántos sudacas viste en la fiesta?
to how-many South Americans$_{PEJ}$ saw.2SG in the party
"How many South Americans$_{PEJ}$ did you see at the party?"
B: #Vi a tres sudacas, pero podrías evitar
saw.1SG to three South Americans$_{PEJ}$ but could.2SG avoid
ese modo de hablar de los sudacas.
that way of speaking of the South Americans$_{PEJ}$
Yo nunca hablo así de ellos.
I never speak so of them
"I saw three South Americans$_{PEJORATIVE}$, but you could avoid that way of speaking about South Americans. I never talk that way."

This is an interesting state of affairs. On the one hand, it shows that ellipsis is an apt strategy to nullify the bias encoded in some lexical items. This follows from the present account that requires lexical insertion in order to make the expressivity salient in the discourse. Alternative accounts that encode the bias in the syntax don't offer a good explanation for why B's answer in (38B) is a non-biased answer. Recall that McCready (2010) proposes lexical entries like the following ones, where a conventional implicature is directly encoded in full lexical items that are manipulated by the syntax and LF:

(40) ⟦sudaca⟧ = $\lambda x.$South American(x) ♦ $Bad(^\cap$South American$)$: $<e,t>^a \times t^s$

Without further ado, ellipsis should not block the conventional implicature that B has a negative attitude toward South Americans. A way of avoiding the problem is assuming with Potts et al. (2009) that identity in ellipsis only refers to descriptive properties of antecedents (see section 1). But note that this claim makes sense if ellipsis doesn't require lexical identity and it is calculated, say, over the focus closures of antecedents and elliptical sites. But if lexical identity is indeed required, such an assumption remains as a controversial stipulation. In this respect, the proposal of deriving expressivity at PF gives better results.

On the other hand, as I have already advanced, the facts in (38) also seem to give additional support for the hypothesis that the expressive dimension in slurs is non-presuppositional. In effect, standard presuppositions are not canceled by ellipsis, as witnessed in cases like the following:[12]

(41) A. Juan dejó de fumar.
     J.   stopped of smoking
  B. Pedro también <dejó de fumar>,
     P.   too   stopped of smoking
     #aunque nunca fumó.
     although never smoked

In sum, slurs behave under ellipsis as predicted by the hypothesis of "late" expressivity. The moral to be extracted from this particular behavior of informal terms and slurs is that expressivity must be expressed (uttered). Putting the type of non-truth-conditional meanings that these terms have in the syntactic-semantic derivation leaves this basic observation unexplained.

A final question is how the stylistic meaning of a given slur can be modeled in the present framework. An important similarity with informal terms is that, in the general case, slurs are also informal. This means that we want to model part of their stylistic meaning as we did for informal terms in section 2.2 (see Díaz Legaspe et al. 2020 on the relation between register and slurs):[13]

(42) *Bias for sudaca:* $c \in CU($sudaca$)$ only if, in c, c_a is a participant in register *informal*

Of course, this is not enough. A concrete use of a slur involves much more than just informal register. Adapting ideas from Orlando and Saab (2020a,b), I would like to suggest that slurs characterize contexts by making salient a certain stereotype of the target group. Concretely, I conjecture that stereotypes can be conceived of as semantic objects ranging over sets of propositions which, taken together, constitute a certain misinformed theory of a given human group. In model-theoretic terms, stereotypes denote in <<s,t>, t>, that is, they denote set of propositions:

(43) 〚Stereotype〛^{g,w} = $\lambda p.\ \exists P_{<e,t>}[P \in C\ \&\ p = [\lambda w.P(\text{Group})(w)]]$

Thus, the stereotype for *"sudaca"* would contain, among other propositions, the propositions that South Americans are prone to laziness, that South Americans are undocumented migrants, and so on. The content of each predicate P is contextually determined by its membership to C, that is, by the large sociocultural context in which a certain stereotype is in force. With this in mind, we can proceed to define the bias dimension of *"sudaca"* as follows:

(44) *Bias for "sudaca"*: $c \in CU(\text{sudaca})$ only if, in c, c_a is a participant in register *informal* and a stereotype about South Americans is in force in c

On this view, slurs serve to the end of conventionally characterizing a certain type of context of use, in which a certain hate ideology is in force. Alternatively, we could describe the dual meaning of a given slur in more neutral terms, using Potts's bullet only to separate the LF (i.e., truth-conditional) and PF (i.e., stylistic) meaning of a certain dual expression:

(45) LF: $\lambda x.$ South American(x) • PF: $\lambda p.\ \exists P[P \in C\ \&\ p = [\lambda w.P(^\cap \text{South American})(w)]]$

At any rate, in both cases, and this is what I would like to stress, the particular stereotype that a given slur makes salient is a property of the vocabulary item in the favored sense of this chapter, that is, a property of a form.

To sum up, I have discussed two important empirical properties of slurs: (i) they are in lexical competition with their corresponding neutral counterparts, and (ii) their expressive content can be eliminated by ellipsis. These two properties make slurs analogous to other expressive parts of the lexicon (lexical pairs opposed only in register), for which I have already argued that the best account is that of constructing the expressive content at PF and not at LF. If this analogy turns out to be substantial, we can conclude that the stylistic semantic approach is the best account of slurs, particularly, of how their expressive content is built.

5. CONCLUSION

I have sketched a general project for what I have called "stylistic semantics." The main goal of this research agenda is to offer a PF account of the expressive content of a subset of biased words, in particular, register terms and slurs. I have proposed that this can be done to the extent the PF interface is capable of introducing stylistic meanings in the favored sense. I have conjectured that PSM, repeated in (46), is responsible for generating PF meanings on the basis of semantic vacuity at LF.

(46) *Principle of stylistic meaning (PSM):* Given a pair of abstract nodes X and Y, taken from List 1, if X and Y are not semantically distinguishable at LF (List 3), they are "semantically" distinguished at PF (List 2).

The proposal captures the two basic properties of a certain type of expressive terms, repeated below, and receives robust evidence from ellipsis and *vesre* speech:

(A) In the general case, expressives form doublets: "*sudamericano*"/"*sudaca*" "South American"/"South American (pejorative)," "*comer*"/"*morfar*," "to eat"/"to eat (pejorative)."
(B) One of the members of these pairs contributes to a certain meaning dimension: style, tone, or expressivity.

The hope is that a proper and more explicit formulation of the conjectures I have discussed here will be extended to other empirical domains in the realm of stylistic semantics.

ACKNOWLEDGMENTS

I have presented different versions of this material at the Facultad de Letras y Ciencias Humanas, Pontificia Universidad Católica del Perú (Lima 2019), *Going Romance XXXII*, Utrecht University (Utrecht 2018), the *IV Congreso Internacional de la Sociedad de Filosofía del Uruguay* (Montevideo 2018), the *IV Issues in Contemporary Semantics and Ontology*: *Modals and Evaluatives: Linguistic and Philosophical Perspectives*, SADAF (Buenos Aires 2018), and the *Comparative Syntax Meeting*, Leiden University (Leiden 2017). I am thankful to these audiences for many interesting and fruitful discussions, in particular, to Ramiro Caso, Nicolás Lo Guercio, Anikó Lipták, Eleonora Orlando, Ana Clara Polakoff, Stefano Predelli, Marco Ruffino, and Ludovic Soutif. I am also in debt to Matthew Barros, with whom I have discussed the hypotheses presented here extensively. I am also grateful to the linguistics and philosophy of language team at the Sociedad Argentina de Análisis Filosófico (SADAF): Eduarda Calado, Ramiro Caso, Sofía Checchi, Eduardo García-Ramírez, Federico Jaimes, Justina Díaz-Legaspe, Nicolás Lo Guercio, Alfonso Losada, Laura Skerk, Matías Verdecchia, and, in particular, to Nicolás Lo Guercio and Eduardo García-Ramírez for many comments and suggestions and to Eleonora Orlando for many years of mutual collaboration and friendship.

NOTES

1. Even if I am only mentioning, not using, slurs and coarse language, I apologize in advance for any unintentional offense I might cause to the reader.

2. As Eduardo García-Ramírez (pers. comm.) observes, the set of items in competition may be more than two. For instance, in Argentina the word "homosexual" has more than one slur as expressive counterpart. This is consistent with all what I will say in what follows. On this point, see also Losada (2020).

3. As Eduardo García-Ramírez pointed out me, this seems to be a too strong claim in view of the fact that there are many possible scenarios in which B could endorse the negative evaluation A conveys with respect to the relevant dog in her utterance. This is correct, but I would say that in those scenarios such an endorsement (i) is not a lexical entailment, and, consequently, (ii) only arises in virtue of some pragmatic mechanism.

4. Note that, in principle, (3) could be analyzed as a standard case of Vehicle Change, where the E-sites are modeled as "see it." However, Thoms (2013) provides the following example that seems to rule out such a possibility:

A: You should *fucking* fire that asshole John!
B: I know you think I should, but I won't as I like him.

Here, "fucking" is an adverbial modifier and, as such, it would not allow for Vehicle Change. However, I am not convinced that the answer in (B) cannot be modeled as a special case of Vehicle Change, where the E-site is modeled as "do it." Whatever the right analysis is, this is orthogonal to the main point I am making here.

5. Following Kaplan (1989), I take the character of any expression E as a function from context to content and the content itself as function from circumstances of evaluation to truth values (i.e., to $<s,t>$ objects on some accounts). Standardly, a Kaplanian context is a tuple consisting at least of the following parameters: $<w, t, a, h, l>$, where w is a possible world, t is a time, a is the agent of the utterance, h the hearer, and l the location.

6. This present test is modeled after Lipták (2020), who discusses a different type of putative mismatch in ellipsis. Here is one of her examples:
A: What are you devouring?
B: A pizza, but I am not devouring it.
B: # I am devouring a pizza, but I am not devouring it!

At first glance, this example does not parallel (18), since in Lipták's example one is tempted to conclude that whatever verb one postulates within the E-site (e.g., "ate") it should contribute a different truth-conditional profile from the one contributed by the verb in the antecedent.

7. Of course, (18B) improves if speaker B adds air quotations or other metalinguistic gestures/devices.

8. The same results obtain in other semantic proposals, like Barros and Kotek's (2019) identity condition.
Redundancy reduction:
XP_E may be reduced (elided or deaccented) provided that it has a salient antecedent, XP_A, and $\bigcup [\![XP_E]\!]^f = \bigcup [\![XP_A]\!]^f$ (Barros and Kotek 2019, 4).

And the same with more flexible approaches (Q-equivalence approaches in Barros and Kotek's terms). I use Merchant's condition just because of the influence it had in the last twenty years.

9. Obviously, with nouns in which there is no gender mismatch one can have the illusion that NP-ellipsis allows bias mismatches (Muñoz Pérez, pers. comm.):
A. ¿Fuiste   al   laburo   de   Pedro   hoy?
   went.2SG   to. the   work   of   P.   today
   "Did you go to Juan's work (informal) today?"
B. No,   al   <trabajo>   de   Juan,   pero   no   tolero   cuando
   No,   to.the   work   of   J.   but   not   tolerate.1SG   when
   hablás   tan   informalmente.   Yo   nunca   lo   hago.
   speak.2SG   so   informally   I   never   it   do.1SG
   "No, to John's, but I don't tolerate when you speak informally. I never do it."

10. This is the core thesis of neutral counterpart theories, supported by Anderson and Lepore (2013a,b), Jeshion (2013a,b), Predelli (2013), Whiting (2013), and McCready (2010), among others. For objections to that thesis, see Hom (2008, 2010), Ashwell (2016), and Losada (2020), among others. See also Díaz Legaspe (2018) for insightful considerations in favor of restricting the thesis in the case of some kind of slurs, the so-called normalizing ones. For a general defense of the Identity Thesis, see Caso and Lo Guercio (2016).

11. See Schlenker (2007) for a presuppositional account, and McCready (2010) for a non-presuppositional approach.

12. But see Schlenker (2007) for arguments in favor that expressive presuppositions are not standard presuppositions, and Lo Guercio (2020) for a recent criticism to presuppositional accounts. One interesting point raised by Lo Guercio (pers. comm.) is that pragmatic accounts of expressivity like those defended in Bolinger (2017) or Nunberg (2018) are immune to the this type of criticism. Indeed, they seem to have a good explanation of why ellipsis can block expressive effects.

13. On the relation between register and slurs, see Díaz Legaspe et al. (2020).

BIBLIOGRAPHICAL REFERENCES

Acquaviva, Paolo. 2008. "Roots and Lexicality in Distributed Morphology." Paper given at the *5th York-Essex Morphology Meeting*. ling.auf.net/lingBuzz/000654.

Anderson, Luvell, and Ernie Lepore. 2013a. "Slurring Words." *Noûs* 47(1): 25–48.

Anderson, Luvell, and Ernie Lepore. 2013b. "What Did You Call Me? Slurs As Prohibited Words." *Analytic Philosophy* 54(3): 350–363.

Arregi, Karlos, and Andrew Nevins. 2012. *Morphotactics: Basque Auxiliaries and the Structure of Spellout. Studies in Natural Language and Linguistic Theory*. Berlin: Springer.

Ashwell, Lauren. 2016. "Gendered Slurs." *Social Theory and Practice* 42(2): 228–239.

Barros, Matthew, and Andrés Saab. 2016. "Implicatures from Silence: A Remark on Chung's Puzzle." Ms., Yale University, CONICET-UBA.

Barros, Matthew, and Hadas Kotek. 2019. "Ellipsis Licensing and Redundancy Reduction: A Focus-Based Approach." *Glossa: A Journal of General Linguistics* 4(1): 1–36. https://doi.org/10.5334/gjgl.811.

Bohrn, Andrea. 2019. "Inversión silábica y realización de género y número: el caso del *vesre* rioplatense." *Rasal* 2015: 29–48.

Bolinger, Renee Jörgensen. 2017. "The Pragmatics of Slurs." *Noûs* 51(3): 439–462.

Caso, Ramiro, and Nicolás Lo Guercio. 2016. "What Bigots Do Say: A Reply to DiFranco." *Thought: A Journal of Philosophy* 5(4): 265–274.

Chomsky, Noam. 1965. *Aspects of the Theory of Syntax*. Cambridge, MA: MIT Press.

Chomsky, Noam. 1995. *The Minimalist Program*. Cambridge, MA: MIT Press.

Chomsky, Noam. 2000. "Minimalist Inquiries: The Framework." In *Step by Step: Essays on Minimalist Syntax in Honor of Howard Lasnik*, edited by Roger Martin, David Michaels, and J. Uriagereka, 89–156. Cambridge, MA: MIT Press.

Chomsky, Noam. 2001. "Derivation by Phase." In *Ken Hale: A Life in Language*, edited by Michael Kenstowicz, 1–52. Cambridge, MA: MIT Press.

Chung, Sandra. 2006. "Sluicing and the Lexicon: The Point of No Return." In *Proceedings of the Annual Meeting of the Berkeley Linguistics Society 31*, edited by Rebecca T. Cover and Yuni Kim, 73–91. Berkeley: University of California, Berkeley Linguistics Society.

Díaz Legaspe, Justina. 2018. "Normalizing Slurs and Out-Group Slurs: The Case of Referential Restriction." *Analytic Philosophy* 59(2): 1–22.

Díaz Legaspe, Justina, Chang Liu, and Robert Stainton. 2020. "Slurs and Register: A Case Study in Meaning Pluralism." *Mind and Language* 35(2): 156–182. https://doi.org/10.1111/mila.12236.

Embick, David. 2000. "Features, Syntax, and Categories in the Latin Perfect." *Linguistic Inquiry* 31(2): 185–230.

Embick, David. 2007. "Linearization and Local Dislocation: Derivational Mechanics and Interactions." *Linguistic Analysis* 33(3–4): 2–35.

Embick, David. 2015. *The Morpheme: A Theoretical Introduction*. Berlin: de Gruyter Mouton.

Embick, David, and Rolf Noyer. 2001. "Movement Operations After Syntax." *Linguistic Inquiry* 32: 555–595.
Fiengo, Robert, and Robert May. 1994. *Indices and Identity*. Cambridge, MA: MIT Press.
Frege, Gottlob. 1918/1956. "The Thought: A Logical Inquiry." *Mind* 65: 289–311.
Grice, H. Paul. 1975. "Logic and Conversation." In *Syntax and Semantics: Speech Acts*, edited by Peter Cole and Jerry Morgan, 43–58. New York: Academic Press.
Gutzmann, Daniel. 2015. *Use-Conditional Meaning: Studies in Multidimensional Semantics*. Oxford: Oxford University Press.
Halle, Morris, and Alec Marantz. 1993. "Distributed Morphology and the Pieces of Inflection." In *The View from Building 20*, edited by Ken Hale and Samuel Keyser, 111–176. Cambridge, MA: MIT Press.
Halle, Morris, and Alec Marantz. 1994. "Some Key Features of Distributed Morphology." In *Papers on Phonology and Morphology* (*MITWPL* 21), edited by Andrew Carnie, Heidi Harley, and Tony Bures, 275–288. Cambridge, MA: MIT Press.
Hankamer, Jorge, and Ivan A. Sag. 1976. "Deep and Surface Anaphora." *Linguistic Inquiry* 7: 391–428.
Harley, Heidi. 2014. "On the Identity of Roots." *Theoretical Linguistics* 40: 225–276.
Hom, Christopher. 2008. "The Semantics of Racial Epithets." *The Journal of Philosophy* 105: 416–440.
Hom, Christopher. 2010. "Pejoratives." *Philosophy Compass* 5(2): 164–185.
Jeshion, Robin. 2013a. "Slurs and Stereotypes." *Analytic Philosophy* 54: 314–325.
Jeshion, Robin. 2013b. "Expressivism and the Offensiveness of Slurs." *Philosophical Perspectives* 27: 231–259.
Johnson, Kyle. 2012. "Pronouns vs. Definite Descriptions." In *Generative Linguistics and Acquisition: Studies in Honor of Nina M. Hyams*, edited by Misha Becker, John Grinstead, and Jason Rothman, 157–184. Amsterdam: John Benjamins Publishing Company.
Kaplan, David. 1989. "Demonstratives." In *Themes from Kaplan*, edited by Joseph Almog, John Perry, and Howard Wettstein, 481–563. Oxford: Oxford University Press.
Kaplan, David. 1999. "The Meaning of 'Ouch' and 'Oops': Explorations in the Theory of Meaning As Use." Ms., University of California, Los Angeles.
Lepore, Ernie, and Matthew Stone. 2018. "Pejorative Tone." In *Bad Words: Philosophical Perspectives on Slurs*, edited by David Sosa, 132–154. Oxford: Oxford University Press.
Lipták, Anikó. 2020. "Fragments with Correction." *Linguistic Inquiry* 51(1): 154–167.
Lo Guercio, Nicolás. 2020. "Slurs and Antipresuppositions." Ms., SADAF.
Losada, Alfonso. 2020. "*Sudaca*: Slurs and Typifying." This volume.
Marantz, Alec. 2013. "Locality Domains for Contextual Allomorphy Across the Interfaces." In *Distributed Morphology Today: Morphemes for Morris Halle*, edited by Ora Matushansky and Alec Marantz, 95–116. Cambridge, MA: MIT Press.
McCready, Elin. 2010. "Varieties of Conventional Implicatures." *Semantics and Pragmatics* 3: 1–57.

Merchant, Jason. 2001. *The Syntax of Silence: Sluicing, Islands, and the Theory of Ellipsis*. Oxford: Oxford University Press.
Merchant, Jason. 2004. "Fragments and Ellipsis." *Linguistics and Philosophy* 27: 661–738.
Merchant, Jason. 2010. "Three Kinds of Ellipsis." In *Context-Dependence, Perspective, and Relativity*, edited by François Recanati, Isidora Stojanovic, and Neftali Villanueva, 141–192. Berlin: Walter de Gruyter.
Nunberg, Geoff. 2018. "The Social Life of Slurs." In *New Work on Speech Acts*, edited by Daniel Fogal, Daniel Harris, and Matt Moss, 237–295. Oxford: Oxford University Press.
Orlando, Eleonora, and Andrés Saab. 2020a. "Slurs, Stereotypes and Insults." *Acta Analytica* (Forthcoming). https://doi.org/10.1007/s12136-020-00424-2.
Orlando, Eleonora, and Andrés Saab. 2020b. "A Stereotype Semantics for Syntactically Ambiguous Slurs." *Analytic Philosophy* 61(2): 101–129.
Potts, Christopher. 2005. *The Logic of Conventional Implicature*. Oxford: Oxford University Press.
Potts, Christopher, Ash Asudeh, Seth Cable, and Yurie Hara. 2009. "Expressives and Identity Conditions." *Linguistic Inquiry* 49(2): 356–366.
Predelli, Stefano. 2013. *Meaning Without Truth*. Oxford: Oxford University Press.
Predelli, Stefano. 2020. "Taboo: The Case of Slurs." This volume.
Reinhart, Tanya. 2006. *Interface Strategies: Optimal and Costly Computations*. Cambridge, MA: MIT Press.
Saab, Andrés. 2008. "Hacia una teoría de la identidad parcial en la elipsis." PhD diss., University of Buenos Aires.
Saab, Andrés. 2019. "Nominal Ellipsis." In *The Oxford Handbook of Ellipsis*, edited by Jeroen van Craenenbroeck and Tanja Temmerman, 526–561. Oxford: Oxford University Press.
Schlenker, Philippe. 2007. "Expressive Presuppositions." *Theoretical Linguistics* 33(2): 237–245.
Thoms, Gary. 2013. "Lexical Mismatches in Ellipsis and the Identity Condition." In *Proceedings of North Eastern Linguistic Society*, vol. 42, edited by Stefan Keine and Shayne Sloggett, 559–572. Amherst, MA: CSLI Publications.
Thoms, Gary. 2015. "Syntactic Identity, Parallelism and Accommodated Antecedents." *Lingua* 166: 172–198.
Trubetzkoy, Nikolai. 1939. *Grundzüge der Phonologie*. Prague: Travaux du Cercle Linguistique de Prague.
Whiting, Daniel. 2013. "It's Not What You Said, It's the Way You Said It: Slurs and Conventional Implicatures." *Analytic Philosophy* 54(3): 364–377.

Chapter 3

The Discursive Dimension of Slurs

Nicolás Lo Guercio

1. INTRODUCTION

Slurs are expressions used to derogate a certain group in virtue of the sexual preferences, gender, ethnicity, nationality, religion, and so on of its members.[1,2] In recent years, they have called the attention of linguists and philosophers interested in their semantics and their social and political significance. On the linguistic side, they stir up interest because of their complex semantic behavior. Consider, for example, the following sentence:

(1)   Johann is a Kraut.

Intuitively, (1) conveys two different contents. On the one hand, it predicates the property of being German (contributed by "Kraut") of Johann; on the other hand, it communicates a content that derogates the group denoted, say, "Germans are despicable."[3] A big part of the literature about slurs has focused on the question of *how* these two pieces of information are conveyed, but although almost every possible theoretical option has been proposed and argued for, no strong consensus has been reached on the matter. Everyone agrees that predication of group membership pertains to truth-conditional content, but there are several proposals regarding the way in which slurs derogate their targets. Some take a pragmatic approach. Anderson and Lepore (2013) and Lepore and Stone (2018) maintain that slurs are prohibited words that trigger open-ended psychological processes of analogy and association in virtue of their history and social significance. Bolinger (2017), in turn, claims that derogation emerges from lexical contrastive preferences based on co-occurring expectations on the part of the agents, while Nunberg (2018) maintains that derogation emerges as a conversational implicature resulting from a violation of the Maxim of Manner. By contrast, some favor a semantic account: Hom (2008) and Hom and May (2013) build both components of meaning into truth-conditional content; Macià (2002), Schlenker (2007), and Cepollaro (2015) defend a presuppositional view; Orlando and Saab (2020) propose that slurs are semantically associated with stereotypes in a parallel meaning dimension; finally, McCready (2010), Predelli (2013), and Gutzmann (2015) defend the idea that slurs' derogatory content is conveyed as a conventional implicature, in the sense developed by Potts (2005).

From another perspective, the interest of slurs rests in their social and political significance: as Langton, Haslanger, and Anderson (2012) point out, uses of slurs are instances of *hate speech* in Matsuda's sense (1993, 36), that is, they typically convey a message of inferiority directed against a historically oppressed group and its uses are persecutory, hateful, and degrading.

In this connection, many authors have noted that speech is socially and politically significant, among other reasons, because it often serves to change permissibility facts. This general idea was initially discussed by Lewis (1979a,b). Presuppositions are a common example: if I say to my friend, "My dog is sick," my utterance requires, in order to be felicitous, that it is part of our common ground that I have a dog. Sometimes, however, I can make an utterance even though I am aware that such a requirement is not fulfilled, in order to bring about what the utterance requires. Lewis calls this process "accommodation." So, if I utter, "My dog is sick" in a context in which it is not part of our common ground that I have a dog, but it is assumed that I am being cooperative and the content in question is not too controversial, the hearer will plausibly incorporate the proposition that I have a dog to our common ground so as to turn my utterance felicitous.

In the previous example, no normative commitment was required by the utterance, but it is easy to imagine other examples in which this happens. Consider the case of orders. If accepted, an order generates an obligation. In order to generate such obligation, however, it is required that the speaker has the relevant authority. Now, suppose that the speaker doesn't have authority, but she still starts giving orders to everyone as if she did. Insofar as no one challenges her, she will thereby obtain such authority. Consequently, her orders will impose obligations on the addressees. As Langton (2015) notes, two relevant events take place in this kind of processes: first, a new social fact comes into being via accommodation, namely the fact that the speaker has now the relevant authority to tell others what to do; second, the addressees have obligations they did not have before.

Arguably, hate speech follows a similar pattern: often a conversational move requires that certain social norms be in force, that some members of the community enjoy privileges while others fulfill subordinated roles, and so on.

Inspired by Lewis and others, Langton (2012, 2015), Langton and West (1999), and McGowan (2004, 2018) provide different accounts of the way in which hate speech changes permissibility facts. According to one of these views (Langton 2015), hate speech's presuppositions are incorporated via accommodation, thereby modifying ulterior permissibility facts: if an utterance somehow presupposes that individuals of a certain group are inferior to other members of the society, and this conversational move is accepted by the interlocutors, it has the double effect of granting the speaker the authority to rank individuals of different groups as inferior or superior to others and of adding the required presuppositions to context, thereby habilitating further conversational and non-conversational moves toward such group in the immediate context, for example, disrespecting or offending them, threatening them, attacking them, and so on. This general phenomenon also applies to the case of slurs, as it has been noted by several authors.[4]

Another feature of hate speech is that it is *harmful*. Matsuda, for example, observes that victims of hate speech

> experience physiological symptoms and emotional distress ranging from fear in the gut, rapid pulse rate and difficulty in breathing, nightmares, post-traumatic stress disorder, hypertension, psychosis, and suicide. [. . .] Victims are restricted in their personal freedom. To avoid receiving hate messages, victims have to quit jobs, forgo education, leave their homes, avoid certain public places, curtail their own exercise of speech rights, and otherwise modify their behavior and demeanor. [. . .] As much as one may try to resist a piece of hate propaganda, the effect on one self-esteem and sense of personal security is devastating. (Matsuda 1993, 24)

But not all hate speech is harmful in the same way. According to an influential line of thought initiated by MacKinnon's work on pornography (1987), there is a distinction between speech that *causes* harm, and speech that *constitutes* harm in and of itself. Inspired by MacKinnon, Langton (1993) articulates this difference in terms of the Austinian distinction between the illocutionary act of an utterance and its perlocutionary effects. On this view, hate speech, in addition to performing an illocutionary act, generates certain perlocutionary effects; thus it is harmful in at least two different ways: on the one hand, it has some indirect effects which ultimately cause harm to certain individuals or groups (the perlocutionary act); on the other hand, it has a particular illocutionary force that is harmful in and of itself, to the extent that it reinforces social norms that prescribe harm to certain groups.

Now, what is the illocutionary profile of hate speech, and specifically of speech involving slurs? In this regard, Langton, Haslanger, and Anderson (2012, 758–759) identify at least three different illocutionary forces related to hate speech: (i) propaganda, (ii) attack/assault, and (iii) authoritative subordinating speech. Propaganda is a kind of speech act that incites or promotes hatred and violence toward the target group. Attack uses are directed toward members of the target group as a raw expression of hate and violence. Through authoritative uses of hate speech, speakers enact certain social norms from positions of authority: in these cases, the point is to deprive members of the target group of some of their rights.[5] In addition to these, I will discuss what McCready and Davis (2017) denominate "complicity" uses, cases in which the slur is used among fellow racists, homophobes, and so on in order to share their negative attitudes toward the target group.

A final challenge for a theory of slurs is that of accounting for *reclamation*. This is the phenomenon whereby a slur starts being used by members of the target group without its derogatory import, maybe to reinforce solidarity or comradeship. Two paradigmatic examples are uses of the N-word between African Americans and uses of "*torta*" in Argentina.[6]

The previous discussion makes it clear that a satisfactory theory of slurs must meet at least four challenges.[7] First, it should tell a story about how the derogatory content associated with slurs is conveyed, whether pragmatically or semantically, and by means of which mechanisms. In the following sections, I will advance a conventional implicature view, although I will introduce significant changes with respect to existing proposals in the same vein (cf. McCready 2010). Second, a theory of slurs should give a general explanation of the way in which slurs manage to change permissibility facts. In this regard, however, slurs introduce an additional difficulty with respect to cases of hate speech not involving slurs, since it seems that the explanation cannot be purely pragmatic (as in Langton's or McGowans's accounts) but must be obtained from a complex interaction between their conventional meaning and general pragmatic mechanisms.[8] Third, a theory of slurs must account for their illocutionary profile. In section 3, I will tackle this issue by relying on a linguistically motivated view of dynamic pragmatics. Finally, a satisfactory account must shed light on the phenomenon of reclamation. I will tackle this problem in the last section, although, admittedly, my view does not provide a definitive answer to this question.

2. THE THEORETICAL FRAMEWORK

2.1. Dynamic Pragmatics

Before introducing my view, it is necessary to briefly present the theoretical framework that I assume throughout this chapter. I adopt a dynamic pragmatic approach along the lines of Stalnaker (1999), Portner (2004), and Roberts (2012), among others.⁹ In addition, I assume that classic illocutionary forces can be derived from semantic content, discursive force, and the context of utterance (see Roberts 2018). Roughly put, the view is the following. Clause-types constitute a universal closed system of grammatically defined sentences. There are three universal clause-types: declaratives, interrogatives, and imperatives. Each one is associated with a specific *sentential force* or *discursive function* (Portner 2004; Roberts 2018). On the view I assume, each clause-type determines a traditional semantic object: declaratives express a proposition, interrogatives express a question, that is, a set of propositions, and imperatives express a property.¹⁰ These clause-types and their corresponding semantic contents are linked by default to specific sentential forces or discursive functions, that is, sentential forces are determined only indirectly, on the basis of these meanings (Portner 2004, 236).¹¹

Discursive functions are then understood as particular ways of updating some component of the conversational context, each being an instance of a universal update function schema: "take a set of *x*'s and another *x*, and add the new *x* to the set" (Portner 2004, 238). Declaratives are associated with the function of assertion. An assertion is a proposal to update the common ground (hereinafter CG), that is, the set of propositions commonly accepted by the participants of the exchange for the purposes of the conversation. A question is a proposal to update the question set (hereinafter QS), namely, the set of issues mutually agreed to be in need of resolution in the context. Finally, a request is a proposal to update the to-do list (hereinafter TDL), namely, a set of properties that certain individual is publicly committed to make true of her (the TDL is indexed to specific participants in the conversation, that is, each participant has its own TDL). A declarative has the discursive function of an assertion, an interrogative has the discursive function of a question, and an imperative is linked to the discursive function of a request. Importantly, the correlation between clause-type/semantic-type and discursive function is default and regular but defeasible. For example, the sentence "You will sit down!" is a declarative; hence it expresses a proposition, but it can be used in the right context as a way of updating the TDL instead of the CG.

Finally, I follow Roberts' (2018, 337–338) view,¹² according to which the speech act performed by an utterance can be predicted as a function of the semantics of the constituent uttered, the specific context of utterance and Gricean-like inferences based on intention recognition and general principles for discourse interpretation (relevance, cooperativeness, rationality). A crucial point for the discussion to come, then, is that I assume that the connection between discursive force and a given speech act type is not semantic but pragmatic.

2.2. Imperatives

The proposal that I will defend in the following section evinces some analogies between uses of slurs and the semantics and pragmatics of imperatives. It will be helpful then to prepare the ground by discussing some features of imperatives that will be relevant later.

According to the dynamic approach introduced in the previous subsection, imperative clauses express a property, that is, a content of semantic type $<e, t>$, and their canonical discursive function is that of adding a property to a public TDL indexed to the addressee. More formally, imperatives update the context as follows:

$$C + \phi_{imp} = \langle CG, QS, T\left[addressee / \left(T\left(addressee \right) \cup \{[[\phi_{imp}]]\} \right) \right] \rangle$$

(Portner 2007, 357)

Imperatives are usually assigned a directive discursive force. Directive force is typically thought of as an attempt to generate in the addressee an intention to act in a certain way. So, it is intuitive to treat properties in the TDL as actions that the addressee is committed to take. But this need not be the case. An utterance with directive discursive force might just be an interpellation to the addressee to get her to adopt certain feelings or affective dispositions, for example, "Calm down!," "Don't be angry with me," and so on. Thus, as Portner notes, the TDL contains properties that the addressee is committed to make true of her, without necessarily specifying what actions need to be taken in order to achieve that goal, if any.[13] Now, formally Portner's semantics for imperatives looks like this:

(2) Leave!
(3) $[\![Leave!]\!]^{w^*,c} = [\lambda w.\lambda x: x = addressee(c). x \text{ leaves in } w]$[14]

As for their pragmatics, Portner argues that the CG and the TDL are intimately related. The former plays a role similar to that of the modal base in Kratzer's semantics (2012, ch. 1–2), namely, it provides the background of relevant possible worlds for interpreting the imperative. The latter plays the role of Kratzer's ordering source: the TDL ranks the worlds of the CG according to how many properties of the TDL are true at those worlds. This view has two advantages. First, it helps explaining the different illocutionary forces that can be associated with an imperative, like ordering, inviting, suggesting, advising, requesting, warning, instructing, among others. On Portner's view, there are several TDLs associated with each participant in the conversation, corresponding to the different types of ordering source in Kratzer's semantics for modals: deontic, bouletic, teleological, among others. All the speech acts previously mentioned emerge from the same canonical force, namely, that of adding a property to the TDL, but they differ with respect to the nature of the TDL involved and plausibly other factors of the context of utterance and the speakers' intentions. For example, an order (besides requiring authority on the part of the speaker as a felicity condition) adds a property to the *deontic* TDL associated with the addressee. Once it is accepted, it becomes a public commitment, that is, a new obligation is imposed on the hearer. Then, the worlds of the CG are ranked according to how many properties of her deontic TDL are satisfied in those worlds.

Second, and related to this, this view of imperatives explains their intimate relation to modals. As several authors have noted, the use of an imperative conversationally licenses an utterance of a corresponding modal, and vice versa:

(4) Sit down! (said to Juan)
(5) Juan should sit down. (deontic)
(6) Have a cookie! (said to Mariana)
(7) Mariana should have a cookie. (bouletic)

Portner's view explains this as follows. Imperatives add a property to the addressee's TDL. In light of this, the addressee adopts a commitment to make the property in question true of her. Crucially, this commitment is public and mutually known; hence it impacts on the CG. So, suppose that I give a certain order and it is accepted by the addressee, who thereby acquires a new obligation. Once this commitment is undertaken, the addressee's new obligation becomes part of our common knowledge; hence it is reflected in the CG, which is updated with a corresponding modal proposition stating that the addressee has a such and such new obligation, namely, the proposition that she ought to do such and such thing. Something analogous happens with invitations, suggestions, advices, and so on and the corresponding flavors of modality.

3. A SEMANTIC-PRAGMATIC PROPOSAL

As it was already indicated, there are several proposals concerning the way in which slurs convey a derogatory content. Since a full discussion of all these theoretical alternatives is beyond the scope of a single chapter, my strategy will be to advance my own take on the issue, a particular implementation of the conventional implicature view, and to show how this approach, together with the version of dynamic pragmatics assumed here, can meet the challenges pointed out in the introduction.

Among those who consider that slurs' derogatory content is part of their conventional meaning, the conventional implicature view (McCready 2010) of slurs is usually motivated by their projection pattern as well as by some conceptual considerations. On the one hand, the derogatory content of slurs projects out of common truth-conditional operators, a prima facie problem for truth-conditional accounts (Hom 2008; Hom and May 2013):[15]

(8)   Johann is a Kraut.
(9)   Johann is not a Kraut.
(10) If you invite a Kraut to the party, I will not go.
(11) How many Krauts are there at your work?
(12) I'm not sure, but he might be a Kraut.

The fact that (8)–(12) convey a derogatory content in spite of the slur being under the scope of a truth-conditional operator suggests that the derogatory attitude is not part of the at-issue content. In light of this, one natural move would be to advocate a presuppositional approach. Yet, presuppositional views also face a difficulty: slurs' projection pattern differs from that of typical presuppositions. For example, slurs' derogatory attitude seems to project when embedded in attitude verbs (the so-called plugs):[16]

(13) John thinks that Johann is a Kraut.

There are also some conceptual reasons for advocating a conventional implicature view. Typically, presuppositions are thought to be backgrounded. On von Fintel's (2008) view, for example, presuppositions are contents that must be already present in the CG so that the at-issue content of an utterance is added to the CG and the said utterance is felicitous: for example, the proposition that I have a dog must be already part of the CG if I am to felicitously add to it the proposition that I took my dog to the vet. But this doesn't seem to be true of slurs. Consider again (1). If the derogatory content were presupposed, according to this view, adding the proposition that Germans are despicable (or that the speaker has negative attitudes toward Germans) to the CG would be a requisite for updating it with the proposition that Johann is German. But this doesn't seem to be so: it is by no means necessary to update the CG with a proposition about Germans' moral status or the speaker's attitudes in order to add to it the proposition that Johann is German. Admittedly, a more detailed discussion is needed in order to settle this issue (see McCready 2010), but this seems sufficient at least to motivate exploring the conventional implicature view.[17]

Now, the most developed conventional implicature view that I am aware of is that of McCready (2010) (inspired by Potts 2005).[18] On this approach, a slur, for example, "Kraut," expresses two dimensions of meaning. At the at-issue level it denotes the property of being German; at the non-at-issue level it expresses a proposition, namely, that Germans are bad:

(14) $[\![Kraut]\!] = \lambda x.\text{German}(x): <e, t>^a \blacklozenge \text{Bad}(^\cap \text{Germans}): t^c$

I will adopt the multidimensional semantic system developed by McCready. However, I propose a modification to the lexical entry of slurs. In my view, the non-at-issue content of slurs expresses a property, that is, something of type $<e, t>$, instead of a proposition. As I will argue in what follows, this stipulation is useful in order to account for the way in which uses of slurs may serve to change permissibility facts, as well as for elucidating their illocutionary profile and the way in which this profile is related to their literal meaning.

Thus, in my proposal a slur like "Kraut" has an at-issue dimension that denotes the property of being German, and a non-at-issue dimension that expresses a different property, that of despising Germans:

(15) $[\![Kraut]\!] = \lambda x: \text{German}(x) \blacklozenge \lambda x: \text{despises}(^\cap \text{Germans})(x): <e, t>^a \times <e^s, t^s>$

This modification requires making some adjustments to McCready's system. First, we need to introduce the required semantic type. Let's call the new system L_{CI}^{++} (based on McCready's system L_{CI}^{+}). The type system itself is identical to L_{CI}^{+} (see the Appendix to McCready 2010) except that

  i. If σ and τ are at-issue types for L_{CI}^{++} and ζ and υ are shunting types for L_{CI}^{++} then $<\sigma, \tau> \times <\zeta, \upsilon>$ is a mixed type for L_{CI}^{++}

Second, we need to introduce new rules for interpreting this type. In effect, L_{CI}^{+} rules cannot interpret expressions with the semantic type we are giving to slurs. To see the point, consider McCready's (2010, 20) relevant rules:

(16) $\dfrac{\alpha \blacklozenge \beta: \langle \sigma^a, \tau^a \rangle \langle \sigma^a, \upsilon^s \rangle, \gamma: \sigma^a}{\alpha(\gamma) \blacklozenge \beta(\gamma): \tau^a \times \upsilon^s}$

(17) $\dfrac{\alpha \blacklozenge \beta: \sigma^a \times t^s}{\alpha: \sigma^a \bullet \beta: t^s}$

The first rule interprets a product type in which the input for the at-issue and the non-at-issue contents are of the same semantic type, that is, both take an at-issue argument. The second rule tells you that once you arrive at something propositional at the shunting level you can pass it to the conventional implicature level. So, in McCready's system, we have expressions that encode a property at both dimensions of meaning but both properties take an at-issue argument. Then we have special rules that interpret these cases. It is clear that these rules cannot interpret the semantic type introduced by the system I defend here, whose non-at-issue meaning takes a non-at-issue argument. In order to preserve McCready's rule we could stipulate that the non-at-issue property encoded in slurs takes an at-issue argument. But this move doesn't work. Consider (1) again, repeated here as (18):

(18)   Johann is a Kraut.

$$\frac{\text{Johann: } e^a \quad \lambda x.\text{German}(x) \blacklozenge \lambda x\colon \text{despises}(^\cap\text{Germans})(x)\colon \langle e, t\rangle^a \times \langle e^a, t^s\rangle}{\text{German(Johann)} \blacklozenge \text{despises}(^\cap\text{Germans})(\text{Johann})\colon t^a \times t^s}$$

$$\text{German(Johann)}\colon t^a \bullet \text{despises}(^\cap\text{Germans})(\text{Johann})\colon t^c$$

This derivation gives the wrong result, since we end up with the proposition that Johann despises Germans. So, we need a rule that allows for mixed types in which the input of the at-issue type and the input of the shunting type are of a different semantic type. More specifically, we need a rule that leaves room for a mixed type in which the input to the shunting type is also a shunting type:

(19)
$$\frac{\alpha \blacklozenge \beta \colon \langle \sigma, \tau \rangle^a \times \langle \zeta^s, \upsilon^s \rangle, \gamma \colon \sigma^a}{\alpha(\gamma) \blacklozenge \beta \colon \tau^a \times \langle \zeta^s, \upsilon^s \rangle}$$

This rule provides the desired result:

$$\frac{\text{Johann: } e^a \quad \lambda x.\text{German}(x) \blacklozenge \lambda x\colon \text{despises}(^\cap\text{Germans})(x)\colon \langle e, t\rangle^a \times \langle e^s, t^s\rangle}{\text{German(Johann)} \blacklozenge \lambda x\colon \text{despises}(^\cap\text{Germans})(x)\colon t^a \times \langle e^s, t^s\rangle}$$

On this view, the shunting property never reaches propositional status, so it is never passed to the conventional implicature level. This solves the previous problem but leads to a new one, related to the tree-interpretation rule of the system. The problem is that, as stated in L_{CI}^+, the tree-interpretation rule collects only *propositional* non-at-issue contents:

Generalized interpretation (L_{CI}^+)
Let Π be a proof-tree with at-issue term $\alpha\colon\sigma^a$ on its root node and distinct terms $\beta_1\colon t^{\{c,s\}}, \ldots, \beta_n\colon t^{\{c,s\}}$ on nodes in it. Then the interpretation of Π is $<[\![\alpha\colon\sigma^a]\!], \{\,[\![\beta_1\colon t^{\{c,s\}}]\!], \ldots, [\![\beta_n\colon t^{\{c,s\}}]\!]\,\}>$.

Let Π be a proof-tree with at-issue term $\alpha{:}\sigma^{\{c,s\}}$ on its root node and distinct terms $\beta_1{:}t^{\{c,s\}}, \ldots, \beta_n{:}t^{\{c,s\}}$ on nodes in it. Then the interpretation of Π is <T, $[\![\alpha{:}\sigma^{\{c,s\}}]\!]$, { $[\![\beta_1{:}t^{\{c,s\}}]\!], \ldots, [\![\beta_n{:}t^{\{c,s\}}]\!]$ }>.[19]

(McCready 2010, 32)

We need to make another amendment to the system. What we do is modify the interpretation-tree rule in order to take into account shunting properties that survive as properties during the derivation:

Generalized interpretation (L_{CI}^{++})
Let Π be a proof-tree with at-issue term $\alpha{:}\sigma^a$ on its root node and distinct terms $\beta_1{:}t^{\{c,s\}}, \ldots, \beta_n{:}t^{\{c,s\}}$, and $\gamma_1{:}<e, t>^{\{c,s\}}, \ldots, \gamma_n{:}<e, t>^{\{c,s\}}$ on nodes in it. Then the interpretation of Π is <$[\![\alpha{:}\sigma^a]\!]$, { $[\![\beta_1{:}t^{\{c,s\}}]\!], \ldots, [\![\beta_n{:}t^{\{c,s\}}]\!]$ }, { $[\![\gamma_1{:}<e, t>^{\{c,s\}}]\!], \ldots, [\![\gamma_n{:}<e, t>^{\{c,s\}}]\!]$ }>.
Let Π be a proof-tree with at-issue term $\alpha{:}\sigma^{\{c,s\}}$ on its root node and distinct terms $\beta_1{:}t^{\{c,s\}}, \ldots, \beta_n{:}t^{\{c,s\}}$, and $\gamma_1{:}<e, t>^{\{c,s\}}, \ldots, \gamma_n{:}<e, t>^{\{c,s\}}$ on nodes in it. Then the interpretation of Π is <T, $[\![\alpha{:}\sigma^{\{c,s\}}]\!]$, { $[\![\beta_1{:}t^{\{c,s\}}]\!], \ldots, [\![\beta_n{:}t^{\{c,s\}}]\!]$ }, { $[\![\gamma_1{:}<e, t>^{\{s\}}]\!], \ldots, [\![\gamma_n{:}<e, t>^{\{s\}}]\!]$ }>.

This rule has the desired effect: it collects all the at-issue contents, all the propositional non-at-issue contents and all the non-propositional non-at-issue contents.

The proposed semantics goes in parallel with a certain pragmatic/conversational dynamics. Recall that I am assuming a view on which semantic types trigger by default a certain discursive function, understood as an update function on a component of context. In my account, a use of a slur like in "Johann is a Kraut" updates two different components of the context, each corresponding to one of its meaning dimensions. At the at-issue level the sentence expresses the proposition that Johann is German. Canonically, a declarative has the discursive force of assertion, so an utterance of "Johann is a Kraut" updates the CG with the proposition that Johann is German. At the non-at-issue level the sentence expresses a property. Consequently, it has the default discursive function of updating the TDL. But who's TDL? In contrast with imperatives, slurs carry no presupposition in this respect. Thus, which participant's TDL is updated (that of the speaker or the addressee, or both) and what kind of TDL is updated (deontic, bouletic, teleological) is in principle open and context-dependent. By default, then, an accepted use of "Kraut" publicly commits some participants in the conversation (determined by context) to make the property in question (despising Germans) true of them. As we saw for the case of imperatives, the updating of the TDL does not necessarily constitute a commitment to perform a determinate action. In the case of slurs it works as an interpellation: the aim is to get the addressee to have certain attitudes or affective dispositions toward the target group. To be sure, it is reasonable to assume that in many cases these attitudes will lead to further actions, but this is not necessary. The updated TDL then ranks the worlds in the CG accordingly: it places all those worlds in which Germans are despised higher in the ranking. Most importantly, since this commitment is mutually known, the CG is also updated with a corresponding modal proposition, namely that Germans should be despised or that Germans are despicable.[20]

The view defended here bears some resemblance with the already discussed semantics and pragmatics of imperatives. My contention is that uses of slurs have, by default, a *directive point:* they encourage certain attitudes, feelings, and emotions that promote hate and violence. This is a consequence of the interaction between their semantic content (the property they express at the non-at-issue level) and the dynamics of conversation. This approach, I will argue, has several advantages.

The proposal entails that some uses of slurs involve somehow a modal element in their interpretation, and this explains how slurs change permissibility facts in a way that acknowledges an important role in their conventional meaning. The idea that there is a modal element involved in some uses of slurs is explicit in Hom and May's view (2013) and it is implicit in other positions, for example, Langton, Haslanger, and Anderson's view (2012) that uses of slurs serve to subordinate its targets, or Swanson (forthcoming) claims that slurs display acceptability implicatures. Moreover, intuitively it seems that the discomfort we feel in the presence of slurs cannot be fully explained if we take these expressions to be merely indicative of the presence of some morally reprehensible beliefs on the speaker's part. Frequently, when presented with an occurrence of a slur we feel the need to clarify that we do not share the speaker's view about the target group. The present proposal captures this intuition by claiming that uses of slurs advocate a viewpoint on which members of the target group should be despised for being inferior to other individuals in the community.

Another reason for recognizing a modal element in the interpretation of slurs is that they license further modal conversational moves, in analogy with what we saw for the case of imperatives:

(20)   a. Johann is a Kraut.
       b. Germans are despicable.
(21)   a. My office is full of spics.
       b. Latinos ought to be despised.[21]

Now, in contrast with Hom and May's view (2013), my proposal is that the modal element is accommodated pragmatically. However, the mechanism by means of which this occurs is different from other proposals (e.g., Langton's or McGowan's). Slurs express properties, so by default they have the discursive function of updating some of the participants' TDLs. In other words, uses of slurs (if accepted) *publicly commit some of the participants in the conversation to make some properties true of them.* The updated TDL then ranks the worlds in the CG according to these commitments: the best worlds are those in which the target group is despised. But updates in the TDLs are public and manifest, so they impact on the CG: a modal proposition is then added to the CG, namely that Ns should be despised, where N denotes the relevant target group. In this way, this account explains how slurs *change permissibility facts* by appealing to their semantic content and the dynamics of conversation: in virtue of their default discursive force, these expressions end up having *an impact on the modal statements present in CG*, thus *modifying the set of norms commonly accepted by the participants in the conversation*. Crucially, if these local enactments of norms in specific conversations become sufficiently widespread and regular they will significantly contribute to the eventual emergence of a global norm within the community according to which members of the target group ought to be despised.

At this point, it is worth pausing to mention two important differences between my view so far and that of Kirk-Giannini (2019).[22] First, according to my account, which TDL is updated by an utterance containing a slur is variable and depends on the context. It could be the TDL of the addressee, that of both the addressee and the speaker, or none. On Kirk-Giannini's view, in turn, everybody's TDLs is updated. Second, on my account, the flavor of the directive speech act triggered by the non-at-issue content of slurs remains open and contextually variable. Sometimes it might be deontic, other times bouletic, and so on. Kirk-Giannini, in turn, argues that the directive content associated with slurs instructs everyone in the conversation to adopt a determinate perspective on the target group. Following Camp (2013), he treats perspectives as ways of cognizing the targeted group. On his account, perspectives determine dispositions to structure and organize information as well as deem certain emotions as appropriate, among other things. In other words, on Kirk-Giannini's view, the directive content instructs everybody to adopt a certain cognitive stance toward the target group (the best one, according to the speaker).

I already presented a semantic/pragmatic theory of slurs and I showed how it accounts for the way in which these expressions manage to modify permissibility facts. My proposal is also well equipped to account for the different illocutionary forces associated with slurs. I already pointed out that slurs possess at least three illocutionary forces: propaganda, complicity, and attack. And there are also reclaimed uses, which do not exhibit either of these illocutionary forces. Let's see how the proposal deals with these issues.

According to my view, illocutionary forces are derived from semantic content, the context of utterance and pragmatic inferences based on intention recognition and general principles of relevance, rationality, and the like. Now, following McCready and Davis (2017), I will assume that the main factor in determining the intention behind the use of a slur is whether the speaker and the hearer are part of the target group. With this in mind, let's analyze different alternatives.

One possible case is that in which neither the speaker nor the hearer is a member of the target group. These situations contain two scenarios: the hearer might be a well-known racist, homophobic, and so on, or just a prospective one.[23] Ultimately, the point of these uses is that of creating or reinforcing certain norms and negative affective dispositions toward the target group. In both cases the basic discursive force is the same; the content of the slur triggers a directive discursive force by default, that is, it updates the participants' TDLs. However, in each case the context favors different interpretations. The most natural interpretation of the latter case is as an exhortation to the addressee: the use serves as an incitement to racism, homophobia, and so on. The directive discursive force of the conversational move, plus the fact that the addressee does not previously share the speaker's commitments with respect to the target group, suffices for stabilizing a *propaganda* interpretation of the utterance.

In the former case, that in which the hearer is a well-known racist, the most natural reading is that of complicity (McCready and Davis 2017, 4–5), that is, the use works as a kind of invitation to share a prejudiced view. But, what is the point of complicity uses? After all, the default discursive force of slurs is that of adding some property to the participants' TDL, and in these cases the property in question (despising members of the target group) is already in the TDLs of both the speaker and the addressee. There are two possibilities. In some of these cases, the point is to add the fact that the speaker and the addressee share a prejudiced view of the CG. Even if both speaker and addressee are racist and each knows that the other is racist, this doesn't mean that it is CG that they are racists. Some complicity uses seek to make this commitment common ground by making these facts explicit. There are other cases, however, in which it is already part of the CG that both speaker and addressee despise members of the target group. In these cases, the point of complicity uses is to maintain the CG that way. Plausibly, some propositions can disappear from the CG in different stages of a conversation, not only because they are explicitly rejected but because they slowly fade out; they are not salient or relevant in the conversation anymore. Insisting with the use of a slur, although it can be somewhat redundant, prevents this; it is a way of guaranteeing that the prejudiced attitudes remain active in the conversation.

Now, in both cases (if the use is accepted) both the speaker's and the addressee's TDLs get updated with the relevant property (despising the target group). As already mentioned, although the update is redundant in the latter case, it serves a conversational function, that is, keeping in force a shared view on the targeted group, with the normative consequences above-mentioned.

Let's consider attack uses now. At first glance, these uses are problematic for my view. Attack uses are mere expressions of hate toward the target group. However, according to the semantic/pragmatic proposal that I am defending, slurs have some kind of directive point by default, that is, their discursive force is that of trying to get others to adopt certain attitudes or affective dispositions toward the target group. How can the theory explain assault uses, then? I claim that these cases are similar to expressive readings of imperatives. If an imperative is uttered in a context in which it is CG that the addressee is not able to carry out the actions required to make the property in question true or, alternatively, it is part of the CG that it is very unlikely that she is willing to make the property in question true, the imperative often receives an expressive reading. Consider (22):

(22) Enjoy the movie!

Something similar occurs, I claim, in attack uses of slurs. The key point is that in these cases the speaker is not a member of the target group, but the addressee is, so plausibly it is part of the CG that it is highly improbable that the latter will form the intention to despise her own group (although this could happen in some very rare cases). Given this assumption the utterance receives a different, expressive interpretation. Since the speaker is employing an expression that encodes a derogatory content toward the addressee's group, it is only reasonable that, once the directive discursive force is discarded for pragmatic reasons, the act is interpreted as an attack. Finally, since the attack speech act is manifest, it impacts on the CG, which is updated with some implicated propositions, as the proposition that the speaker despises the members of the target group.

Finally, variability with respect to membership of speaker and hearer in the target group helps explaining reclaimed uses. In these uses, as in attack examples, the directive force is blocked: since the addressee is a member of the target group there is no expectation that she will add the required property to her TDL. If what I have claimed in the previous paragraph is correct, this licenses an expressive interpretation. However, the attack interpretation is also typically cancelled in this case: being a member of the target group, it is implausible that the speaker is insulting the addressee because of her belonging to the relevant group. These facts, plus further contextual information concerning the social history of the words, license the use of the slur as an expression of solidarity or camaraderie.

Here, again, it is worth commenting on Kirk-Giannini's position. He motivates his account by arguing against speaker-oriented expressivism about slurs (cf. Jeshion 2013), that is, the view that slurs' primary function is to express a negative mental state of the speaker (it might be a belief or a different kind of attitude). Roughly speaking, he maintains that expressivism has two problems: first, it fails to account for the fact that utterances that convey the same information as an utterance involving slurs lack the correspondent derogatory potential; second, speaker-oriented expressivism fails to account for the fact that uses of slurs are offensive even in contexts in which the attitudes of the speaker are already known. My view deals with these two problems in a similar way. The former is taken care of by the fact that slurs have a directive discursive force, so they are not only a means of expressing information about the mental states of the speaker. Concerning the latter, I argued that in some cases (attack and reclaimed uses) slurs serve as mere ways of expressing an attitude of the speaker. However, if my view is correct, they do this in a way that avoids the problems that Kirk-Giannini observes for speaker-oriented expressivist accounts. More precisely, they do this only in some contexts and the content in question is expressed pragmatically, and not encoded in the conventional meaning. In fact, some of these uses are challenging for Kirk-Giannini's view: on his proposal, uses of slurs are always directives to adopt a certain cognitive perspective toward the targeted group. However, there seem to be some uses of slurs against members of oppressed groups that look more like pure insults, raw expressions of hate and anger, and not like directives to such individuals to cognize themselves differently (e.g., "F--- you, you f---ing N!").

4. CONCLUSION

I have argued that slurs have two dimensions of meaning, an at-issue dimension that encodes a descriptive property denoting the relevant group, and a non-at-issue one that encodes the property of despising the target group. Thus, a complete sentence containing a slur expresses two contents: at the at-issue level, a proposition that predicates group membership of the subject; at the non-at-issue level, the property of despising the target group. Within an independently motivated view of dynamic pragmatics, it follows that sentences containing slurs have two different discursive functions by default, that is, they update two different components of the context. On the one hand, they update the CG; on the other hand, they update the TDL, that is, the set properties that a certain participant in the conversation is publicly committed to making true of her in the context. This means that slurs possess at some level a directive discursive force by default, that is, they are specially fitted for attempting to make people adopt certain attitudes.

The proposal has several advantages. First, it provides a pragmatic account of the way in which slurs serve to change permissibility facts by showing how they might have a modal impact on the CG. Moreover, it manages to do that by giving the semantic content of those expressions a key role in the process. Second, it explains the illocutionary profile of slurs: propaganda and complicity uses exploit the directive discursive force of slurs with different purposes, exhorting the addressee to despise the target group in the former case, making it CG that there is such a commitment, or keeping it that way, in the latter. The view also sheds light on attack and reclaimed uses. In these cases, the directive discursive force is typically blocked in virtue of features of the context having to do with the belonging (or not) of the speaker and addressee to the target group, thus receiving an expressive interpretation of a different kind in each case.

Let me end the chapter by briefly discussing the distinction between speech that *causes harm* and speech that *constitutes harm* in and of itself. As I pointed out in the introduction, a given speech constitutes harm in and of itself insofar as it creates or reinforces social norms that prescribe harm, while it merely causes harm when the harmful consequences of the speech act are just an indirect result thereof. The proposal I defended seems compatible with this distinction. On the one hand, consider propaganda uses. In my view, these uses instantiate the default directive discursive force of slurs. Hence, they change permissibility facts (in a defeasible way) in virtue of their semantic content and the way in which they update context. Put differently, they have a normative impact on the conversational record, licensing in this way further conversational and non-conversational moves. Although the immediate effect of this process is local and circumscribed to the conversation, it is plausible that global social norms depend in part on these local enactments. So, on my account, at least some uses of slurs often serve to create or reinforce social norms which prescribe harm toward certain individuals and groups by virtue of their default discursive force. But that is to say that at least some uses of slurs *constitute* harm.

Attack uses are different. In those cases, the default directive force of slurs is typically blocked by contextual considerations, so the speech act ends up with a merely expressive function. It is clear that these uses are harmful, but it seems that the way in which they are is different from propaganda uses. Probably the speaker's expression of hate toward the target group ends up moving others to hate and violence. For example, attack speech acts might be used by highly admired individuals or persons who enjoy special moral authority within the community, and this might lead others to imitate them.

But this mechanism of dissemination of hate does not depend on the linguistic features of the speech act: they can be considered perlocutionary effects of the utterance. If this is correct, then attack uses do not constitute harm but merely *cause* it.

ACKNOWLEDGMENTS

I want to thank specially Eleonora Orlando and Andrés Saab for their helpful objections, comments, and suggestions. They have been a great support in my academic life. The chapter greatly benefited from discussion with the members of the BA-LingPhil group in Buenos Aires: Ramiro Caso, Matías Verdecchia, Sofía Checchi, Eduarda Calado, Eduardo García-Ramirez, Federico Jaimes, and Laura Skerk, to whom I am thankful. I must also express my gratitude to the audiences of the III workshop CLE-SADAF held in Buenos Aires in 2019, and the work in progress seminar of the BA-Logic group. After submitting this chapter it came to my knowledge the work of Kirk-Giannini (2019), who recently published a paper defending very similar ideas to the ones I pursue here. I want to thank Kirk-Giannini for helpful comments and for pointing out to some interesting differences between our accounts.

NOTES

1. Throughout the chapter I will discuss examples that contain slurs. Although I tried to keep these to a minimum, and they are only mentioned and not used, I want to make it clear that they serve academic purposes only. I do not share any of the attitudes commonly associated with them.

2. I will assume that slurs have "neutral counterparts," that is, synonymous expressions that lack derogatory content. The claim has been criticized by Hom (2008), Ashwell (2016), and DiFranco (2015), among others. See Caso and Lo Guercio (2016) for a defense of the neutral counterpart thesis against some of these objections.

3. We must distinguish here derogation from offense (Hom 2012). Derogation is an objective feature of the utterance, while offense is a possible subjective/psychological effect. See Orlando and Saab (2020) for a further defense of this distinction.

4. Swanson (forthcoming) maintains that slurs trigger acceptability implicatures, namely, implicatures about what is acceptable in some relevant sense (socially, legally, conversationally, etc.). In the same vein, Kukla (2018) argues that slurs serve to create, but also to enact/reinforce ideologies, understood (very roughly) as a set of social norms, roles, and identities.

5. Authoritative subordinating speech is hate speech that is made from a position of authority, for example, a white Pretorian legislator that utters "Blacks are not

permitted to vote" during the apartheid (Langton 1993, 302). See Maitra (2012) for discussion. I will not discuss these uses in detail in this article.

6. "*Torta*" is a common Argentinian slur for lesbians.

7. Admittedly, the following list does not exhaust the problems a theory of slurs must solve. One problem I will not discuss, for example, is that of accounting for the expressive gradation of slurs, that is, the fact that some slurs are stronger than others.

8. For reasons of space, I cannot discuss Bolinger's and Nunberg's purely pragmatic accounts here. See Cepollaro (2017) for objections to these approaches.

9. There are different implementations of this approach. I follow mostly Portner's view.

10. See Kaufmann (2011) for an alternative view, according to which imperatives express a modal proposition.

11. We assume what Portner (2018, 153–157) denominates "the compositional approach."

12. I do not adopt Roberts' specific proposal for imperatives, only her idea that one can derive speech act types from discourse function and the context of utterance.

13. See Portner (2007, fn. 2).

14. Here the condition that the property be true of the addressee is included as a presupposition. The imperative denotes then a partial function that returns neither true nor false if the individual is not the addressee.

15. Hom (2008) and Hom and May (2013) are perfectly aware of this apparent problem. They attempt to deal with it (i) by distinguishing between offense and derogation, and (ii) by relativizing the problem in virtue of a series of alleged non-projective, non-reclaimed uses of slurs. See Sennet and Copp (2015) and Cepollaro and Thommen (2019) for discussion of other problems with Hom and May's truth-conditional view.

16. Although see Caso (2020) for discussion on this topic. See also Macià (2002), Schlenker (2007) and Cepollaro (2015) for defenses of the presuppositional view. See Lo Guercio (2020) for an argument against presuppositional views based on the idea of anti-presupposition.

17. See also Saab (2020) for an argument against the pressupositional view.

18. See also Gutzmann (2015). See Hom (2008) and Hom and May (2013) for a critique of the conventional implicature view. See also Kratzer (1999) and Anand (2007) for some alleged counter-examples.

19. The second part of the rule is there to take care of cases in which there is no at-issue content involved.

20. Two important points must be clarified. First, the view is neutral with respect to the conditions under which a use of a slur counts as "accepted." Plausibly, this is a highly contextual matter: in some contexts, lack of verbal rejection could count as acceptance, but in other contexts an awkward silence might be sufficient for rejection. Second, the "acceptance" in question is acceptance *for the purposes of conversation*; it does not necessarily mean that the subject morally agrees with the user of the slur. Although accepting a use of a slur, even for the purposes of conversation, might be morally impermissible, this need not be the case: there could be contexts in which explicitly rejecting the use of the slur is not morally mandatory, for example, if rejection puts the life or the physical integrity of the individual or others in risk (to choose the most dramatic example).

21. That the modal is conversationally licensed can be further motivated by noticing the oddness of a sentence like "Spics should not be despised."

22. Stanley (2015, ch. 4) also proposes a view that directly links the semantics of imperatives to that of subordinating speech, including pejoratives. However, he does not present an explicit semantics for slurs.

23. I am assuming that the use is sincere, that is, that the speaker is a bigot.

BIBLIOGRAPHICAL REFERENCES

Anand, Pranav. 2007. "Re-expressing Judgment." *Theoretical Linguistics* 33(2): 199–208.

Anderson, Luvell, and Ernest Lepore. 2013. "Slurring Words." *Noûs* 47(1): 25–48.

Ashwell, Lauren. 2016. "Gendered Slurs." *Social Theory and Practice* 42(2): 228–239.

Bolinger, Renee Jörgensen. 2017. "The Pragmatics of Slurs." *Noûs* 51(3): 439–462.

Camp, Elizabeth. 2013. "Slurring Perspectives." *Analytic Philosophy* 54(3): 330–349.

Caso, Ramiro. 2020. "A Bidimensional Accounts of Surs." This volume.

Caso, Ramiro, and Nicolás Lo Guercio. 2016. "What Bigots Do Say: A Reply to DiFranco." *Thought: A Journal of Philosophy* 5(4): 265–274.

Cepollaro, Bianca. 2015. "In Defense of a Presuppositional Account of Slurs." *Language Sciences* 52: 36–45.

Cepollaro, Bianca. 2017. "The Semantics and Pragmatics of Slurs and Thick Terms." PhD dissertation. https://tel.archives-ouvertes.fr/tel-01508856/document.

Cepollaro, Bianca, and Tristan Thommen. 2019. "What's Wrong with Truth-Conditional Accounts of Slurs?" *Linguistics and Philosophy* 42(4): 333–347.

DiFranco, Ralph. 2015. "Do Racists Speak Truly? On the Truth-Conditional Content of Slurs." *Thought: A Journal of Philosophy* 4(1): 28–37.

Gutzmann, Daniel. 2015. *Use-Conditional Meaning*. Oxford: Oxford University Press.

Hom, Christopher. 2008. "The Semantics of Racial Epithets." *Journal of Philosophy* 105(8): 416–440.

Hom, Christopher. 2012. "A Puzzle About Pejoratives." *Philosophical Studies* 159(3): 383–405.

Hom, Christopher, and Robert May. 2013. "Moral and Semantic Innocence." *Analytic Philosophy* 54: 293–313.

Jeshion, Robin. 2013. "Expressivism and the Offensiveness of Slurs." *Philosophical Perspectives* 27: 232–259.

Kaufmann, Magdalena. 2011. *Interpreting Imperatives*. Dordrecht: Springer Science & Business Media.

Kirk-Giannini, Cameron Dominico. 2019. "Slurs Are Directive." *Philosophers' Imprint* 19(48): 1–28.

Kratzer, Angelika. 1999. "Beyond 'Ouch' and 'Oops': How Descriptive and Expressive Meaning Interact." Handout for *Cornell Conference on Theories of Context Dependency*, Amherst.

Kratzer, Angelika. 2012. *Modals and Conditionals*. Oxford: Oxford University Press.
Kukla, Rebecca. 2018. "Slurs, Interpellation, and Ideology." *The Southern Journal of Philosophy* 56: 7–32.
Langton, Rae. 1993. "Speech Acts and Unspeakable Acts." *Philosophy & Public Affairs* 22(4): 293–330.
Langton, Rae. 2012. "Beyond Belief: Pragmatics in Hate Speech and Pornography." In *Speech and Harm: Controversies Over Free Speech*, edited by Ishani Maitra and Mary Kate McGowan, 72–93. Oxford: Oxford University Press.
Langton, Rae. 2015. "How to Get a Norm from a Speech Act." *The Amherst Lecture in Philosophy* 10: 1–33.
Langton, Rae, and Caroline West. 1999. "Scorekeeping in a Pornographic Language Game." *Australasian Journal of Philosophy* 77(3): 303–319.
Langton, Rae, Sally Haslanger, and Luvell Anderson. 2012. "Language and Race." In *Routledge Companion to Philosophy of Language*, edited by Gillian Russell and Delia Graff Fara, 753–767. Dordrecht: Routledge.
Lepore, Ernest, and Mathew Stone. 2018. "Pejorative Tone." In *Bad Words: Philosophical Perspectives on Slurs*, edited by David Sosa, 132–154. Oxford: Oxford University Press.
Lewis, David Kellog. 1979a. "Scorekeeping in a Language Game." *Journal of Philosophical Logic* 8(1): 339–359.
Lewis, David Kellog. 1979b. "A Problem About Permission." In *Essays in Honour of Jaakko Hintikka*, edited by Esa Saarinen, Risto Hilpinen, Ikka Niiniluoto, and Merrill Provence Hintikka, 163–175. Dordrecht: Reidel.
Lo Guercio, Nicolás. 2020. "Slurs and Antipresuppositions." Ms., SADAF. https://semanticsarchive.net/Archive/DE0ODk4M/SlursandAntiPresuppositions.pdf.
Macià, Josep. 2002. "Presuposición y significado expresivo." *Theoria* 17(3): 499–513.
MacKinnon, Catherine Alice. 1987. *Feminism Unmodified: Discourses on Life and Law*. Cambridge, MA: Harvard University Press.
Maitra, Ishani. 2012. "Subordinating Speech." In *Speech and Harm: Controversies Over Free Speech*, edited by Ishani Maitra and Mary Kate McGowan, 94–120. Oxford: Oxford University Press.
Matsuda, Mari. 2018. "Public Response to Racist Speech: Considering the Victim's Story." In Words *That Wound: Critical Race Theory, Assaultive Speech, and the First Amendment*, edited by Mary Matsuda, 17–51. Boulder, CO: Westview Press.
McCready, Elin. 2010. "Varieties of Conventional Implicature." *Semantics and Pragmatics* 3: 1–57.
McCready, Elin, and Christopher Davis. 2017. "An Invocational Theory of Slurs." *Proceedings of LENLS14*. https://semanticsarchive.net/Archive/TdmNjdiM/mccready-davis-LENLS14.pdf
McGowan, Mary Kate. 2004. "Conversational Exercitives: Something Else We Do with Our Words." *Linguistics and Philosophy* 27(1): 93–111.
McGowan, Mary K. 2018. "On Covert Exercitives." In *New Work on Speech Acts*, edited by Daniel Fogal, Daniel Harris, and Matt Moss, 185–201. Oxford: Oxford University Press.

Nunberg, Geoffrey. 2018. "The Social Life of Slurs." In *New Work on Speech Acts*, edited by Daniel Harris, Daniel Fogal, and Matt Moss, 237–295. Oxford: Oxford University Press.

Orlando, Eleonora, and Andrés Saab. 2020. "Slurs, Stereotypes and Insults." *Acta Analytica*. https://doi.org/10.1007/s12136-020-00424-2.

Portner, Paul. 2004. "The Semantics of Imperatives Within a Theory of Clause Types." In *Proceedings of Semantics and Linguistic Theory 14*, edited by K. Watanabe and R. B. Young, 235–252. Ithaca, NY: CLC Publications, Cornell University Linguistics Department.

Portner, Paul. 2007. "Imperatives and Modals." *Natural Language Semantics* 15(4): 351–383.

Potts, Christopher. 2005. *The Logic of Conventional Implicatures*. Oxford: Oxford University Press.

Predelli, Stefano. 2013. *Meaning Without Truth*. Oxford: Oxford University Press.

Roberts, Craige. 2012. "Information Structure: Towards an Integrated Formal Theory of Pragmatics." *Semantics and Pragmatics* 5: 1–69.

Roberts, Craige. 2018. "Speech Acts in Discourse Context." In *New Work on Speech Acts*, edited by Daniel Harris, Daniel Fogal, and Matt Moss, 317–359. Oxford: Oxford University Press.

Saab, Andrés. 2020. "On the Locus of Expressivity: Deriving Parallel Meaning Dimensions from Architectural Considerations." This volume.

Schlenker, Philippe. 2007. "Expressive Presuppositions." *Theoretical Linguistics* 33(2): 237–245.

Sennet, Adam, and David Copp. 2015. "What Kind of a Mistake is It to Use a Slur?" *Philosophical Studies* 172(4): 1079–1104.

Stalnaker, Robert Culp. 1999. *Context and Content: Essays on Intentionality in Speech and Thought*. Oxford: Oxford University Press.

Stanley, Jason. 2015. *How Propaganda Works*. New Jersey: Princeton University Press.

Swanson, Eric. Forthcoming. "Slurs and Ideologies." In *A Volume on Ideology*, edited by Robin Celikates. Oxford: Oxford University Press.

von Fintel, Kai. 2008. "What Is Presupposition Accommodation, Again?" *Philosophical Perspectives* 22(1): 137–170.

Chapter 4

A Bidimensional Account of Slurs

Ramiro Caso

1. INTRODUCTION

In this chapter I propose an account of slurs according to which they have both a truth-conditional semantic dimension and a non-truth-conditional one. I will work within the two-dimensional, use-conditional semantic framework developed by Gutzmann (2015), where the non-truth-conditional dimension is modeled in terms of restrictions placed on context by felicity conditions. Following an insight by Kirk-Giannini (2019) and Lo Guercio (2020), I take it that the semantic type of a slur's non-truth-conditional dimension is a property, or more properly a particular kind of *de se* proposition. My account, however, differs from theirs in both technical implementation and substantial issues and has an independent justification.

A methodological remark is in order. I will be paying attention to the interpretation of slurs in Rioplatense Spanish as spoken in Buenos Aires, as well as more customary examples, coming from American English (AE). While most literature on slurs is focused almost exclusively on AE slurs and AE speaking communities, it will prove instructive to pay attention to the interpretation of slurs in Rioplatense Spanish, as being sensitive to data collected from other languages and linguistic communities may help us in better understanding which aspects of the use of slurs are genuinely semantic, and which ones are pragmatic or sociological in nature.[1] Thus, a minor dialectical contention of this chapter is that prohibitionism (understood as the social practice of prohibiting the use of slurs) may obscure data concerning the proper semantic account of slurs.

The plan is as follows. First, I introduce slurs and review some well-known facts concerning their projection behavior. Then, I deploy the semantic framework to be used throughout the discussion, a subsystem of Gutzmann's (2015) bidimensional logic $\mathscr{L}_{TU}$, and I show how slurs are captured. After that, some data points concerning projection in Rioplatense Spanish are reviewed. In particular, I focus on an apparent *de dicto/de re* effect concerning attitude ascription, pointing out that, in this variety of Spanish, indirect speech reports are systematically ambiguous between speaker-oriented and ascribee-oriented attributions of the derogatory attitude connected with the use of a slur. I use embedded questions in order to show that this ambiguity is only a pseudo-*de dicto/de re* effect. Then, I put forward the main contribution of the chapter, the idea that a slur's non-truth-conditional semantic dimension consists in a specific kind of *de se* proposition that, by a defeasible pragmatic default, is generally ascribed to the speaker.

2. SLURS AND SCOPING OUT

Slurs are expressions systematically used to derogate and/or express negative attitudes toward (the members of) certain groups purely on the basis of being (members of) those groups. The groups in question may be based on social criteria ("trailer trash," "redneck"), ethnicity ("chink," "spic"), religion ("kike"), nationality ("wop," "spic"), political ideology ("libtard," "repugnican"), sexual orientation ("faggot"), and sadly possibly many more criteria. My working hypothesis is that this derogatory or expressive dimension is a conventional, thus properly semantic, feature of slurs.

Slurs possess two clearly independent dimensions of meaning. On the one hand, they exhibit a *truth-conditional dimension*, responsible for the fact that sentences like (1) have determinate truth conditions:

(1) Juan is a spic.

I assume that the truth-conditional contribution of a slur is such that it is identical to that of its neutral counterpart, if such an expression exists, which makes for the truth-conditional equivalence of sentences like:

(2) I bet you, no spic will finish the race.
(3) I bet you, no Hispanic will finish the race.

(Hom and May 2013, 2014, 2018 notwithstanding, there is a fairly extended consensus to the effect that something like the Identity Thesis holds more or less generally for slurs, where applicable.[2]) On the other hand, slurs exhibit a *non-truth-conditional dimension*, responsible for their derogatory potential, and which accounts for the fact that (2) is pejorative in a sense in which (3) is not (of course, (3) may be pejorative because despicable, but not in virtue of systematic or conventional reasons, as is the case with (2)).

Following Gutzmann (2015), I settle for an interpretation of slurs' non-truth-conditional dimension in terms of the expression of an attitude. Thus, a sentence like (1) conveys the non-truth-conditional meaning that the speaker has a derogatory attitude toward Hispanics. As for derogation, I take it that the expression of a derogatory attitude is itself an act of derogation, capable of harming the slur's targets.

One of the most distinctive linguistic behaviors of slurs is the fact that they seem to scope out of most, if not all, linguistic contexts, in the sense that their slurring effect is achieved even if there is no assertion of their truth-conditional content at all:

(4) Juan is not a spic.
⇒ The speaker has a derogatory attitude toward Hispanics.
(5) If Susan marries that spic, Peter will be shocked.
⇒ The speaker has a derogatory attitude toward Hispanics.
(6) Peter thinks that Juan is a spic.
⇒ The speaker has a derogatory attitude toward Hispanics.

Indeed, what is distinctive of constructions like (4), (5), and (6) is that, contrary to what happens in (1), the slur is not asserted of anyone, but the act of slurring takes place nonetheless.

In the following sections, I present the formal bidimensional system $\mathscr{L}_S$, a subsystem of Gutzmann's $\mathscr{L}_{TU}$ (Gutzmann 2015, ch. 4), in terms of which I attempt to capture the specificity of the linguistic behavior of slurs.

3. A USE-CONDITIONAL SEMANTICS FOR SLURS

Gutzmann (2015) develops a bidimensional semantic system $\mathscr{L}_{TU}$ where the non-truth-conditional dimension of expressions in general, and of slurs in particular, is captured as a use-conditional meaning (UC-meaning, for short). In particular, slurs are interpreted as denoting use-conditional propositions, modeled, following Kaplan (1999), as sets of contexts of use. In this section, I review Gutzmann's bidimensional system and explain how slurs are introduced in that framework. I start with the informal idea behind Gutzmann's $\mathscr{L}_{TU}$, stemming from Kaplan's (1999) work on expressives. Then, I focus on a fragment of $\mathscr{L}_{TU}$, which I call $\mathscr{L}_S$, suitable for the semantic account of slurs.

3.1. Kaplan's Use-Conditional Conceptual Framework

The informal interpretation of Gutzmann's bidimensional semantics is provided by Kaplan's (1999) insights concerning expressives like "ouch" and "oops." The main thrust behind Kaplan's use-oriented approach to meaning is that the meaning of certain expressions may be determined by asking under which circumstances they would be felicitously used, the answer being rendered in something closely resembling the Tarskian clauses for truth. For example, "Oops!" may be felicitously used when the speaker observes a minor mishap (or something in the vicinity of that), and "Ouch!" when the speaker experiences a mild pain (or something in the vicinity of that). What we get is:

(U_{oops}) "Oops!" is felicitously used at c iff the speaker of c observes a minor mishap.
(U_{ouch}) "Ouch!" is felicitously used at c iff the speaker of c experiences a mild pain.

Following these meaning specifications, the UC-meanings of sentence-level expressives like "ouch" and "oops" may be understood as sets of contexts of use, that is, as restrictions on context regarding felicitous use.

This general idea may be extended to other, non-sentence-level UC-expressions, like "damn" and "spic." Thus, for example, an utterance at a context c containing the complex expression "damn Kermit" is felicitously used just in case the speaker of c has negative feelings toward Kermit. And an utterance of a sentence like (1), repeated here for convenience:

(1) Juan is a spic

is felicitous at a context c just in case the speaker of c has a derogatory attitude toward Hispanics. Following Gutzmann, sets of contexts are called *use-conditional propositions*, or *u*-propositions, for short.

Gutzmann classifies UC-expressions in terms of two binary feature sets, [±2-dimensional], according to whether the expression in question has both truth-conditional (TC) and UC-meaning (+), or only UC-meaning (-), and [±functional], according to whether the UC-meaning of the expression takes a TC-argument to yield a UC-meaning (+), or is fully saturated (-). The fact that an utterance of "Ouch!" has no truth-conditional content makes it [-2-dimensional]. The fact that, by its own, it expresses a *u*-proposition (the *u*-proposition that the speaker of the context has a mild pain) makes it [-functional]. The fact that "damn" doesn't contribute anything to the truth-conditional content of the sentences in which it occurs makes it [-2-dimensional], as well. The fact that it takes a truth-conditional argument (e.g., Kermit) to yield a *u*-proposition (that the speaker of the context doesn't like Kermit) makes it [+functional]. And the fact that slurs like "spic" make both kinds of contribution makes them *hybrid* expressions, that is, expressions whose complete semantic specification is given in terms of two substantive, independent dimensions of conventionally encoded meaning. Thus, they are [+2-dimensional]. The fact that they do not take any argument in order to yield a *u*-proposition (e.g., the *u*-proposition that the speaker of the context has a derogatory attitude toward Hispanics) makes them [-functional].

3.2. The $\mathscr{L}_S$ Bidimensional System

Gutzmann (2015) develops Kaplan's insights in a rigorous, formal semantic framework. Following Potts (2005, 2007a,b), Portner (2007), and McCready (2010), he puts forward a bidimensional semantic system, the logic $\mathscr{L}_{TU}$, capable of accounting for the UC-meaning of a wide range of expressions. Here, I present a fragment of $\mathscr{L}_{TU}$ adequate for the treatment of slurs, which I call $\mathscr{L}_S$.

As an intermediate step toward $\mathscr{L}_{TU}$, Gutzmann adopts (and then reformulates) the compositional system of Portner (2007), which has the advantage of making Potts's (2005) $\mathscr{L}_{CI}$ system fully compositional. I present $\mathscr{L}_S$ in both Potts's and Portner's style, as they are more straightforward than Gutzmann's own final sequent notation, whose full complexity isn't needed for a bidimensional account of slurs. For ease of comparison, and to see the innovation involved in bidimensional systems, $\mathscr{L}_S$ also encodes UC-expressions like "damn," which provide an instructive contrast for slurs.

3.2.1. Semantic Types

Since the UC-meanings of [-functional] UC-expressions are sets of contexts of use, we may think of adding c as a basic UC-type for contexts, and then define sentential level UC-semantic values as $\langle c, t \rangle$. However, Gutzmann opts for adopting a primitive sentence-level UC-type u. Thus, the type definition of $\mathscr{L}_S$ is:

1. e, t are the basic TC-types.
2. u is the basic UC-type.
3. If σ and τ are TC-types, then $\langle \sigma, \tau \rangle$ is a TC-type.
4. If σ is a TC-type and τ is a UC-type, then $\langle \sigma, \tau \rangle$ is a UC-type.

3.2.2. Lexical Entries

A bidimensional semantic system has two dimensions of meaning to deal with. Following Portner (2007), these two dimensions are systematized by means of two different interpretation functions, $[\![\cdot]\!]^t$ and $[\![\cdot]\!]^u$, for TC and

UC-content, respectively. Lexical entries are specified in terms of the two functions for each lexical item:

1. $[\![Juan]\!]^t = juan : e$
   $[\![Juan]\!]^u = \emptyset$
2. $[\![Hispanic]\!]^t = \lambda x.hispanic(x) : \langle e, t \rangle$
   $[\![Hispanic]\!]^u = \emptyset$
3. $[\![spic]\!]^t = \lambda x.hispanic(x) : \langle e, t \rangle$
   $[\![spic]\!]^u = bad(^\cap hispanic) : u$
4. $[\![damn]\!]^t = \emptyset$
   $[\![damn]\!]^u = damn : \langle e, u \rangle$

As we can see, slurs like "spic" are of TC-type $\langle e, t \rangle$, that is, functions from entities to truth values (i.e., properties of individuals), and of UC-type u. Expressions like "damn" are of UC-type $\langle e, u \rangle$, that is, functions from entities (like Kermit) to u, and they have an empty TC-dimension. And neutral terms like "Hispanic" are of TC-type $\langle e, t \rangle$, and they have an empty UC-dimension. Proper names are of type e, and they lack UC-meaning. The UC-semantic value of "spic," rendered here as $bad(^\cap hispanic)$, is a shorthand for the following u-proposition:

$\{c : c_s$ has a derogatory attitude toward Hispanics at $c_w\}$,

where c_s is the speaker of c, c_w is the world of c, bad encodes the derogatory attitude, and $^\cap$ is an operator taking from the TC-semantic value of "spic," the property $\lambda x.hispanic(x)$, to its extension.

3.2.3. Semantic Parsetrees

$\mathscr{L}_S$ represents the semantic structure of sentences in terms of *semantic parsetrees*, which encode the semantically relevant features of linguistic structures. In a unidimensional semantic framework (e.g., Heim and Kratzer 1998), the parsetree for a sentence like:

(7) Mary sings.

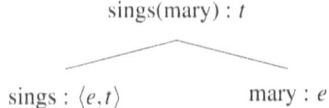

Figure 4.1 Unidimensional semantic parsetree for (7), "Mary sings." Image Credit: Ramiro Caso.

is given in figure 4.1, where the *e* type expression, *mary*, provides an argument for the ⟨*e, t*⟩ type expression, *sings*, whose combination yields a *t* type expression, the (abstractly represented) sentence *sings(mary)*. In ordinary unidimensional semantics, the semantic operation that corresponds to constituent merge is functional application (FA), which in tree form may be rendered as in figure 4.2.

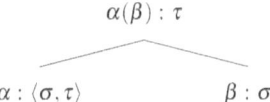

Figure 4.2 **Unidimensional Functional Application (FA).** Image Credit: Ramiro Caso.

That is, by FA, an expression of semantic type ⟨σ, τ⟩ is combined with an expression of semantic type σ in order to yield an expression of semantic type τ. If we want an inline notation, we may adopt the customary double brackets:

FA: for all nodes α, β, if $[\![\beta]\!]$ is in the domain of $[\![\alpha]\!]$, then $[\![\alpha\beta]\!] = [\![\alpha]\!]([\![\beta]\!])$.

$\mathscr{L}_s$ modifies unidimensional parsetrees by allowing multidimensional expressions, that is, expressions with more than one dimension of meaning. Following Potts (2005), these independent semantic dimensions are at the same time bundled together and kept distinct by a metalogical operator • (called *bullet*). The bidimensional parsetree corresponding to (7) is shown in figure 4.3. As a convention, TC-meanings are specified above the bullet, and UC-meanings are specified below. Since no expression in (7) is use-conditional, all UC-meanings in the parsetree are set to ∅.

Since we have two independent interpretation functions, and UC-expressions with very different semantic properties, FA is divided into two different rules (cf. Portner 2007):

- *Ordinary Functional Application (OFA)*: for all nodes α, β, if $[\![\beta]\!]^t$ is in the domain of $[\![\alpha]\!]^t$, then
    1. $[\![\alpha\beta]\!]^t = [\![\alpha]\!]^t([\![\beta]\!]^t)$
    2. $[\![\alpha\beta]\!]^u = [\![\alpha]\!]^u \cup [\![\beta]\!]^u$
- *Expressive Functional Application (EFA)*: for all nodes α, β, if $[\![\beta]\!]^t$ is in the domain of $[\![\alpha]\!]^u$, then
    1. $[\![\alpha\beta]\!]^t = [\![\beta]\!]^t$
    2. $[\![\alpha\beta]\!]^u = \{[\![\alpha]\!]^u([\![\beta]\!]^t)\} \cup [\![\beta]\!]^u$

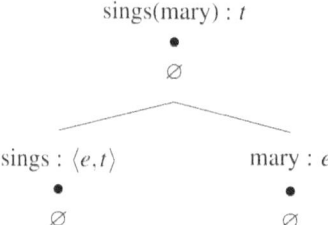

Figure 4.3 Multidimensional semantic parsetree for (7), "Mary sings." Image Credit: Ramiro Caso.

Note that the final output of the function $[\![\cdot]\!]^u$ is a *set* of u-propositions, not a single proposition, as it is for $[\![\cdot]\!]^t$. This allows us to collect all the different possible UC-meanings corresponding to a single (complex) expression in a single semantic value.

It is useful to represent these rules in parsetree format as well, see figure 4.4. In OFA, the TC-meaning of $\alpha\beta$ is computed in the customary way, and the UC-meaning is formed simply by collecting any u-propositional meanings in a single set. In EFA, the TC-value of β is returned unmodified as the TC-value of $\alpha\beta$, and a novel UC-meaning is generated by applying the UC-semantic value of α to the TC-value of β.

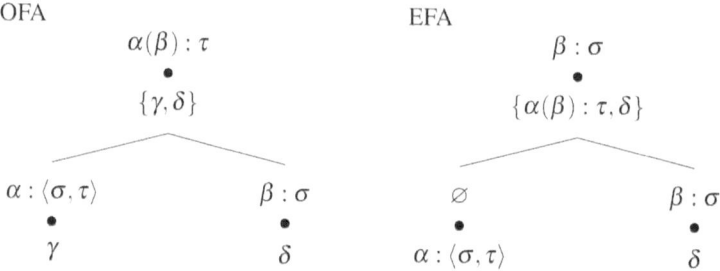

Figure 4.4 Ordinary Functional Application (OFA) and Expressive Functional Application (EFA). Image Credit: Ramiro Caso.

3.2.4. UC-Content Lowering

Finally, let's introduce the idea of *UC-content lowering* (Gutzmann 2015, 24). This is a way of getting a possible-worlds proposition from a u-proposition, relative to a context of use c. Briefly, the idea of lowering is to replace all the variables for contextual parameters in a u-proposition with constants for the values of the corresponding parameters of c, except for the possible world. Thus, for a context c' where c'_s = Peter:

$\{w :$ Peter has a derogatory attitude toward Hispanics at $w\}$

is the lowering of the u-proposition $\{c : c_s$ has a derogatory attitude toward Hispanics at $c_w\}$ relative to c'.

3.3. Representing Slurs in $\mathscr{L}_s$

Now we are able to represent UC-expressions like "damn" and, in particular, "spic." I will use both the inline notation of Portner (2007), and a version of Potts's (2005) semantic parsetrees suitably modified to reflect the two interpretation functions. Let's start with a neutral sentence like:

(8) Juan is Hispanic.

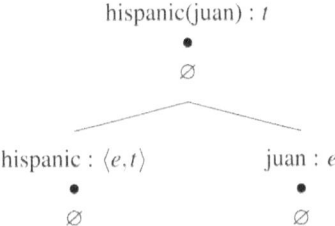

Figure 4.5 Multidimensional semantic parsetree for (8), "Juan is Hispanic." Image Credit: Ramiro Caso.

The semantic parsetree for (8) is shown in figure 4.5. We calculate the semantic values of (8). Since $[\![Hispanic]\!]^u = \varnothing$, $[\![Juan]\!]^t$ is not in its domain, so EFA doesn't apply. But since $[\![Juan]\!]^t$ *is* in the domain of $[\![Hispanic]\!]^t$, semantic composition is obtained *via* OFA:

- $[\![Hispanic(Juan)]\!]^t = [\![Hispanic]\!]^t([\![Juan]\!]^t) = $ T/F
- $[\![Hispanic(Juan)]\!]^u = [\![Hispanic]\!]^u \cup [\![(Juan)]\!]^u = \varnothing$

Here, the interpretation is in agreement with usual unidimensional frameworks (*modulo* the presence of the UC-meaning dimension).

Now we move on to sentences with slurs:

(9) Juan is a spic.

The semantic parsetree for (9) is shown in figure 4.6. In this case, even though "spic" is [+2-dimensional], $[\![Juan]\!]^t$ is not in the domain of $[\![spic]\!]^u$ (for "spic" is [-functional]), so EFA doesn't apply. But, since $[\![Juan]\!]^t$ is in the domain of $[\![spic]\!]^t$, OFA does apply, and we get:

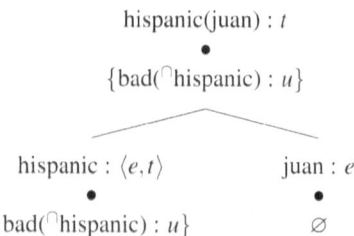

Figure 4.6 Multidimensional semantic parsetree for (9), "Juan is a spic." Image Credit: Ramiro Caso.

- $[\![spic(Juan)]\!]^t = [\![spic]\!]^t([\![Juan]\!]^t) = \text{T/F}$
- $[\![spic(Juan)]\!]^u = [\![spic]\!]^u \cup [\![(Juan)]\!]^u = \{bad(^\cap Hispanic) : u\}$

As expected, the UC-meaning of "spic" is preserved as a UC-meaning of (9).

Up to now, we have seen how semantic composition works with purely TC-expressions, and with [+2-dimensional] expressions. Now, we move to a purely UC-expression like "damn," which is [-2-dimensional] and [+functional], thus requiring a truth-conditional argument to apply to at the UC-level:

(10) That damn Juan is Hispanic.

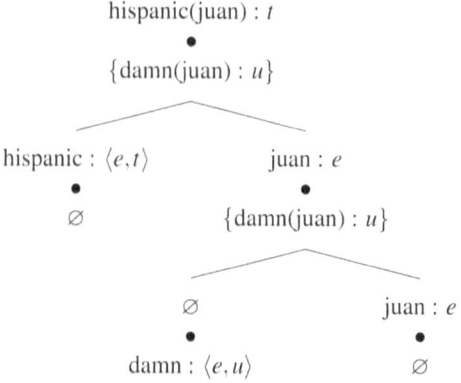

Figure 4.7 Multidimensional semantic parsetree for (10), "That damn Juan is Hispanic." Image Credit: Ramiro Caso.

The semantic parsetree for (10) is shown in figure 4.7. Let's start with "That damn Juan." Recall that "damn" is of UC-type $\langle e, u \rangle$. Since $[\![damn]\!]^t = \emptyset$, OFA doesn't apply. But EFA does, since $[\![Juan]\!]^t$ is in the domain of $[\![damn]\!]^u$, so that:

- $[\![damn(juan)]\!]^t = [\![Juan]\!]^t$
- $[\![damn(juan)]\!]^u = \{[\![damn]\!]^u([\![Juan]\!]^t)\} \cup [\![Juan]\!]^u = \{damn(juan) : u\}$

And the composition of *damn*(*juan*) with *hispanic* proceeds *via* OFA, since $[\![damn(Juan)]\!]^t = [\![Juan]\!]^t$ is in the domain of $[\![Hispanic]\!]^t$, so that:

- $[\![Hispanic(damn(Juan))]\!]^t = [\![Hispanic]\!]^t([\![Juan]\!]^t) = T/F$
- $[\![Hispanic(damn(Juan))]\!]^u = [\![damn(Juan)]\!]^u \cup [\![Hispanic]\!]^u = \{damn(juan): u\}$

Again, as expected, the UC-meaning of "that damn Juan" is preserved as a UC-meaning of (10).

This is enough to get a taste of $\mathscr{L}_S$ (and a preview of $\mathscr{L}_{TU}$). Let's move on to scoping out.

3.4. Capturing Scoping Out

Capturing the scoping out behavior of slurs in $\mathscr{L}_S$ is strikingly easy. This is no surprise, since such scoping out is built into $\mathscr{L}_S$. Let's start by recalling the examples:

(4) Juan is not a spic.
(5) If Susan marries that spic, Peter will be shocked.
(6) Peter thinks that Juan is a spic.

The relevant expressions here are "not," "if," and "thinks." None of these expressions have UC-meanings, so the UC-interpretation function assigns them the empty set. The negation, "not," is a function from truth values to truth values, hence of TC-type $\langle t, t \rangle$. The conditional "if" is treated as heading a restrictor, and is of type $\langle t, \langle t, t \rangle \rangle$, that is, it takes a sentential argument and yields a function from truth values to truth values. Finally, "think" is of type $\langle \langle s, t \rangle, \langle e, t \rangle \rangle$, that is, it takes a propositional complement and yields a property of individuals (provisionally, though not officially, the basic TC-types of $\mathscr{L}_S$ will be enlarged with a primitive type *s* for states or possible worlds). These operators are designed to be transparent with respect to the UC-content of their arguments, so scoping out is warranted by the semantics of $\mathscr{L}_S$, in the sense that whatever UC-meanings the arguments to these operators have, they are passed up the parsetree.

Let's start with the semantic representation of (4) as shown in figure 4.8. Here, we leave *hispanic*(*juan*) unanalyzed, as it has been parsed before;

after that, *hispanic(juan)* is combined with "not" by means of OFA, to yield the root node. The way OFA works ensures that whatever UC-meaning *hispanic(juan)* has is passed to the entire clause.

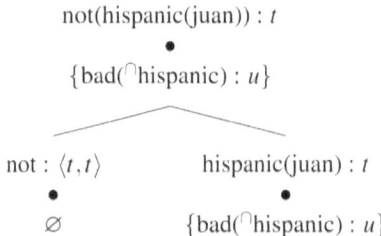

Figure 4.8 Multidimensional semantic parsetree for (4), "Juan is not a spic." Image Credit: Ramiro Caso.

For the purposes of representing (5), let *p* abbreviate "Susan marries that spic," and *q* abbreviate "Peter will be shocked." The parsetrees for these clauses are relatively unproblematic. The only thing to note is that we assume the parsetree in figure 4.9 for "that spic." That is, "that spic" is analyzed as of type *e*, unapologetically dropping any mention to context of use or assignments to free variables in the interpretation functions. Combination is done

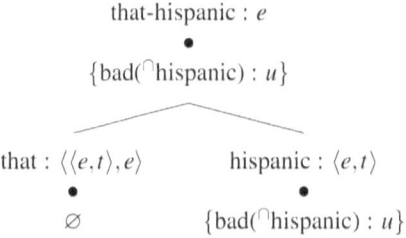

Figure 4.9 Multidimensional semantic parsetree for "that spic." Image Credit: Ramiro Caso.

by OFA. OFA also warrants that the UC-meaning of "spic" is passed all the way up the parsetree of "Susan marries that spic." With these elements in mind, the parsetree for (5) is shown in figure 4.10. Here again, the properties of OFA, and the fact that "if" operates only on the TC-dimension of its argument clause, accounts for the projection of slurs under conditional embeddings.

A Bidimensional Account of Slurs 79

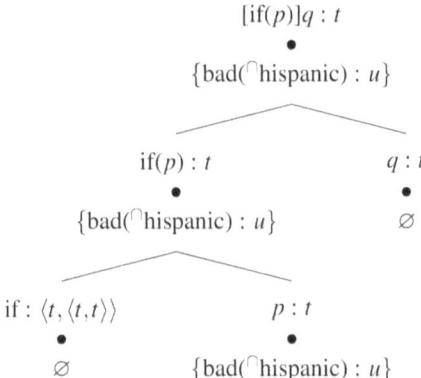

Figure 4.10 Multidimensional semantic parsetree for (5), "If Susan marries that spic, Peter will be shocked." Image Credit: Ramiro Caso.

Finally, the parsetree of (6) is given in figure 4.11. We assume that, in the context of verbs that take propositional complements, an abstraction operation lifts the t type clause *hispanic(juan)* to a corresponding $\langle s, t \rangle$ complement. Since type lifting is triggered by the TC-type mismatch between *hispanic(juan)* and *think*, it is safe to assume that it doesn't affect the UC-meaning of the complement clause. And, since "think" is sensitive only to the TC-dimension of its argument clause, the UC-meaning of *hispanic(juan)* is passed by OFA all the way up the parsetree.

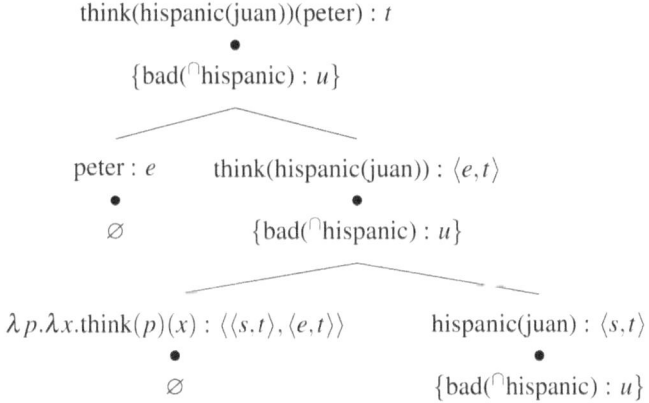

Figure 4.11 Multidimensional semantic parsetree for (6), "Peter thinks that Juan is a spic." Image Credit: Ramiro Caso.

4. SLURS AND SCOPING OUT IN RIOPLATENSE SPANISH

The projection behavior of slurs is, as we have seen, quite liberal, in the sense that slurs scope out of most, if not all, constructions, even of the so-called presupposition plugs, like propositional attitude verbs, as in (6). Interestingly, they are able to scope out of speech reports as well, though there are some subtleties involved here. From now on, I will focus on slurs in Rioplatense Spanish, as the scoping out behavior of slurs in speech reports is easier to appreciate there. This is a detour from usual discussions. Indeed, in the literature on slurs, examples almost invariably come from American English speaking communities. Since this faces the methodological danger of obscuring which aspects of the interpretation of a slur are distinctively semantic, and which ones are of a more pragmatic nature, I propose to focus on slurs as they are used in Rioplatense Spanish, as this may shed light on phenomena that are present in AE speaking communities but that may not be as easy to appreciate there.

4.1. Slurs in Rioplatense Spanish

Rioplatense Spanish is, sadly, very prolific in the generation of slurs, and all the main varieties of slurs are attested: social slurs ("*negro*," "*cheto*," "*villero*"), ethnic slurs ("*colla*," "*boliguayo*"), religious slurs ("*moishe*"), slurs based on nationality ("*bolita*," "*paragua*," "*peruca*," "*brazuca*," "*chilote*"), on ideology ("*globoludo*," "*kuka*," "*gorila*," "*peroncho*"), on sexual orientation ("*puto*," "*marica*"), and so on. Since I am mostly concerned with scoping out data, I will focus on the interpretation of one particular slur, "*bolita*." There is nothing distinctive about this expression, as the data points can be reproduced with respect to any other slur we may choose. As expected, no changes need to be introduced in $\mathscr{L}_s$ in order to capture the basic syntax and semantics of Rioplatense Spanish slurs, save for the addition of new lexical entries of the same kind as before.

4.2. Scoping Out in Rioplatense Spanish

What is interesting of Rioplatense Spanish is that the scoping out behavior of slurs is more clearly nuanced there. For indirect speech reports in Rioplatense Spanish speaking communities exhibit a clear and systematic ambiguity with respect to the ascription of the derogatory attitude associated with a slur:

(11) María dijo que nunca se casaría con un bolita.

María said that she would never marry a bolita.
⇒ The speaker has a derogatory attitude toward Bolivians.
⇒ María has a derogatory attitude toward Bolivians.

Indeed, a speech report like (11) exhibits a clear and systematic ambiguity between an ascription of the derogatory attitude to the speaker and an ascription of that attitude to the ascribee (in this case, María).

I pause to note that the possibility of ascribing a conventionally associated expressive attitude to someone else besides the speaker has been noted before in American English, for epithets by Kratzer (1999, 14), as in (12), and for slurs by Schlenker (2003, 109), as in (13):

(12) My father screamed that he would never allow me to marry that bastard Webster.
(13) I am not prejudiced against Caucasians. But John, who is, thinks/claims that you are the worst honky he knows.[3]

However, these findings have been resisted, for example, by Potts (2005, ch. 5.3), who provides a quotative analysis for these examples: embedding contexts would not provide for a shift of the subject of the attitude, but for some sort of direct quotation effect. But the quotative analysis doesn't seem correct for Rioplatense Spanish, since the ambiguity is actually reminiscent of a typical *de dicto/de re* effect and is readily present without the need of any special linguistic or pragmatic context.

The quotative analysis doesn't strike me as correct for AE either, but there is a more subtle issue here. It is instructive to observe that Schlenker's example involves a quite explicit qualification to the effect that the speaker doesn't actually have the derogatory attitude connected with the slur. This is instructive in the sense that prohibitionism may be responsible for this, insofar as treating slurs as prohibited words may make it too hard a task for a speaker to separate herself from the slur's derogatory potential. In Rioplatense Spanish, there are generally no such problems, the ambiguity pointed out being accepted by most speakers.[4]

In this section and the next, I argue that this systematic ambiguity cannot be captured in Gutzmann's framework without introducing modifications, insofar as the *u*-propositions expressed by slurs place constraints on context based on the attitudes of the *speaker* of the context. So, this leaves open the question of how to account for this ambiguity. In section 6, I introduce a non-trivial modification to $\mathscr{L}_s$ that provides for an elegant explanation of this ambiguity in attitude ascription.

The first thing to notice about examples like (11) is that the ambiguity in attitude ascription is reminiscent of a *de dicto/de re* effect: under the would-be *de dicto* reading, the attitude would be attributed to the ascribee, whereas under the would-be *de re* reading, it would be attributed to the speaker. This may generate the following train of thought: if this ambiguity could be explained in terms of a genuine *de dicto/de re* ambiguity, there could be a way of incorporating it into Gutzmann's bidimensional framework without any need to modify the semantic analysis of slurs. I will argue that this cannot be done, for the ambiguity that exists in attitude ascription is an entirely different phenomenon, and is not reducible to a *de dicto/de re* ambiguity. (It should be noted that, even on the assumption that the ambiguity in attitude ascription were due to a *de dicto/de re* ambiguity of some sort, slurs could not be incorporated into Gutzmann's $\mathscr{L}_{TU}$ without the need of substantial modifications. Indeed, on this assumption, slurs could no longer be seen as encoding a saturated UC-meaning: they would have to take a TC-argument that varied according to the would-be *de dicto* or would-be *de re* reading, thus becoming unsaturated UC-expressions of some sort. The *de se u*-propositions approach could be used in order to avoid making slurs unsaturated UC-expressions in that event.)

That the ambiguity in attitude ascription doesn't actually pattern with a genuine *de dicto/de re* ambiguity may be shown by paying attention to speech reports done by means of indirect questions, where the *de dicto/de re* effect is clearly attested, yet there is no ambiguity in attitude ascription. For, consider a sentence involving an expressively neutral term, like "student":

(14) John told me which students came to the party.

Sentence (14) has two readings: a *de dicto* reading under which John must know, not only the identity of certain partygoers, but also that they are students; (ii) a *de re* reading under which John may be ignorant with respect to that last piece of knowledge, but the speaker isn't. Let's suppose that the students who went to the party are Mary and Peter. Under the *de dicto* reading, (14) is true just in case John told the speaker that Mary and Peter went to the party and John knows that they are students. Under the *de re* reading, (14) is true just in case John told the speaker that Mary and Peter went to the party, but John need not know that they are students.

Now contrast an indirect speech report that uses a *that*-clause involving a slur, like (15), and two indirect reports reporting the same speech act, but in terms of embedded questions, like (16) and (17):

(15) Juan dijo que tres bolitas vinieron a la fiesta.
      Juan said that three bolitas *came to the party.*
      ⇒ The speaker has a derogatory attitude toward Bolivians.
      ⇒ Juan has a derogatory attitude toward Bolivians.

(16) Juan dijo cuántos bolitas vinieron a la fiesta.
Juan said how many bolitas *came to the party.*
⇒ The speaker has a derogatory attitude toward Bolivians.
(17) Juan me dijo cuántos bolitas vinieron a la fiesta.
Juan told me how many bolitas *came to the party.*
⇒ The speaker has a derogatory attitude toward Bolivians.

Noticeably, (15) exhibits the systematic ambiguity in attitude ascription present in Rioplatense Spanish, that seems to pattern with the *de dicto/de re* ambiguity with respect to the use of "*bolita.*" However, neither (16) nor (17) exhibits this ambiguity, even though they exhibit a parallel *de dicto/de re* ambiguity with respect to the TC-component of "*bolita*" (i.e., the nationality of the partygoers). So, despite this genuine *de dicto/de re* ambiguity, according to which Juan is, or is not, credited with knowledge of the nationality of the partygoers, there is no corresponding *de dicto/de re* effect with respect to attitude ascription: (16) and (17) are consistently interpreted in terms of a speaker-oriented attitude ascription. In order to see why this is so, I will briefly review the semantics of embedded questions.

5. THE SEMANTICS OF EMBEDDED QUESTIONS

There are several semantic theories of questions, and different ideas on how to integrate interrogatives and declaratives in a single semantic theory.[5] For definiteness, I assume Dayal's theory of questions (Dayal 2017). In this framework, questions are interpreted as denoting Hamblin sets, that is, sets of propositions. More precisely, a question denotes the set of its *possible* answers (Hamblin 1973). This holds of both polar (18) and constituent (19) questions, whether direct or indirect:

(18) a. Did Bill dance? / whether Bill danced
b. $\lambda p[p = \,^\wedge\text{danced(bill)} \lor p = \,^\wedge\neg\text{danced(bill)}]$
c. {^bill danced, ^b-30 ptill didn't dance*}
(19) a. Who danced? / who danced
b. $\lambda p.\exists x[\text{person}(x) \land p = \,^\wedge\text{danced}(x)]$
c. {^susan danced*, ^bill danced, ^john danced*}

Here, the Hamblin set of the question in (a) is given in (b) in intension, as a property of propositions, and in (c) in extension, as a set of propositions (where ^ is an operator taking from sentences to the propositions they express, with the true propositions in the set marked by *).

As for the syntactic structure of questions, it is assumed that, in constituent questions, wh-phrases move to the position of SpecCP when C⁰ is marked [+wh]. Again, this holds for both direct and indirect questions. For (19), a basic syntactic analysis would then be as shown in figure 4.12.

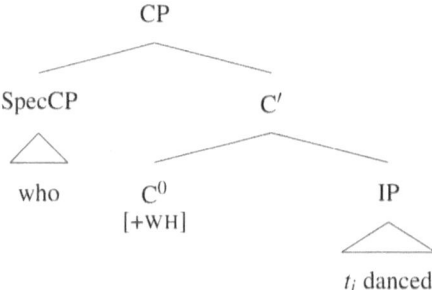

Figure 4.12 Syntactic tree for (19), "Who danced?/who danced." Image Credit: Ramiro Caso.

From the semantic standpoint, questions are interpreted as in figure 4.13. In this parsetree, *danced*(x_i) is the question nucleus, of type t. It contains a variable of type e, corresponding to the trace left by the wh-expression. The question nucleus combines with C⁰, a function $\lambda q[p = q]$ of type $\langle\langle s, t\rangle, \langle s, t\rangle\rangle$ that takes a propositional argument and yields a proposition as value. Type mismatch generates the promotion of the nucleus from type t to type $\langle s, t\rangle$. As a consequence, we get $\lambda q[p = q](^\wedge danced(x_i))$, which resolves to $p = {^\wedge}danced(x_i)$. This combines in turn with the wh-phrase, of type $\langle\langle e, t\rangle, t\rangle$, thus yielding $\lambda P \exists x[person(x) \wedge P(x)](\lambda x_i[p = {^\wedge}danced(x_i)])$. Here, abstraction over x_i is triggered during the combination, and the resulting semantic value resolves to $\exists x[person(x) \wedge p = {^\wedge}danced(x)]$. Finally, the propositional variable p is abstracted over to get the property of propositions expressed by a question, $\lambda p \exists x[person(x) \wedge p = {^\wedge}danced(x)]$. Thus, a question like (19)

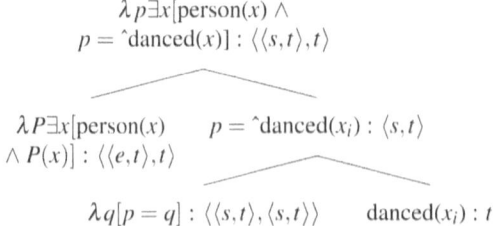

Figure 4.13 Unidimensional semantic parsetree for (19), "Who danced?/who danced." Image Credit: Ramiro Caso.

denotes the set of all propositions of the form *x danced*, for some value of *x*, with *x* a person.

Indirect questions embedded under verbs that induce veridicality effects, like "tell" and "*decir*," are interpreted as denoting the maximally informative proposition of their corresponding Karttunen sets, that is, the sets of their *true* answers (Karttunen 1977).[6] This is done *via* an answerhood operator Ans introduced in the context of the embedding predicate (cf. Heim 1994). Thus, for example, a sentence like,

(20) Juan dijo cuáles estudiantes vinieron a la fiesta.
Juan told [me] *which students came to the party*,

is semantically parsed as in figure 4.14 (with Q standing for *which students came to the party*).

The *de dicto*/*de re* ambiguity of (20) is accounted for in terms of an ambiguity in Q itself, with (21a) giving the *de dicto* reading of the question, and (21b) giving the *de re* reading:

(21) a. $Q_1 = \lambda p \exists x[\text{student}(x) \wedge p = {^\wedge}\text{came.to.the.party}(x)]$
 b. $Q_2 = \lambda p \exists x[p = {^\wedge}[\text{student}(x) \wedge \text{came.to.the.party}(x)]]$

When Q_1 is plugged into the answerhood operator Ans, yielding Ans(Q_1), the ascribee is reported as having asserted a proposition of the form *x came to the party*, and the identification of the value of *x* as (a mereological sum of) students is entirely on the part of the speaker. When Q_2 is plugged into Ans, yielding Ans(Q_2), the ascribee is reported as having asserted, or as having knowledge of, a proposition of the form *x is a student and x came to the party*, where the identification of the value of *x* as (a mereological sum of) students is entirely on the part of the ascribee.

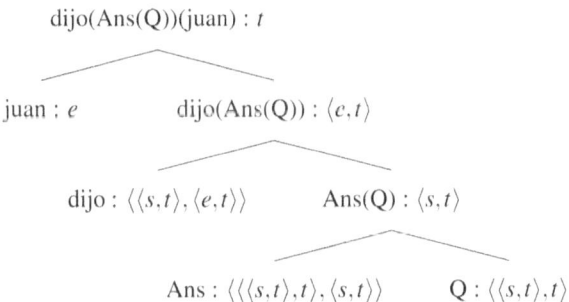

Figure 4.14 Unidimensional semantic parsetree for (20), "Juan dijo cuáles estudiantes vinieron a la fiesta." Image Credit: Ramiro Caso.

The same holds for a report like (16), which receives basically the same analysis:

(16) Juan dijo cuántos bolitas vinieron a la fiesta.
Juan said how many bolitas *came to the party.*

Where Q is the ambiguous question *cuántos bolitas vinieron a la fiesta*, (16) is characterized by the parsetree in figure 4.15 (now in a bidimensional framework). Again, the *de dicto/de re* ambiguity with respect to the TC-content of "*bolita*" is explained as in (21). However, as the parsetree for (16) makes clear, the UC-content of "*bolita*" is not affected by this ambiguity in the question itself.

So, the ambiguity concerning attitude ascription doesn't reflect a genuine *de dicto/de re* ambiguity. This seems to block the possibility of explaining projection data in terms of a *de dicto/de re* ambiguity affecting the interpretation of the slur's UC-content. The most natural explanation of the ambiguity in Gutzmann's semantic framework for slurs is thus blocked as well. How may we account for this peculiar projection of derogatory content? In the next section, I introduce a modification into $\mathscr{L}_S$ regarding the UC-type of slurs, that allows for an elegant representation of the systematic ambiguity attested in speech reports in Rioplatense Spanish.

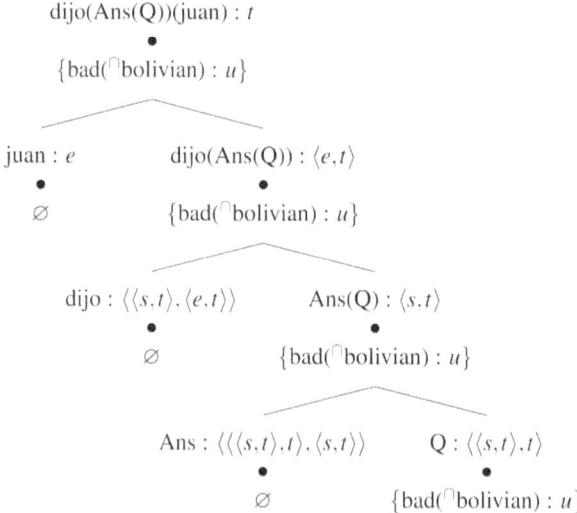

Figure 4.15 Multidimensional semantic parsetree for (16), "Juan dijo cuántos bolitas vinieron a la fiesta." Image Credit: Ramiro Caso.

6. *DE SE U*-PROPOSITIONAL CONTENT

In order to deal with the systematic ambiguity concerning speech reports, I'd like to take up an idea by Kirk-Giannini (2019) and Lo Guercio (2020), and make the following suggestion. On the semantic side, slurs have a *sui generis* UC-semantic type. In particular, they express *u*-properties, or rather *de se u*-propositions, that is, agent-relative *u*-propositions. On the pragmatic side of the interpretation of slurs, the conversational effect of a slur's UC-dimension at a context c is to demand an application of the lowering of the corresponding *de se u*-proposition relative to c, to an agent relevant at c. As a matter of pragmatic interpretation, the application of the lowered *u*-proposition defaults to the speaker, unless there are overriding factors. For example, this pragmatic default may be contextually overridden by a pragmatic fidelity maxim, thus explaining both why, in the majority of cases, attribution is to the speaker, and why violations of the default interpretation are limited mostly (but not exclusively) to indirect speech reports.

Integrating this semantic idea into a UC-framework is not as straightforward as it may seem, however. For the hierarchy of UC-types has provision for eternal *u*-propositions only (i.e., only of type *u*). However, we need *de se u*-propositions, hence of an agent-relative UC-type. But agent-relative UC-types, or something close to them, already have the job of being *u*-properties, as witnessed by the UC-semantic value of expressions like "damn," which are of type $\langle e, u \rangle$. So, we seem to have a type problem: we need some distinction where we seem to have none.

There are at least two ways of integrating *de se u*-propositions in $\mathscr{L}_S$. The first involves introducing a new, primitive TC-type, a, for agents. Once we have this new type, *de se u*-propositions may be modeled as semantic values of type $\langle a, u \rangle$, and *de se* (*t*-)propositions as semantic values of type $\langle a, t \rangle$. Accounting for the relativity of propositional truth to an agent requires a relativization of the interpretation functions to an agent parameter, in the same way we would add a world parameter in intensional semantics. So, $[\![\bullet]\!]^t$ and $[\![\bullet]\!]^u$ receive an agent parameter, thus yielding $[\![\bullet]\!]^{t\langle a \rangle}$ and $[\![\bullet]\!]^{u\langle a \rangle}$. Since we have no object language operator capable of shifting this new parameter, OFA and EFA remain the same, *modulo* the extra parameter. As a consequence of this modification, $\mathscr{L}_S$ has room for [-functional] UC-expressions of type *u*, and [-functional] UC-expressions of type $\langle a, u \rangle$. If we want a uniform semantic representation for saturated UC-types, we may assign $\langle a, u \rangle$ UC-type to all [-functional] UC-expressions, allowing some of them to be agent-sensitive, some agent-insensitive, according to whether the agent parameter features non-trivially to the right of the identity symbol in the corresponding lexical entries.

The second way of incorporating *de se u*-propositions into $\mathscr{L}_S$ stems from the consideration that agents are entities, so it also makes sense to treat them as of type e. Under this construal, *de se u*-propositions are of type $\langle e, u \rangle$, and *de se* (*t*-)propositions are of type $\langle e, t \rangle$. This forces a type collapse with *u*-properties of individuals and (*t*-)properties of individuals, respectively. As before, the interpretation functions may be relativized to a further, object parameter (different, though, from the eventual assignment function required for the interpretation of traces, indexicals, and like expressions). As before OFA and EFA remain the same, *modulo* the newly added parameter. The problem that now arises is different: we now have expressions of UC-type $\langle e, u \rangle$ that are [+functional], like "damn," and expressions of UC-type $\langle e, u \rangle$ that are [-functional], like "spic" and "*bolita*." And the saturated or unsaturated nature of these expressions cannot be derived (exclusively) from their semantic types. This way of construing *de se* propositions seems to require that certain $\langle e, u \rangle$-type expressions be lexically marked as [-functional], and some as [+functional], independently of their UC-types.

Is there a way of deciding between these two construals of *de se* propositions? Maybe the following consideration can tip the scale in favor of the former. Being bearer of an attitude is a property only agents can instantiate. It makes no sense to apply these properties to non-agentive entities in a literal way. Hence, it is more in line with the properties attributed by these *de se* propositions to construe them as properties of a special kind of entities, namely, agents.

Hence, I will proceed under the former construal of *de se* propositions.[7] Being agent-sensitive, *de se u*-propositions no longer place restrictions on contexts of use alone, but on agent-context pairs. Thus, for example, in the case of "*bolita*," instead of:

$$\{c : c_S \text{ has a derogatory attitude toward Bolivians at } c_W\}$$

we have

$$\{\langle c, a \rangle : a \text{ is salient at } c \text{ and } a \text{ has a derogatory attitude toward Bolivians at } c_W\}$$

Now, what does putting forward a *de se u*-proposition amount to? Formally, a *de se u*-proposition encodes the idea that, for an utterance U involving a slur like "*bolita*" to be felicitous, there must be a context c and an agent a such that (i) U takes place in c, (ii) a is conversationally relevant at c, and (iii) a is bearer of the derogatory attitude encoded by the slur at the world of c. The full conversational effect of sentential UC-type meanings in general, and of *de se u*-propositions in particular, is explained in terms of their lowering. Recall that the lowering of a *u*-proposition relative to a context c is the result of setting all the contextual variables to the values of the respective parameters of c, save for the possible world parameter, which is replaced by a free world variable, bounded by the set abstractor. In the case of *de se u*-propositions, the lowering is a truth-conditional *de se* proposition. For a sentence containing "*bolita*," the lowering amounts to the following *de se* proposition:

$$\{\langle w, a \rangle : a \text{ is salient at } c \text{ and } a \text{ has a derogatory attitude toward Bolivians at } w\}$$

Since no contextual parameter beyond c_w features in the original *de se u*-proposition, the resulting *de se t*-proposition very closely resembles the original *de se u*-proposition.

The conversational effect of the use of a slur under the new semantics can now be fully appreciated. In virtue of their UC-semantic value, the use of a slur puts forward, *via* lowering, a *de se t*-proposition. *De se t*-propositions demand application to an agent before they can be properly evaluated as true or false. So, the use of a slur at a context c demands the identification of an agent to which to attribute the possession of the relevant derogatory attitude. Which agent this is, is no longer encoded in the semantics of the slur. It is only by a pragmatic default that the relevant agent is generally identified with the speaker. This pragmatic default may be motivated by the fact that slurs like "*bolita*" have a conventionalized derogatory effect. The free choice of a slur by the speaker makes for a conversational point: bringing to salience a derogatory attitude toward the members of the slur's extension. On account of that free choice, the speaker has to answer for her choice of words, and absent any other, suitably salient agent, the attitude is ascribed to her.

The upshot of this proposal is that slurs invariably project in essentially the same fashion regardless of sentential context (contexts of direct quotation aside), any difference in attitude ascription being traceable to a pragmatic operation, be it in terms of a default speaker-oriented ascription, or in terms of an ascribee-oriented application. The general prediction is that attitude ascriptions are speaker-oriented unless there is a different, contextually salient agent apt for being the bearer of the derogatory attitude (apt in the sense that there are good contextual grounds for pinning the derogatory attitude on her). If there is such an agent, but the speaker doesn't distance herself from the attitude, this may result in either a speaker-oriented or an ascribee-oriented attribution. If the speaker successfully distances herself from the derogatory attitude, the ascription is then unambiguously ascribee-oriented.

The existence of the pragmatic default constraining the application of the resulting *de se t*-proposition may now be used to account for the fact that, in most cases, projection results in speaker-oriented attitude ascriptions. As we saw in section 3.4., lexical entries and functional application principles conspire to ensure that whatever saturated UC-meaning a subsentential expression may have, it is passed all the way up the parsetree, and becomes a UC-meaning of the entire clause. As a result, the *de se u*-propositions expressed by slurs project out of embedding constructions. The general unavailability of a suitably salient object besides the speaker, apt for being the bearer of the corresponding derogatory attitude, warrants, *via* the pragmatic default, the well-attested speaker-oriented attribution.

The systematic ambiguity of reports like (11):

(11) María dijo que nunca se casaría con un *bolita,*

on the other hand, may be easily explained in terms of the default attribution being contextually overridden. For indirect speech reports are special contexts, in the sense that free choice of words is compatible with a cancellation of the default pragmatic interpretation. This may be due to the operation of a fidelity principle that enables the speaker to use words the ascribee used, or would use, in making the speech report. The speech report itself is enough to bring the ascribee to contextual salience. The presumption that the speaker's free choice of words may operate under fidelity, on the other hand, is enough to make the ascribee contextually apt for being the bearer of the derogatory attitude. In Rioplatense Spanish communities, the speaker usually need not do anything else to distance herself from the derogatory attitude, which accounts for the fact that both ascribee-oriented and speaker-oriented attitude ascriptions are readily available in the interpretation of speech reports.

As highlighted by Schlenker-cases like (13):

(13) I am not prejudiced against Caucasians. But John, who is, thinks/ claims that you are the worst honky he knows.

the suspension of the pragmatic default is not restricted to indirect speech reports, but to attitude reports in general, provided the speaker is able to distance herself from any derogatory attitude, and provides for the contextual identification of a suitable agent to be the bearer of the conventionally expressed derogatory attitude.[8]

An interesting data point is provided by the unambiguous:

(22) Juan dijo quiénes le pegaron al bolita.
Juan said who beat the bolita.
(23) Juan me dijo quiénes le pegaron al bolita.
Juan told me who beat the bolita.

As we saw, speech reports like (16):

(16) Juan dijo cuántos bolitas vinieron a la fiesta.
Juan said how many bolitas *came to the party.*

which employ indirect questions, have only speaker-oriented attitude ascriptions. This is easily explained insofar as the slur occurs in the wh-expression, for then free choice of words cannot sensibly be taken to follow any fidelity principle (indeed, the ascribee could not have used a wh-expression in her direct speech). But, in (22) and (23), the slur occurs in a part of the indirect question that may in principle be affected by fidelity.[9] So, why is there no ambiguity here? The reason why the fidelity principle doesn't override the pragmatic default in these cases seems to be that, in speech reports done by means of indirect questions, the proposition asserted by the ascribee is identified in a purely descriptive way, as the proposition identical to the maximally informative answer to the relevant question, whatever it turns out to be. So, in making this indirect, descriptive identification, there is no presumption to the effect that the free choice of words is tracking words the ascribee would in principle subscribe.

7. CONCLUSION

Following an insight by Kirk-Giannini (2019) and Lo Guercio (2020), I presented a bidimensional semantic system $\mathscr{L}_S$ which resulted from incorporating *de se u*-propositions into Gutzmann's logic $\mathscr{L}_{TU}$, and from allowing slurs to express *de se u*-propositional contents as their UC-meanings. Slurs have their full conversational effect *via* UC-content lowering, whereby they contextually express a *de se t*-proposition, which requires the contextual identification of a suitable agent on which to pin the derogatory attitude associated with the use of the slur. Projection data points concerning slurs in both American English and Rioplatense Spanish linguistic communities were then explained in terms of (i) a pragmatic default that warrants the application of the resulting *de se t*-proposition to the speaker and (ii) clearly defined override conditions, which allow for the explanation of cases where the attribution is made to a contextually salient agent different from the speaker herself.

NOTES

1. Due to the nature of the examples I will use, I should explicitly state that slurs will always be mentioned, and never used, throughout the discussion.

2. Argentinian speakers are unusually productive in the generation of slurs, and they have coined the term "*boliguayo*," which is a slur directed at

(ethnically diverse) populations of Amerindian origin from countries at the north of Argentina. Though, for this particular slur, there is no neutral counterpart which is linguistically as simple as the slur itself, this doesn't mean that it is not possible to find a way of describing the extension of "*boliguayo*" in purely descriptive, non-pejorative terms, as I have done in the previous sentence. So, we are not forced to have a pejorative way of singling out the slur's truth-conditional contribution in our metalanguage.

3. Schlenker (2003) introduces this example in the course of arguing in favor of the existence of monsters, that is, operators that shift the context of utterance, and not merely the circumstance of evaluation.

4. It should be noted that certain Rioplatense Spanish speakers are not sensitive to the ambiguity, and some even claim that using slurs under direct quotation is derogatory. These judgments seem to be elicited by a prohibitionistic take on slurs some Rioplatense Spanish speakers have. But this is actually not the norm in Rioplatense Spanish linguistic communities.

5. Here, and in what follows, I use "interrogative" and "declarative" to refer to syntactic types. I reserve "question" and "question denotation," on one the hand, and "proposition," on the other hand, for the semantic objects denoted by interrogatives and declaratives, respectively.

6. This requires that the domain of objects have a mereological structure (Link 1983). Then, the maximally informative true answer to a constituent question Q of the form $wh[\varphi(t)]$ is the proposition $\varphi(s)$, with s the mereological sum of all the individuals x such that $\varphi(x)$ is a true answer to Q. For example, in the case of the question "Who danced?," and assuming that the corresponding Hamblin set is {^john danced*, ^mary danced*, ^bill danced}, the maximally informative true answer to Q is the proposition ^*j+m danced* (with *j+m* the mereological sum of John and Mary).

7. Everything that follows could be recast in terms of the construal of *de se u-* and *t-*propositions as of type $\langle e, \ldots \rangle$.

8. Schlenker puts forward this example in the course of an argument in favor of the existence of Kaplanian monsters in natural languages. A point in favor of the present proposal is that it can account for Schlenker's data without the need to posit these curious semantic entities.

9. I am grateful to Matías Verdecchia for pointing out these cases to me, and for helping me out, together with Eleonora Orlando and Andrés Saab, in sorting out the issue.

BIBLIOGRAPHICAL REFERENCES

Dayal, Veneeta. 2017. *Questions*. Oxford: Oxford University Press.
Gutzmann, Daniel. 2015. *Use-Conditional Meaning: Studies in Multidimensional Semantics*. Oxford: Oxford University Press.
Hamblin, Charles Leonard. 1973. "Questions in Montague English." *Foundations of Language* 10(1): 41–53. https://doi.org/10.1016/B978-0-12-545850-4.50014-5.

Heim, Irene. 1994. "Interrogative Semantics and Karttunen's Semantics for 'Know.'" In *Proceedings of the Israeli Association for Theoretical Linguistics*, vol. 1, edited by Rhonna Buhalla and Anita Mittwoch, 128–144. Jerusalem: Akademon.

Heim, Irene, and Angelika Krazter. 1998. *Semantics in Generative Grammar*. Oxford, Cambridge, MA: Blackwell.

Hom, Christopher, and Robert May. 2013. "Moral and Semantic Innocence." *Analytic Philosophy* 54(3): 314–329. https://doi.org/10.1111/phib.12020.

Hom, Christopher, and Robert May. 2014. "The Inconsistency of the Identity Thesis." *ProtoSociology* 31: 113–120. https://doi.org/10.5840/protosociology20143110.

Hom, Christopher, and Robert May. 2018. "Pejoratives As Fiction." In *Bad Words*, edited by David Sosa, 108–131. Oxford: Oxford University Press.

Kaplan, David. 1999. "The Meaning of 'Ouch' and 'Oops': Explorations in the Theory of Meaning As Use." Ms., University of California, Los Angeles.

Karttunen, Lauri. 1977. "Syntax and Semantics of Questions." *Linguistics and Philosophy* 1(1): 3–44. https://doi.org/10.1007/BF00351935.

Kirk-Giannini, Carlo Domenico. 2019. "Slurs Are Directives." *Philosopher's Imprint* 19(48): 1–28.

Kratzer, Angelika. 1999. "Beyond 'Ouch' and 'Oops': How Descriptive and Expressive Meaning Interact." Unpublished manuscript. https://semanticsarchive.net/Archive/WEwNGUyO/Beyond%20%22Ouch%22%20and%20%22Oops%22.pdf.

Link, Gödehard. 1983. "The Logical Analysis of Plurals and Mass Terms: A Lattice-Theoretical Approach." In *Meaning, Use and the Interpretation of Language*, edited by Rainer Bäuerle, Christoph Schwarze, and Armin von Stechow, 303–323. Berlin, New York: Walter de Gruyter.

Lo Guercio, Nicolás. 2020. "The Discursive Dimension of Slurs." This volume.

McCready, Elin. 2010. "Varieties of Conventional Implicature." *Semantics and Pragmatics* 3(8): 1–57. https://doi.org/10.3765/sp.3.8.

Portner, Paul. 2007. "Instructions for Interpretation As Separate Performatives." In *On Information Structure, Meaning and Form*, edited by Kerstin Schwabe and Susanne Winkler, 407–426. Amsterdam, Philadelphia: John Benjamins.

Potts, Christopher. 2005. *The Logic of Conventional Implicature*. Oxford: Oxford University Press.

Potts, Christopher. 2007a. "The Centrality of Expressive Indices." *Theoretical Linguistics* 33(2): 255–268. https://doi.org/10.1515/tl.2007.019.

Potts, Christopher. 2007b. "The Expressive Dimension." *Theoretical Linguistics* 33(2): 165–197. https://doi.org/10.1515/tl.2007.011.

Schlenker, Philippe. 2003. "A Plea for Monsters." *Linguistics and Philosophy* 26(1): 29–120. https://doi.org/10.1023/A:1022225203544.

Chapter 5

Expressives and the Theory of Bias

Ludovic Soutif and Carlos Márquez

Language puts at our (i.e., the speaker's) disposal a full range of lexical items, morphological devices, and syntactic constructions to convey our (her) emotional states and evaluative attitudes toward world happenings. These are known in both the philosophy and the linguistics' literatures as *expressives*.[1] Whether expressives form among themselves a unified natural semantic class picked out by a set of distinctive properties is a controversial issue.[2] We won't get into it here. We will simply assume they do for argument's sake. The claim that expressives have a fairly stable conventional meaning—across contexts of use—is comparatively less contentious. After all, all one needs to do to get a rough idea of their socially established meaning is to look up in the dictionary. One can find there, if not a nominal definition in conceptual terms, at least an account of their linguistic meaning in terms of circumstances of use-types.

In this chapter, we set ourselves the task of reviewing a semantic framework due to Predelli's book *Meaning without Truth* (2013). Let's coin it, following the author's suggestion, the Theory of Bias (hereafter, TB).[3] As Predelli views it, TB is not solely meant to account for the meaning of expressives: it is intended, rather, as a general framework to account for various possible manifestations of the non-truth-conditional phenomenon, expressives being but one possible manifestation of it.[4] Since TB is not intended, unlike other frameworks—notably, Potts (2007a)—to account for the distinctive semantic behavior of expressives, claiming that its predictive power is limited is stating the obvious. It is like claiming (in a complaining tone of voice) of a knife that it is not completely fit to perform certain tasks such as the tightening of a screw. A more interesting and relevant question to ask is this: to what extent can the theory be used to account for the specific semantic properties of expressives? Our aim here is twofold. First, it is to show that the theory is more resourceful than it seems, for it gives a consistent semantic explanation even for the most challenging syntactic constructions in which expressives occur. Second, it is to show that the theory's predictive power reaches its limits precisely at the point where differences among instances of non-truth-conditional meaning become relevant.

More precisely, the chapter is framed as follows. Having outlined TB's key features (section 1), we show how they can be brought to bear on the analysis of a standard type of expressive sentence featuring sentential interjections (section 2). Sections 3 and 4 turn to less standard types of expressive sentences, one being an instance, following Predelli's (2013) coinage, of *settled* expressive sentences, while the other involves a (seeming) contradiction. As for the latter, we argue that, appearances notwithstanding, its analysis along TB lines is compatible with one of the premises of the argument it rests upon. Finally, section 5 argues that TB's predictive power breaks down at the point where the type of sentence or illocutionary act performed in uttering it and methodological issues like the issue as to which syntactic embedding is to be considered as the crucial test for expressive content come to the fore.

1. AN OUTLINE OF TB

Semantically speaking, TB singles out as a two-tiered account. This means that the meaning of *any* linguistic expression whatsoever, including that of expressive words and morphemes, is analyzed within the framework along a truth-conditional and a non-truth-conditional tier. The former pertains to the truth-conditions of the sentence the expression occurs in. In harmony with the Principle of Compositionality, the expression's meaning (semantic value) is analyzed in terms of its contribution to the truth-conditions of the sentence. The latter is, as its name suggests, truth-conditionally otiose. It pertains to further aspects of the expression's meaning, such as its contribution to the conditions of use of the sentence it occurs in, as a whole.[5]

The features of the expression's linguistic meaning responsible for its truth-conditional contribution are called by Predelli (2010, 2013), following Kaplan (1989), its *character*, while the features of its linguistic meaning responsible for its use-conditional contribution are called its *bias*. Formally speaking, the former can be represented as a function from contexts to intensions (contents), while the latter is represented as a proper subclass (subset) of the class (set) of all contexts, picked out by a constraint derived from the expression's conventional meaning.[6] On this view, the linguistic meaning of any expression e is representable as a pair featuring, on the one hand, e's *character*, responsible for e's truth-conditional profile and, on the other hand,

e's bias, responsible for its non-truth-conditional or use-conditional profile; in short, as follows: $meaning(e) = <char(e), bias(e)>$.

The point of the pair notation is that it easily generalizes over all types of linguistic expressions, for e need not make any difference to the truth-conditions of the (uttered) sentence it occurs in to be endowed with a character. Likewise, it need not make any (positive or negative) contribution to the (uttered) sentence's conditions of use to be endowed with a bias. A trivial or even dummy character (or bias) is still a character (or bias). Its contribution is merely null.

As far as the so-called pure expressives are concerned, Predelli's general insight is that their truth-conditional contribution being null, their non-truth-conditional one can be represented by a nontrivial bias. Thus, the linguistic meaning of lone interjections like "Hurray!" is depicted as a character-bias pair "where *char*(hurray) is presumably some sort of 'dummy' character reflecting the idea that 'hurray' is not truth apt" (Predelli 2013, 66) and *bias*(hurray) a nontrivial bias determined by a meaning-encoded constraint on its appropriate use—something like: "Hurray!" is appropriately used only if the agent of the context approves of something in the context (Predelli 2013, 65). The linguistic meaning of sentential interjections like "Hurray s" is, in turn, depicted as a character-bias pair where *char*(Hurray s) is trivial (rather than dummy), while *bias*(Hurray s) isn't. The latter is roughly the same as *bias*(hurray!) except that the agent's attitude is targeted in this case at s's content (Predelli 2013, 73). The linguistic meaning of pejorative epithets and attributive adjectives—like "damn" in "that damn dog"—although not topically discussed, is liable to be dealt with along the same lines.[7]

One thing, however, is to have an insight that generalizes over members of the category of expressives, another is to provide an argument in support of the introduction of a new semantic (non-truth-conditional) tier into a framework that is, on the whole, Kaplanian. Predelli (2010, 164) provides an argument running, basically, as follows.

Consider sentences (1), (2), and (3)—(3) being the neutral counterpart of the expressive sentences (1) and (2).

(1) Alas s
(2) Hurray s
(3) S

The sentences in (1)–(3) are, arguably, truth-conditionally equivalent: assuming that the only relevant sameness criteria are model-theoretic structures featuring extensions (sets) and elements, assertive utterances thereof are true in exactly the same circumstances, namely, in the circumstances required for (3) to be true. Yet, (1), (2), and (3) do not have the same meaning, being appropriately used in different circumstances.[8] Since the semantic differences between the three sentences are presumably due to the occurrence of different expressive prefixes in (1) and (2) and the absence thereof in (3), it follows that their respective semantic contributions are explainable not only at the level of the sentences' truth-conditions but also at some non-truth-conditional level; for example, at the level of their conditions of appropriate use. If the argument is sound, we seem to be justified in accommodating a new tier—in addition to the truth-conditional tier—along which the semantic contribution of any expressive can be analyzed. Let's see how this can be done, starting with the analysis of a standard type of expressive sentence.

2. SOME STANDARD EXPRESSIVE SENTENCES

Consider the following substitution instances of, respectively, (1), (2), and (3):

(4) Alas, Trump was elected.
(5) Hurray, Trump was elected.
(6) Trump was elected.

Sentences (4)–(6) are truth-conditionally equivalent, for they are true (or false) in just the same circumstances, namely, if and only if Trump—that is, the proper name's semantic value—belongs to the extension of the predicate "elected" (i.e., to the set of elected things) in the possible world of the context at some earlier time than the time of the context. Less informally, this is so in virtue of the following semantic rules for a non-fully interpreted language involving the constant prefix "alas":

Rule 1. $[\![s]\!]_{M,c} = [\![ex]\!]_{M,c} ([\![s_1]\!]_{M,c})$—where s is an expressive sentence of the form $ex\ s_1$, ex is an expressive prefix, and s_1 is a simple (non-expressive) sentence.
Rule 2. $[\![alas]\!]_{M,c} = id^9$

Rule 1 says that the truth-conditional semantic value of the expressive sentence s in a model M with respect to a context c (c being a member of the non-empty set of contexts of M) is a function of the truth-conditional semantic value (in M with respect to c) of the expressive prefix that takes as argument the truth-conditional semantic value (in M with respect to c) of the simple, non-expressive sentence s_1. Rule 2 says that the truth-conditional semantic value of "alas" (in M with respect to c) is the identity function. By Compositionality, we get that the semantic value of (4) in M with respect to c just is the semantic value of (6) in M with respect to c. The same holds mutatis mutandis for (5) in relation to (6). This being so, assuming that the semantic value of (6) in M with respect to c is the True, the semantic values in M with respect to c of (4) and (5) also are the True.

Yet, (4), (5), and (6) aren't use (i.e., non-truth)-conditionally equivalent: whereas (4) and (5) are subject to meaning-encoded constraints for their appropriate use, this is not the case with (6), due to the occurrence of biased expressions in (4) and (5) and the lack thereof in (6). In conformity with the dictionaries' definitions, TB renders the meaning-encoded constraint for "alas" as a necessary condition for membership in the class of its appropriate uses. So, one gets something like the following clause as bias for (4):

(i) $c \in CU(4)$ only if at c_t and c_w, c_a is unfavorably disposed toward $Cont_c(s)$—where "c" stands for a context, "CU" for the class of contexts of (appropriate) use, subscripted "t," "w," and "a" for contextual parameters (i.e., c's time, possible world and agent), and "$Cont_c$" for the expressive sentence's content in c.

Since the bias difference with respect to (4) is owed to the fact that "hurray" in (5) meaning-encodes just the opposite constraint on its use, TB renders the bias for (5) as follows:

(ii) $c \in CU(5)$ only if at c_t and c_w, c_a is favorably disposed toward $Cont_c(s)$[10]

"Alas" and "hurray" being the only biased expressions in (4) and (5), it is safe to assume that (i) and (ii) provide necessary *and* sufficient conditions for membership in the class of their appropriate use, so that the use of a biconditional in lieu of a conditional in (i) and (ii) would do here. Accordingly, the biases for (4) and (5) can be represented in set-theoretic terms as *proper* subclasses of the class of all contexts; namely, respectively, as follows:

$CU(4)$:{c: at c_t and c_w, c_a is unfavorably disposed toward $Cont_c(s)$}[11]
$CU(5)$:{c: at c_t and c_w, c_a is favorably disposed toward $Cont_c(s)$}

While the non-truth-conditional difference between (4) and (5) gets explained by their meaning-encoding different constraints on their appropriate (non-defective) use, the non-truth-conditional difference of either one with respect to (6) gets explained by the lack of any similar constraint on the use of (6), which means that the class of contexts of use for (6) is just the class of all contexts whatsoever—at least, as far as meaning-encoded constraints are concerned.

So, if one uses TB to account for the meaning of the sentential expressives featuring in (4) and (5), it turns out that one gets just the expected result in step with the argument scheme sketched above. There are indeed semantic differences between (4), (5), and (6) compositionally captured by the theory at the level of the expressions' respective (negative, positive, or null) biases—that is, with respect to *one* feature of their linguistic meanings. Yet, these differences are represented in the theory as truth-conditionally otiose or, as Predelli puts it, "character-idle." This is as it should be since the semantic value of sentential expressives being the identity function, the expressive sentences containing them return their argument as semantic value, that is, the semantic value of the non-expressive sentence. No more no less is needed, so it seems, to explain the truth-conditional equivalence holding between (4), (5), and (6).

Now, let's see if the theory has the resources to deal with less standard types of expressive sentences. We start with an instance of the so-called settled expressive sentences before proceeding to an instance of (seeming) expressive contradiction (section 4).

3. SETTLED EXPRESSIVE SENTENCES

Consider the following couple of sentences:

(7) Alas, I am unfavorably disposed toward something.
(8) I am unfavorably disposed toward something.

How does TB explain the relevant semantic difference between (7) and (8)? Pretty much along the same lines as it explains the differences between (4), (5), and (6), namely, by the occurrence of a biased expression ("alas") in (7) and the lack thereof in (8). However, a new element gets into the picture here: although (4)–(5) and (7) instantiate the same syntactic structure—they all are of the form $ex\ s_1$, where ex belongs to the class of expressive prefixes and s_1 is a simple sentence, that is, a sentence that contains no occurrence of an expressive prefix (Predelli 2010, 165; Predelli 2013, 114)—(7) exhibits a penchant for truth not exhibited by (4) and (5) above: it tends to be true *whenever* the expressive prefix is appropriately used, that is, whenever it is used in conformity with its bias. In Predelli's terminology, (7) is (merely) *settled*.[12]

To get the point, it is useful to contrast (7) with another instance of an expressive sentence that also contains a reference to the speaker's disposition within the prefixed simple sentence. Consider the following instance:

(9) Alas, I am unfavorably disposed toward Trump's election (i.e., toward the fact that Trump was elected).

The appropriate contexts of use of (9) are presumably those in which the agent of the context is unfavorably disposed toward her being unfavorably disposed toward Trump's election, for the meaning-encoded constraint on the (appropriate) use of "alas" in an expressive sentence of the form "Alas *s*" states that its appropriate contexts of use are those in which the agent of the context is unfavorably disposed toward the content of *s* with respect to *c* and the content of *s* in (9) with respect to *c* is not (the fact) *that Trump was elected* but (the fact) *that the agent of the context is unfavorably disposed toward this fact*. As awkward as this sounds, such context is available or, at least, thinkable as a context of use for (9).

Suppose the agent of the context *is* a fan of Donald Trump (i.e., she is *not* unfavorably disposed toward Trump's election), yet for some reasons, she does not feel that way. Suppose she is a thwarted Trump fan. As a result, she feels unhappy with the fact that she is unhappy with (or unfavorably disposed toward) Trump's election. Being a fan of Donald Trump, she ought to feel happy with the fact that he was elected, but since she is not in the appropriate emotional state—so goes the story—the fact that she isn't makes her unhappy. In such a circumstance, uttering (9) would be expressively appropriate.[13] Yet, the sentence can hardly be considered as settled. (9) is not true for all contexts of use since in the case at hand *s* is clearly *false*. Contrast this with (7). Here, in all appropriate contexts of use the agent of the context is unfavorably disposed toward something, which makes the sentence true. (7), in contrast to (9), is settled.[14] Moreover, assuming (8) is true, (7) and (8) are truth-conditionally indistinguishable, which is just what the argument in support of non-truth-conditional meaning requires.

4. (SEEMING) EXPRESSIVE CONTRADICTIONS

Now consider the following couple of sentences:

(10) That stupid Trump isn't stupid.
(11) Trump isn't stupid.

The sentence in (10) seems to point toward the following fact: an expressive adjective ("stupid") can be used within the same sentence both as an epithet in subject position *and* predicatively, in such a way that an utterance of the sentence sounds like an instance of a contradictory statement. The same fact is, so it seems, evidenced by easily conceivable exchanges wherein a speaker contradicts another who uses the same expressive adjective in predicate position (see Geurts 2007, 210–211).[15] If one grants the contradiction, one must be ready to acknowledge that the first occurrence of "stupid" in (10) *entails*

Trump's lack of intelligence, a feature denied in the predicative part of the sentence. The problem is that this interpretation looks incompatible with the argument's premise to the effect that (10) is truth-conditionally equivalent to (11), since a contradictory statement like (10) is, by definition, false in all possible worlds, whereas a statement like (11) is either true or false depending on whether Trump lacks intelligence or not. We are faced, so it seems, with a dilemma here: either (10) is truth-conditionally equivalent to (11), yet if this is the case (10) cannot be—contrary to facts—a contradictory statement; or (10) is a contradictory statement, but if this is so, the truth-conditional premise in Predelli's argument is false.

Fortunately, the dilemma supposedly faced here is not a *real* dilemma—we are not forced to choose one horn—since, on any reading of (10), Predelli's argument goes through. Predelli (2010, 176) rightly points out that expressive sentences of the form "That [ADJ] *NP* is *F*" are ambiguous between two readings: an expressive and a non-expressive one, and that the contrast between the two readings is syntactically detectable in some (notably, Romance) languages under the following form: "That [ADJ] *of a* [NP] is *F*."[16] He skips over a further non-expressive reading that is worth considering and that we also take to be unproblematic.

On the only expressive reading available for "that stupid Trump," (10) involves no contradiction because the adjective expresses the speaker's contemptuous attitude or unfavorable disposition toward the proper name's semantic value without *entailing* that Trump lacks intelligence, since the adjective on its epithetical occurrence makes no contribution to the truth-conditions of the sentence. On one of the non-expressive readings available for the complex demonstrative—the one apparently considered by Predelli[17]—the occurrence of the adjective in argument position *does* entail Trump's lack of intelligence and the adjective itself behaves like a standard predicate. It follows that a contradiction *is* involved in stating (10), since the truth-conditional contribution of the adjective is non-null—after all, if no predication were involved, statements like (11) would hardly make sense. Another non-expressive reading, however, is available on which the occurrence of the adjective in the complex demonstrative *need not* entail Trump's lack of intelligence provided it is used the way Donnellan's definite descriptions are sometimes used to pick out their denotation; namely, non-attributively.[18] On this other non-expressive reading, no contradiction is involved either in asserting (10), since no lack of intelligence is predicated in the subject part of the sentence. Just like on the expressive reading, the truth of the truth-conditional equivalence premise in Predelli's argument is secured and the contradiction is only a seeming one.

All in all, Predelli's argument goes through on each of these readings either because no real contradiction is involved—on the expressive and the second of the non-expressive readings of (10)—thereby securing its truth-conditional equivalence with (11), or because a contradiction *is* involved—on one of the non-expressive readings—thereby turning (10) and (11) non-truth-conditionally equivalent. In the latter case, the argument still goes through because this is not a case in which the premise(s) could be true and the conclusion false: in *no* world (be it actual or possible) a contradiction is equivalent to a contingent statement.

5. TB'S PREDICTIVE POWER

We saw that TB has the resources to deal with instances of expressive sentences of different kinds, be they settled or (seemingly) contradictory expressive statements. In that respect, it displays no limitations. But how does it fare when it comes to modeling distinctive semantic properties of expressive content such as its independence (vis-à-vis truth-conditional content) and non-displaceability in syntactic embeddings? In this section, we argue that TB's predictive power breaks down where significant differences among instances of non-truth-conditional meaning come to the fore. We start with the so-called property of independence.

5.1. Independence

Some expressions make a contribution along a semantic tier that remains separate from (or inaccessible to) the descriptive or truth-conditional tier, as evidenced by the fact that the expression can be removed or changed without affecting the sentence's truth-conditional (or "*at issue*") content. This is known as the *independence* property. Expressives are often considered as paradigmatic examples of linguistic expressions that instantiate that property. Cruse (1986, 272), for instance, writes that "expressive meaning carried by a lexical item in a statement plays no role in determining its truth-conditions," and gives as example the truth-conditional equivalence between two sentences one of which contains an expressive attributive adjective ("blasted") and the other, its neutral counterpart, has no such adjective in it. Potts (2005, 156–158, 2007a, 167–169) takes, in turn, independence to be one of the defining features of expressive content.

If this is so—that is, if independence is paradigmatically exemplified by expressive content—it is tempting to extend the list by appending lexical items such as discourse particles like the (unstressed) German particles "*ja*," "*doch*," and "*wohl*." For discourse particles not only serve, like all discourse markers, as discourse-structuring elements, they also convey information about the epistemic states or attitudes of discourse participants toward the propositional content of an utterance (Zimmermann 2011; Gutzmann 2013, 2015; Döring 2013). Functionally speaking, they may be, and have indeed been, considered as expressives, in the broad sense of linguistic devices whose role is to let the others know the speaker's states and attitudes toward the propositional content of an utterance rather than to describe some state(s) of the world. Semantically speaking too: it has been argued that they make no contribution to the truth-conditional content of the sentence they occur in (Gutzmann 2015, 220), but contribute, instead, to its expressive content along a separate tier (see Kratzer 1999).

Consider the following illustration due to Zimmermann (2011, 2013):[19]

(12) Max ist *ja* auf See.
(13) Max ist *doch* auf See ⎬ Max is PRT at sea
(14) Max ist *wohl* auf See.

(15) Max ist auf See.   Max is at sea.

It turns out that the same previously mentioned kind of argument in support of a separate, non-truth-conditional dimension of meaning can be rehearsed for the occurrence of discourse particles—symbolized in the English translation above by PRT (PRT = 'particle'). Sentences (12)–(15) are, indeed, truth-conditionally equivalent: they are true (or false) in just the same circumstances, namely, if and only if ⟦*Max*⟧ belongs to ⟦*ist auf See*⟧ at the time of the utterance. Yet, they do not have the same meaning and are correctly (felicitously) used in different circumstances. Roughly, (12) is appropriate if the speaker assumes that the hearer is aware of the fact that Max is at sea. (13) is appropriate if the speaker assumes that the hearer is *not* aware of this fact at the time (13) is uttered. (14) is appropriate if the speaker is unsure of the truth of the proposition expressed at the time of the utterance. By contrast, (15) is appropriate in all contexts. Since, as Zimmerman (2011, 2013) points out, "a difference in the choice of the particle ('*ja*,' '*doch*,' '*wohl*') leads to a difference in felicity conditions [. . .] such that each sentence will be appropriate in a different context," it follows that the difference in semantic contribution must be explained at a level different from the truth-conditional level, namely, at the use-conditional (or felicity conditions) level.

That TB is able, like any multi-tiered theory, to predict the independence feature shared by these putative instances of expressive meaning is pretty straightforward here. Just as the substitution of "alas" by "hurray" in (5) or its removal in (6), though expressively significant, had no impact on the truth-conditions of the sentences, the substitution of "*ja*" by "*doch*" in (13), "*doch*" by "*wohl*" in (14), and the removal of the particle in (15), albeit expressively significant, has no bearing on the sentences' truth-conditions. This is explained in the theory by the fact that it accommodates a separate dimension of meaning, the hallmark of which is to remain inaccessible (at least, in some cases) to the sentences' descriptive or truth-conditional content. Now, the fact that TB and the argument it rests upon easily generalize over items whose membership in the category of expressives is questionable is not necessarily a good sign. There are, indeed, significant differences among the phenomena often gathered under the same *expressives* or *expressive content* heading that are easily overlooked when the focus is on non-truth or use-conditionality. Consider the following examples owed to Zimmermann (2007, 253):

(16) Ihr   Tierarzt hat den verdammten Köter wohl schon
     your   vet   has the damn   cur   PRT   already
     eingeschläfert.
     put.down
     "I suppose your vet has already put down that damn cur."

(17) Hat Ihr   Tierarzt den verdammten Köter wohl schon
     has your vet   the damn   cur   PRT   already
     eingeschläfert?
     put.down
     "Tell me your suspicion: has your vet already put down that damn cur?"

In contrast to the expressive "*den verdammten Köter*" ("that damn cur") and the pronoun of address "*Ihr*" ("your"), which also happen to be biased expressions that instantiate the independence property,[20] the use-conditional meaning of the discourse particle (PRT) "*wohl*" is sensitive to the type of sentence, declarative or interrogative, it occurs in.[21] In (16) it gives cues about the epistemic state of the speaker who turns out to be unsure of the truth of the proposition expressed ("*I suppose* your vet already put down that damn cur"), whereas in (17) the epistemic reference point with respect to which the non-truth-conditional content of the whole sentence is evaluated shifts to the addressee ("*Tell me your suspicion*: has your vet already put down that damn cur?").[22] Nothing analogous can be expected from other kinds of expressives, except in cases in which the syntactic embedding brings about a shift in the context of evaluation (see section 5.2). The discourse particles' sentence-type (or, more specifically, sentence mood) sensitivity seems to be a peculiar phenomenon. The uses of both the expressive adjective and the formal pronoun in (16) and (17) are constrained by the same meaning-encoded restrictions: in both cases, the sentences are felicitously used if the speaker displays a somehow contemptuous attitude toward the modified noun's referent and stands in the appropriate social relationship with the addressee. In contrast, the uses of "*wohl*" in (16) and (17) are not subject to the same meaning-encoded restriction: (16) is infelicitous if *the speaker* knows (or is pretty sure) that the proposition is true, whereas (17) is infelicitous if *the addressee* knows the answer for sure, as it happens in some expert contexts wherein the addressee is the authority on the issue. In other words, discourse particles in the narrow sense allow for bias shifts depending on the mood of the sentence and the kind of illocutionary act (claiming or asking) performed in uttering it, whereas the bias of other kinds of expressives remains insensitive to that kind of feature.[23]

Although it structurally predicts the independence feature shared by all kinds of expressives, TB says nothing about what turns them into *different* instances of expressive/use-conditional content; in particular, it does not say anything specific concerning features such as the sensitivity of the bias of discourse particles versus the insensitivity of the bias of other kinds of expressives, like interjections and epithets, to sentence mood and illocutionary force. But why on earth, it might be objected, should it say anything at all? Being what it is—namely, a vanilla multi-tiered theory of meaning, TB is not even *meant* to do so. And, in any event, it certainly does *not* predict all types of expressive meaning to exhibit the same range of features. However, if TB is to be ever *used* as a theory of *expressive* meaning, a story needs to be told concerning features that single out expressives (in the narrow sense) as a distinctive kind of non-truth-conditional content. The insensitivity of their bias to sentence mood and illocutionary force is one. Our claim is *not* that this feature cannot be accommodated by the theory. It is, rather, that that cannot be done without suitable adjustments. This in itself indicates that TB qua theory of expressive meaning is in need of complementation.

5.2. Non-Displaceability

One thing not to be conflated with the unshiftability of the bias of expressives (in the narrow sense) is their non-displaceability in syntactic embeddings. The former concerns differences in semantic behavior owing to the expression's sensitivity to illocutionary acts performed in uttering the sentence; the latter, differences in semantic behavior owed to the expression's sensitivity to the semantic properties of the operator of the embedding clause. Illocutionary acts are often viewed as unembeddable, with a few possible exceptions (Krifka 2014). If this is the case, one can easily understand why one should be mindful not to conflate them: they just aren't the same phenomena.

The non-displaceability property can be defined as that of remaining semantically unembedded in syntactic embeddings. This means that the expressions the content of which is left untouched by the embedding operator "always tell us something about the [present or actual] situation of utterance" (Potts 2007a, 169). They "cannot [. . .] be used to report on past events, attitudes, or emotions, nor can they express mere possibilities, conjectures, or suppositions" (Potts 2007a, 169). Non-displaceability, so understood, is often considered as the hallmark of expressives and expressive content.[24] Cruse, for instance, points out that "a characteristic distinguishing expressive meaning from propositional meaning is that it is valid only for the utterer, at the time and place of utterance" (1986, 272); and Potts (2007a) takes this to be evidenced by the pragmatic infelicity of continuations in sentential constructions like (18)–(20) below:[25]

(18) That stupid Trump is not fit to be president of the United States. (#He doesn't lack intelligence.)
(19) If that stupid Trump enters the room, I leave. (#He doesn't lack intelligence.)
(20) Maybe that stupid Trump will enter the room. (#He doesn't lack intelligence.)

Again, having located the meaning-encoded constraints on the appropriate use of expressives at the non-truth-conditional tier, TB turns out to have just the right predictive power when it comes to the non-displaceability of expressive content in syntactic embeddings such as (18)–(20). In (18), the speaker's contemptuous or, at least, negative attitude toward Trump scopes out of negation, as testified by the infelicity of the continuation between parentheses. In (19), the same kind of (pragmatic) infelicity indicates that the content expressed by the epithet is not conditionalized by its occurrence in the antecedent clause; and in (20), its syntactically falling into the scope of the modal operator does not turn it into a mere possibility. This is accounted for in TB by the following structural feature of the theory: since the meaning-encoded constraints operate at a level that is different from the level truth-functional and modal operators operate at, they are expected to remain unaffected by the expressive's syntactic embeddings. This is just what happens here: "that stupid Trump" keeps on expressing, while syntactically falling into the scope of negation, the conditional, and the modal operator, the speaker's negative attitude toward Trump, the speaker's attitude being part of the meaning-encoded constraint to be met for the context to be an appropriate context of use for the epithet. The same holds for embeddings of expressives in attitude verbs and indirect speech reports (see Predelli 2013, 75–78; 87–89): unless the context is quotational or the use metalinguistic or/and echoic as in (21) and (22) below, the expressive content inflicted by the speaker on the hearer is left untouched and the expressive's bias remains unaffected while the effect of such embeddings is, usually, to cancel content projection.

(21) That "stupid" Trump is not fit to be president of the United States. (He doesn't lack intelligence.)

(22) That stupid Trump is not fit to be president of the United States. (He doesn't lack intelligence.) [Uttered by a Trump fan with an ironical overtone to mock her political opponents]

In (21) and (22), the displacement effects achieved by mentioning (rather than using) the epithet or by using it ironically with an appropriate tone of voice are testified by the pragmatic *felicity* of the continuations in parentheses. Now, such an approach, albeit entirely correct, strikes us as insufficiently specific, since not all non-displaced content is expressive.[26]

Consider the following sentence:

(23) It's possible that Trump's son has colluded with the Russians.

"It's possible that"—just like "not" in (18) and "maybe" in (20)—belongs to the group of predicates that act as "holes" (Karttunen 1973), that is, as predicates (operators) that pass the presuppositions of the embedded sentences up the tree without altering or canceling them. Whoever utters (23) presupposes that Trump has a son, which is just the presupposition of its embedded part—that is, of the sentence "Trump's son has colluded with the Russians." So, it seems that we are in presence of an instance of non-displaced content (in the relevant sense) that is not an instance of expressive content, since no attitude or emotional state of the speaker is expressed or displayed in uttering (23). If this is true, to say that expressives are expressions whose content is left untouched by their syntactic embedding by means of operators like "maybe" in (20) or "not" in (18) is not to say anything specific about that kind of content as opposed to, say, presuppositional content.

For a non-displaced content to qualify as expressive, it must be such that *it cannot be displaced in syntactic embeddings that normally act as "plugs"* (Karttunen 1973), that is, as predicates that block off all the presuppositions of the embedded sentence(s). "Believes" in (24) acts as a plug—the speaker of (24) may yet *need not* presuppose that Trump has a son—while the embedded epithet in (25) keeps on conveying that, to put it mildly, the speaker of (25) does not think too highly of Trump, as testified by the pragmatic infelicity of the continuation in parentheses:

(24) *New York Times* journalists believe that Trump's son has colluded with the Russians.
(25) *New York Times* journalists believe that that stupid Trump has colluded via his son with the Russians. (# I believe he is not stupid.)

The different semantic behaviors of the presupposition trigger and the expressive in constructions like (24) and (25) has been construed as testifying, if not a difference in kind between the corresponding contents, at least "an important contrast between presuppositional and expressive content" (Potts 2007a, 170). It can be construed, instead, as showing that *the crucial test for a non-truth-conditional content to qualify as expressive is its unpluggability in the syntactic scope of non-factive verbs like "believe" in (25) and the so-called verbs of saying*. The fact that some cases—like (26) below—allow for spectacular displacements of expressive content need not be taken to undermine this construal, since they are easily accommodated by conceding that the context with respect to which the expressive content is evaluated *need not be* the actual utterance situation (see Potts 2007a, 172–176; Schlenker 2007, 244):

(26) My father screamed that he would never allow me to marry that prick. [Uttered by Ivana Trump][27]

The further fact that variations are observed within the category of expressives with respect to their (un)pluggability in forms of speech (direct, indirect, free indirect) need not be taken to undermine it either. This should be understood as pointing, instead, toward the need for a more flexible account along the lines of Sauerland (2007).

TB fails to pinpoint unpluggability as the crucial test for expressive content, presumably because it is designed to account for the semantic properties *shared* by the different manifestations of the non-truth-conditional phenomenon rather than the distinctive properties of expressives. Having emphasized that his own analysis of expressive content in terms of non-truth-conditional features of the expression's meaning (i.e., of the expression's *bias*) "goes hand in hand" (Predelli 2013, 76) with the widely noted non-displaceability property of expressives, Predelli gives as example the semantic unembeddedness of the epithet "bastard" in the scope of the truth-functional operator of negation:

> For instance, if the occurrence of "that bastard Kresge" in ["It is just false that that bastard Kresge is late for work. # He is a good guy"] is indeed within the area of semantic influence for "it is just false that," and if what this latter expression contributes is merely the truth-function of negation, it follows from the anomaly of the continuation "He is a good guy" that Kresge's unpleasant features remain truth-conditionally "off the record." (Predelli 2013, 76)

What is true for expressions (or constructions) of the same category is also true for expressions belonging to different categories: it is important to test several types of embedding—in the case at hand, embeddings in attitude verbs and verbs of saying in addition to embeddings in truth-functional and modal operators—before drawing any conclusion about the kind of content that is being tested. Otherwise, it will be no proper testing, but the valueless confirmation of what was thought to be the case ahead of any investigation of the semantic behavior of the expressions at hand. Because TB does not fit the methodological bill, it ends up overlooking significant semantic differences within the range of non-truth-conditional phenomena, thereby failing to be sufficiently specific about their semantic behavior.

6. CONCLUDING REMARKS

Blakemore once made the following observations:

> Given the range of non truth-conditional phenomena and the theoretical differences between the various people who have studied them, it is not really surprising that no single theory of non truth-conditional meaning has emerged. But then, again, it is not clear that we should want a unitary account of all the different phenomena which have been identified as examples of non truth-conditional meaning: perhaps the only thing that the expressions [illocutionary and attitudinal adverbials, discourse connectives, particles] in (1–7) have in common is that they don't contribute to the truth conditions of the utterances that contain them. (Blakemore 1997, 92)

With the emergence of TB, the situation has dramatically changed. Not only do we have now a unitary semantic framework to account for a variety of non-truth-conditional phenomena, but, more importantly, we have a positive rather than a purely negative account of those phenomena. So, it would be false from the standpoint of the new framework to claim that "*the only thing* that the [relevant] expressions [. . .] have in common is that they don't contribute to the truth-conditions of the utterances that contain them." A property shared by all biased expressions is that they contribute, in virtue of some features of their linguistic meaning, to the felicity conditions of the utterances that contain them. This is accounted for within TB by the bias tier and one of its merits is to show that this is so even when the expression's use is subject to no meaning-encoded restriction—the class of its contexts of use being in that case the class of all contexts. Moreover, *pace* Blakemore, it is also clear that such an account is needed. Without it or an equivalent framework, one would be left with unrelated subclasses of truth-conditionally otiose expressions and, as Zimmermann aptly puts it, "as many formal analyses as there are classes of non-descriptive elements traditionally recognized by descriptive grammarians" (2007, 254). In that respect, TB allows us to take an important step toward a general and positive grasp of the semantic behavior of the members of a *whole class* of use-conditional phenomena. Now, we hope to have cogently shown that more is required of the framework for it to be used as an explanatory model of expressive meaning, even taken in its full generality.[28] For one thing, the expression's *bias* should be depicted as being possibly sensitive to the kind of illocutionary act performed in uttering the sentence it occurs in, even when no such sensitivity is actually displayed. For another, unpluggability should be pinpointed as the crucial test for expressive content. This is not to say that Predelli's Theory of Bias could not deal with the relevant semantic and pragmatic phenomena while fitting the methodological bill. This is just to say that a suitable extension is needed for the theory to be fully applicable to the cases under scrutiny.

ACKNOWLEDGMENTS

Research for this chapter has benefited from the financial support of the Conselho Nacional de Desenvolvimento Científico e Tecnológico (Research Productivity Grant-Level 2; Junior Post-Doctoral Fellowship, 2016–2017, process #152155/2016-3), the Coordenação de Aperfeiçoamento de Pessoal de Nível Superior (CAPES-COFECUB research project #813-14), and the Fundação de Amparo à Pesquisa do Estado de São Paulo (Post-Doctoral Fellowship, 2018–2020, process #2018/04058-7), Brazil. We are grateful to these institutions. We also thank Stefano Predelli, Eleonora Orlando, and Andrés Saab for helpful comments on earlier drafts; Marco Ruffino, Eros Corazza, Nicolás Lo Guercio, Sébastien Gandon, Henri Galinon, Dirk Greimann, Célia Teixeira, and Guido Imaguire for challenging discussions.

NOTES

1. A tentative list is provided by Kaplan (1999) featuring adjectives like "damn," interjections like "oh," "ouch," "alas," diminutives like "*Tütchen*" ("baggie" in German), nicknames like "Liz," and ethnic slurs like "chink." An updated list would surely encompass colored expressions like "cur," derogatory terms targeted at nonethnic groups like "faggot" or "whore," and exclamatives like "what a tall dog!" All these may be said to be "expressives in the narrow sense" (Gutzmann 2013, 4) just spelled out. Appending, following Kratzer's (1999) and Potts et al.'s (2009) suggestions, honorifics (like "*san*" in Japanese) and discourse particles (like "*ja*" in German) to the list is debatable, for, as Cruse (1986, 274) rightly points out, "the meaning they express is not necessarily so distinctively emotive"; nor is, unlike the meaning of expressives in the narrow sense, "prosodically gradable."

2. See Geurts's (2007) objections to Potts (2007a) and Potts's (2007b) reply. For further evidence in support of a semantic type distinction between expressives and descriptives, see Potts et al. (2009).

3. 2013: viii and *passim*.

4. Further manifestations include vocatives, dates, and signatures. The effect of their respective biases on the character of indexical expressions is analyzed in the third part of the book under the heading of *obstinacy*.

5. It is now common in semantics (and pragmatics) to describe this further layer of meaning as *use-conditional*. See Recanati (2004, 47–50), Gutzmann (2013, 2015), Predelli (2013), Rami (2014). The idea stems from Kaplan (1989, 1999).

6. Predelli (2013, 61–64) draws a distinction between two kinds of constraints on an expression's use: universal constraints derivable from general facts about types of use (e.g., face-to-face vs. delayed contexts of communication) or linguistic production and general constraints derivable from regularities encoded in the expression's meaning. The constraint encoded by the meaning of expressives is of the latter kind.

7. Of course, not all expressive adjectives lack a truth-conditional dimension. For instance, "stupid" presumably makes a nontrivial contribution to the truth-conditions of the sentences in which it occurs. This means that not all expressives are pure expressives.

8. It is assumed here for the sake of argument that the right way to construe the meaning of expressions such as "alas" or "hurray" and the sentences in which they occur is in terms of rules (or circumstances) of appropriate use. This is fairly uncontroversial. See, for example, Recanati (2004, 447).

9. Predelli (2013, 115). The same rules hold for "hurray."

10. Predelli (2013, 73).

11. Predelli (2013, 113).

12. "A sentence s is settled iff $\text{true}_c(s)$ for all $c \in \text{CU}(s)$" (Predelli 2013, 70).

13. Another circumstance in which uttering (9) would be expressively appropriate is one in which the agent of the context is self-deceived.

14. We owe this point to S. Predelli (personal communication, December 27, 2017).

15. Geurts gives the following example: speaker A assertively utters: "That bastard Schmidt is a bastard," while speaker B assertively utters: "Schmidt is not a bastard." Here, it seems OK to claim that B contradicts A.

16. Predelli (2013, 97) gives the following example: "Quello stupido *di un* capo di governo sarà rieletto" in Italian; rendered in English as: "That stupid *of a* prime minister will be re-elected." We gather the ambiguity is still there when it is *not* detectable in the surface structure, as it is the case with non-Romance languages. For a full defense of the thesis of the syntactically grounded semantic ambiguity of some pejoratives (namely, prototypical slurs), see Orlando and Saab (2020).

17. Predelli (2010, 176) is not explicit, but we can infer this from the parallel he draws with the entailment relation that holds between the definite description and its restrictive-relative-clause paraphrase ("the prime minister *who is stupid*") in "the stupid prime minister will be re-elected" on its non-expressive reading.

18. Does the *demonstratum need* to have whatever descriptive property is associated with the pejorative adjective "stupid"? We believe the answer is no! Think of a case wherein the speaker mistakenly believes that the *demonstratum* is *the* Trump she

has in mind (say, Donald, as opposed to Eric or Barron) and whom she judges stupid. We take it that in this case the complex demonstrative refers to the *demonstratum* even though the latter turns out to have none of the properties the intended referent is meant to have, in particular that of lacking intelligence. Kaplan (1989, 515) interestingly points out that Donnellan's distinction between referential and attributive uses of definite descriptions "seems to fit [. . .] the case of demonstrations," but does not bother explaining how it does. Our suggestion that the occurrence of the complex demonstrative in (10), therefore (10) itself is amenable to a further non-expressive reading goes some way toward explaining it.

19. We simply added (15), (12)–(14)'s neutral counterpart. See Gutzmann (2013, 11–12) and Döring (2013) for further illustrations featuring "*ja*," "*doch*," and "*wohl*."

20. One caveat: the bias of some instances of register (e.g., formal and informal pronouns of address) is sensitive to the properties of the expression's semantic value—see Predelli (2013, 84–86) on addressee-directed biases. This means that it must be acknowledged that interactions occur in some cases between the bias- and the character-level and that the non-truth-conditional level is not completely insulated from the truth-conditional one, at least as far as expressives other than expletives are concerned. Such interactions are, nevertheless, limited and easily handled by a theory of expressives that gives pride of place to the property of independence. On this, see Potts (2007a).

21. More precisely, the non-truth-conditional contribution of the modal particle interacts with the *mood* of the sentence. Since sentence mood constrains the illocutionary force of the utterance, a change in sentence mood may lead to a change in illocutionary force. On this, see Gutzmann (2015, 229–230).

22. On the notion of an epistemic reference point and the sentence-type sensitivity of discourse particles, see Zimmermann (2011, 3.1). For arguments in support of the claim that German modal particles allow for shifts in the context of interpretation, see Döring (2013).

23. Alternatively, the difference might be accounted for in terms not of a bias shift, but of a double (as opposed to single) constraint on the sets of appropriate contexts of use for the discourse particle. Thanks to Eleonora Orlando for pointing this out.

24. In what follows, we remain neutral about the substantive issue as to whether expressive content is *always* non-displaceable. Empirical evidence supports the view that they are *not* (Amaral, Roberts, and Smith 2007; Harris and Potts 2009). Our interest here is more methodological than substantive and our argument can be adequately put in the form of a conditional: if—as predicted by TB in virtue of its formal structure—expressive content is always non-displaceable, then further theoretical features are needed to account for the contrast between expressive and, for example, presuppositional content since presuppositional content also projects out. Remember that a conditional with a false antecedent is true. This is all we need for the argument's sake.

25. The examples are ours.

26. We do not mean that Predelli is himself committed to the view that all non-displaceable content is expressive. He rather seems to hold the contrary (i.e., that all expressive content is non-displaceable); which is *apparently* more palatable (see note

22 for qualifications, though). Our point is that, regardless of Predelli's own commitments, TB is, methodologically speaking, insufficiently specific.

27. Adapted from Kratzer (1999). See also Schlenker (2003) and Geurts (2007) for further examples. None of these examples need to be taken to express the authors' opinion.

28. Our point about the incompleteness of TB presumably generalizes over further members of the family of multidimensional accounts of non-truth-conditional meaning (e.g., Potts's account) to the extent that they do not tackle the issues raised in this paper. A possible exception is Gutzmann's, as it takes on board sentence mood (see footnote 20).

BIBLIOGRAPHICAL REFERENCES

Almog, Joseph, John Perry, and Howard Wettstein, eds. 1989. *Themes from Kaplan*. New York: Oxford University Press.

Amaral, Patricia, Craige Roberts, and E. Allyn Smith. 2007. "Review of the Logic of Conventional Implicatures by Chris Potts." *Linguistics and Philosophy* 30(6): 707–749.

Blakemore, Diane. 1997. "On Non-Truth Conditional Meaning." In *Pragmatik: Implikaturen und Sprechakte*, edited by Eckard Rolf, 92–102. New York: Springer.

Cruse, David Alan. 1986. *Lexical Semantics*. Cambridge: Cambridge University Press.

Döring, Sophia. 2013. "Modal Particles and Context Shift." In *Beyond Expressives: Explorations in Use-Conditional Meaning*, edited by Daniel Gutzmann and Hans-Martin Gärtner, 95–123. Leiden, Boston: Brill.

Geurts, Bart. 2007. "Really Fucking Brilliant." *Theoretical Linguistics* 33(2): 209–214.

Gutzmann, Daniel. 2013. "Expressives and Beyond: An Introduction to Varieties of Use-Conditional Meaning." In *Beyond Expressives: Explorations in Use-Conditional Meaning*, edited by Daniel Gutzmann and Hans-Martin Gärtner, 1–55. Leiden, Boston: Brill.

Gutzmann, Daniel. 2015. "Use-Conditional Meaning: Studies in Multidimensional Semantics." In *Oxford Studies in Semantics and Pragmatics 6*. Oxford: Oxford University Press.

Gutzmann, Daniel, and Hans-Martin Gärtner, eds. 2013. *Beyond Expressives: Explorations in Use-Conditional Meaning*. Leiden, Boston: Brill.

Harris, Jesse A., and Christopher Potts. 2009. "Perspective-Shifting with Appositives and Expressives." *Linguistics and Philosophy* 32(6): 523–552.

Horn, Laurence R., and Gregory Ward, eds. 2004. *The Handbook of Pragmatics*. Oxford: Blackwell.

Kaplan, David. 1989. "Demonstratives: An Essay on the Semantics, Logic, Metaphysics, and Epistemology of Demonstratives and Other Indexicals." In *Themes from Kaplan*, edited by Joseph Almog, John Perry, and Howard Wettstein, 481–563. New York: Oxford University Press.

Kaplan, David. 1999. "The Meaning of 'Ouch' and 'Oops': Explorations in the Theory of Meaning as Use." Manuscript, UCLA.

Karttunen, Lauri. 1973. "Presuppositions of Compound Sentences." *Linguistic Inquiry* 4(2): 169–193.

Kratzer, Angelika. 1999. "Beyond 'Ouch' and 'Oops'. How Descriptive and Expressive Meaning Interact." Comment on Kaplan's paper at the Cornell Conference on Context Dependency. March 26. http://semanticsarchive.net/Archive/WEwNGUyO/.

Krifka, Manfred. 2014. "Embedding Illocutionary Acts." In *Recursion: Complexity in Cognition*, edited by Thomas Roeper and Margaret Speas, 59–87. Heidelberg, New York, London: Springer.

Maienborn, Claudia, Klaus von Heusinger, and Paul Portner, eds. 2011. *Semantics*. Berlin: Mouton de Gruyter.

Orlando, Eleonora, and Andrés Saab. 2020. "A Stereotype Semantics for Syntactically Ambiguous Slurs." *Analytic Philosophy* 61(2): 101–129.

Potts, Christopher. 2005. *The Logic of Conventional Implicatures*. Oxford: Oxford University Press.

Potts, Christopher. 2007a. "The Expressive Dimension." *Theoretical Linguistics* 33(2): 165–198.

Potts, Christopher. 2007b. "The Centrality of Expressive Indices." *Theoretical Linguistics* 33(2): 255–268.

Potts, Christopher, Ash Asudeh, Seth Cable, Yurie Hara, Elin McCready, Luis Alonso-Ovalle, Rajesh Bhatt, et al. 2009. "Expressives and Identity Conditions." *Linguistic Inquiry* 40(2): 356–366.

Predelli, Stefano. 2010. "From the Expressive to the Derogatory: On the Semantic Role for Non- Truth-Conditional Meaning." In *New Waves in Philosophy of Language*, edited by Sarah Sawyer, 164–185. New York: Palgrave Macmillan.

Predelli, Stefano. 2013. *Meaning Without Truth*. Oxford, NY: Oxford University Press.

Rami, Dolf. 2014. "The Use-Conditional Indexical Conception of Proper Names." *Philosophical Studies* 168(1): 119–150.

Recanati, François. 2004. "Pragmatics and Semantics." In *The Handbook of Pragmatics*, edited by Laurence R. Horn and Gregory Ward, 442–462. Oxford: Blackwell.

Roeper, Thomas, and Margaret Speas, eds. 2014. *Recursion: Complexity in Cognition*. Heidelberg, New York, London: Springer.

Rolf, Eckard, ed. 1997. *Pragmatik: Implikaturen und Sprechakte*. New York: Springer.

Sauerland, Uli. 2007. "Beyond Unpluggability." *Theoretical Linguistics* 33(2): 231–236.

Sawyer, Sarah, ed. 2010. *New Waves in Philosophy of Language*. New York: Palgrave Macmillan.

Schlenker, Philippe. 2003. "A Plea for Monsters." *Linguistics and Philosophy* 26(1): 29–120.

Schlenker, Philippe. 2007. "Expressive Presuppositions." *Theoretical Linguistics* 33(2): 237–245.

Zimmermann, Malte. 2007. "I Like That Damn Paper - Three Comments on Christopher Potts' the Expressive Dimension." *Theoretical Linguistics* 33(2): 247–254.

Zimmermann, Malte. 2011. "Discourse Particles." In *Semantics*, edited by Claudia Maienborn, Klaus von Heusinger, and Paul Portner, 2012–2038. Berlin: Mouton de Gruyter.

Chapter 6

Taboo

The Case of Slurs

Stefano Predelli

In this chapter, I provide an informal introduction to the idea of *taboo*, with particular attention to the case of *slurs*. In section 1, I briefly summarize the central tenets of the dominant multidimensional approach to slurs, according to which a slur's *semantic contribution* exhaustively involves a truth-conditional and an expressive component. In section 2, I sketch the general methodological background for the semantic treatment of semantic contributions—that is, in the case of slurs, of the truth-conditional and expressive parts of their meanings. In section 3, I introduce the idea of taboo as an independent dimension of meaning, focusing on the occurrences of *coarse* expressions in quotational contexts. In section 4, I extend these considerations to the case of slurs, and I address a few objections against the idea of taboo as an aspect of meaning.

This chapter's final section gestures toward some philosophical and meta-semantic consequences of taboo. In contrast with the aspects of meaning included in an expression's semantic contribution, taboo is inextricably encoded in an expression's *form* and directly pertains to its tokening. Accordingly, the study of taboo is of interest beyond the analysis of slurs and of expressives, and it affects the scope of the *representationalist* stance described in section 2. My closing sentences mention a few promising topics which may benefit from the token-directed methodology invoked by the taboo dimension.

1. THE STATE OF THE ART: AN OPINIONATED SUMMARY

In the last two decades, the study of slurs has occupied a central role in the analysis of expressive devices. In particular, David Kaplan's influential notes on *meaning and use* (Kaplan 1999) have spurred what may be characterized as the dominant approach to slurring and expressivity in general—an approach that has systematically been developed and modified in Christopher Potts's influential *The Logic of Conventional Implicature* (Potts 2005) and in the considerable literature it engendered.[1]

The initial hypotheses in this approach seem uncontroversial: unlike cries or sneezes, slurs are meaningful expressions, whose meaning is partly characterizable in terms of a *derogatory* dimension. And so, at least as a first approximation, competent users of, say, "wop" employ that slur as an English noun and they do so in order to express some sort of negative attitude toward their target.[2]

At least as rough preliminaries, these assumptions are intended to be consistent with the elusive characteristics of the derogatory dimension. Admittedly, the disdain semantically associated with a slur may be difficult to describe, it may vary in subtler ways than other conventionally entrenched aspects of meaning, and it may anyway display vague and negotiable boundaries. As a result, the description of a slur's derogatory contribution may remain a fertile topic of contention from the viewpoint of sociolinguistics, of political discourse, and of the theory of communication. Yet, *modulo* a few cautionary *caveats*, semanticists may legitimately leave these subtleties aside, and they may settle for decent approximations invoking not better specified negative attitudes or properties.

With these caveats in place, it is tempting to present these approximations in *contentful* terms: part of the meaning of, say, "wop" may have to do with the notion *that* Italians are intrinsically unworthy of respect, or with the idea *that* they are generically and/or stereotypically describable in terms of certain undesirable features, or with the view *that* the speaker bears an unfavorable attitude toward them. In this respect, then, a slur's expressive dimension appears to be no worse off than that of similarly elusive exemplars, as in Kaplan's description of "oops" in terms of the notion *that* the speaker has witnessed a minor mishap, or in analyses of "bunny" as encompassing the requirement *that* the addressee is a child.[3]

My cursory mention of contentful regimentations also indirectly indicates a widespread generosity toward analogies and theoretical unifications. Surely, only a relatively distant perspective may legitimately assimilate the peculiarities of "wop" with the characteristics of "oops," with the idiosyncrasies of "bunny," or, in the case of Potts's even wider outlook, with the compositional complexities of relative clauses and nominal appositives. Yet, one important trait presumably applies to all of these cases, and it provides at least partial justification for a unified approach. As I am about to explain, it is a trait having to do with the *role* of the aforementioned contentful outcomes, rather than with their exact substance.

The role in question comes to the foreground in the study of the interactions between truth-conditional content and those other contentful elements. The buzzwords are familiar: the latter *project*, they are *non-displaced*, or they *scope-out*, in the sense that they remain indifferent to the truth-conditional effects of negations, modals, conditionals, and (at least to some extent) attitude reports.[4] And so,

(1) If that is a bunny, it likes his carrots.

is unconditionally child-directed, and, in Potts's wider outlook,

(2) It is not the case that the teachers, who are underpaid, will go on strike.

is positively committed to the teachers' lack of adequate remuneration.

When it comes to slurs, this projective behavior comes to light with particular clarity when the hypotheses with which I began this chapter are accompanied by another widespread assumption, namely, the idea that slurs are also endowed with straightforward (and straightforwardly displaceable) truth-conditional content.[5] For instance, in this view, "wop" is truth-conditionally indistinguishable from "Italian," in the sense that "wop" is the *charged* version of "Italian," or, in more common parlance, in the sense that "Italian" is the *neutral counterpart* of "wop." And so, the contrast between run-of-the-mill contents and derogatory contributions results in a neat division of labor: for instance,

(3) If Mario is a wop, he likes his pasta al dente.

unconditionally derogates Italians, but only conditionally describes Mario's nationality. In the jargon from the foregoing paragraph: the derogatory dimension of "wop" remains unaffected by "if" and by other devices of truth-conditional displacement.

Accordingly, the standard take on slurs has generated a variety of *multidimensional* semantic approaches, designed so as to isolate the slurring dimension from the sort of content that remains on the truth-conditional record. Probably the most influential approach in this respect, namely Potts's approach to conventional implicature, enshrines this duality within a type-theoretic framework which distinguishes between classic *at issue* types and the CI-type t^c, and which accounts for non-displaceability with opportune tree-admissibility conditions and interpretive clauses.[6] Others opt for a presentation couched in terms of a divide among parameters of semantic evaluation: for instance, "Mario is a wop" ends up being true with respect to all *points of evaluation* in which it is true that Mario is Italian, whereas it is deemed to be licensed in all *contexts* whose speaker believes that Italians are intrinsically despicable (or something in that vein).[7]

To summarize: according to a standard approach, slurs (not unlike analogous candidates, such as simple interjections or instances of child-directed speech) are endowed with a peculiarly expressive dimension of meaning. *Modulo* a few independently important admonitions, this dimension may be glossed in terms of contentful requirements, variously having to do with the speaker's attitude, with the characteristics of her addressee, or with certain properties of a targeted group. In turn, these requirements bear a distinctive semantic relation to a slur's (or a child-directed noun's, or an appositive's) truth-conditional content, as testified by the phenomenon of non-displaceability. And so, for instance, (3) conditionally attributes to Mario the property of being an Italian, but it unconditionally derogates Italians.

In the remainder of this chapter, I adopt the general traits of this picture without further ado: as it will turn out, what I am after is not its adequacy, but its completeness. Before I suggest what I take to be a necessary *addition* to the semantics of slurs (and of a variety of other charged expressions), I pause on certain methodological requirements for the study of the aforementioned traditionally accepted parts of a slur's meaning. The representationalist viewpoint that emerges shall provide a useful point of contrast when I finally tackle taboo in sections 3 and 4.

2. REPRESENTATIONALISM

My emphasis on the contentful dimensions of a slur's meaning need not be sacrosanct. For some, the apparently inevitable difficulty in pinpointing a slur's derogatory features in terms of neat and precise glosses indirectly indicates that what is at issue is not straightforward content, but some less easily specifiable negative attitude toward the relevant targets.[8] For others, less cognitively oriented features must anyway enter the picture, including vague invitations to adopt a hostile posture or generic promotions of unsympathetic courses of action. The differences among these proposals are independently interesting, but they should not obscure an important underlying commonality—one which indirectly justifies my pedagogical focus on contentful affairs. I refer to this common assumption in terms of a shared commitment to *representationalism*, in a sense, I am about to discuss. I start, as part of a relatively uncontroversial background, by putting slurs (and interjections, and child-directed speech, and all the rest) on the backburner, and by focusing on more familiar cases of semantic analysis.

It is customary to conceive of an expression as an affair involving at least two features, roughly characterizable in terms of that expression's *form* and what I call (with some hesitation, see the comments in section 4) its *semantic contribution*. For instance, the common English noun for certain flying mammals shares its monosyllabic form, but not its semantic contribution, with an equally common noun for hitting devices: expressions articulated as "bat" are alternatively associated with pipistrelles or with something of greater interest from the viewpoint of baseball or cricket. Or else, the two-letter form "he" occurs side by side with a semantic contribution pertaining to the contextually salient male in the case of the third-person pronoun, but flanks a different affair in the case of the name of the fifth letter of the Hebrew alphabet. Conversely, the nouns "attorney" and "lawyer" arguably share their semantic contribution, something having to do with being a law practitioner, though they obviously display forms of a very different nature: the former, for instance, begins with "a" but the latter does not.

The divide between form and semantic contribution is neatly reflected in a traditional division of labor within traditional linguistics. Surely, forms are of primary importance from the viewpoint of phonology or, if written languages are accepted as objects of genuine linguistic interest, from the viewpoint of orthography or scriptology. Semantics, on the other hand, is unsurprisingly entirely devoted to the study of what I noncommittally encompassed under the label of "semantic contribution": "bat" or "he" or "lawyer," the forms, may well enter the semanticist's textbook, but they do so exclusively as pointers for the semantic traits with which they are allegedly associated. That is, they serve the role of useful stand-ins or *representatives* for those traits.

Admittedly, given that natural-language semantics is an empirical discipline, it must eventually be concerned with competent speakers' semantic intuitions, or at least with those intuitions that are deemed to be of relevance on the basis of this or that methodological viewpoint. Since our intuitions deal with the effects engendered by particular acts of speaking, it is inevitable that, one way or another, semantics will eventually need to come to grips with the effects achieved by particular utterances, with all their Janus-faced profiles. And so, one's favorite theory of pronouns will eventually need to be tested vis-à-vis scenarios involving certain tokens of the form "he," and one's hypotheses about English synonymies will need to withstand our intuitions about particular instances of the forms "attorney" and "lawyer." And yet, it is crucial that this methodological attention to tokens do not degenerate into a lethal enamorment with the nitty-gritty of the articulation process. If representation and *representatum* are to be kept apart, the study of meaning must inevitably *abstract away* from that which carries that meaning, namely, the forms that echo in the circumstances of speaking.

This sort of abstraction is commonly reflected within the traditional semantic clauses by appealing to this or that result *with respect to* a parameter of the appropriate kind. The choice of such parameters will obviously depend on the details of one's favorite semantic apparatus. One well-known framework serves particularly well here, one which approaches (truth-conditional) meaning in terms of Kaplan-style *characters* (Kaplan 1989a). And so, the semantic contribution of, say, one sense for "bat" may be the constant character which yields, with respect to any context c and circumstance w, the class of pipistrelles in w. Or else, the semantic contribution of the more familiar usage of "he" is the indexical character whose value, with respect to any c and w, is the salient male individual in c. Or something of this sort—the details are irrelevant for my purposes here. What is relevant is that these semantic contributions are rendered with no requirements pertaining to the occurrences of the forms "bat" or "he" in those circumstances or contexts: uttering "bat" or "he" may well be necessary for making a conversational point, but that point will inevitably have to do with certain animals and certain males, rather than with the token of any form.

From the viewpoint of truth-conditional semantics, there are very good reasons for a representationalist strategy of this sort—that is, in Kaplan's apt slogan, for being clear about the divide between the *verities of meaning* and the *vagaries of action* (Kaplan 1989b, 585).[9] Or, at least, there are very good reasons for keeping the two apart as long as semantics is traditionally conceived as the study of "entailment, contradiction, and so on" (Dowty et al. 1981, 2), that is, as the source of a *logic*. The disastrous results of failing to do so are familiar enough. For instance, it is inevitable that whenever "John is a lawyer" is uttered truly, "It is not the case that John is not a lawyer" ought to be true as well. But it is equally inevitable that, on any such occasion, a six-letter expression is being tokened, and that there exist exemplars of a noun beginning with the letter "l." And yet, the former is an instance of a genuinely semantic phenomenon, namely, mutual entailment, whereas the latter is not: one ensues from the semantic contributions of the expressions at issue, whereas the other appeals to the tokening of their forms.

All of this, thus far, left expressives and their multidimensional semantics on the backburner and focused on the simpler instance provided by what I took to be expressively neutral expressions such as "lawyer," "he," and the like. Hence, thus far, I focused on a representationalist approach to semantic contribution in cases in which semantic contributions may safely be assumed to pertain only to the truth-conditional dimension (that is, in my simple model, to character). Yet, crucially, a similar methodological stance characterizes the classic approach to slurs, register, interjections, and the rest, that is, it equally applies, mutatis mutandis, to the *expressive dimension* of meaning. In this respect, the contentful glosses sketched in section 1 profitably (though not inevitably) highlight the methodological parallelism between the truth-conditional and expressive aspects of an expression's semantic contribution—in the case of slurs, the methodological parallelism between the character of, say, "wop," and its derogatory dimension. And so, just as

(4) Mario is a wop.

is said to be true *with respect to* all and only those contexts and circumstances in which Mario is Italian, it is also defined as being licensed *with respect to* all and only those contexts whose agent despises Italians (or something of that sort).[10]

The point of the locution "with respect to" is often left implicit but is relevant, here as in the truth-conditional case: what is at issue is the evaluation of the expressive part of an expression's semantic contribution, given a certain parameter as argument. In particular, what are now of significance are those aspects in the meaning of, say, "wop" that interact with the relevant aspects of their arguments, presumably (though not necessarily) contexts: the expressive dimension of "wop" requires contexts of a particular kind, those involving generically despicable Italians, unsympathetic agents, or whatever your favorite take on this particular example demands. And so, the expressive part of the semantic contribution of "wop" is rendered by means of functions sensitive to this or that feature, but utterly indifferent to the actual tokening of that noun, and hence a fortiori to its form.

The logic, once again, follows suit: (4) bears certain meaning-grounded relationships with

(5) I deem Italians to be unworthy of respect.

or with "Italians are intrinsically despicable," or with whatever other gloss appropriately reflects the derogatory dimension of "wop."[11] But these turn out to be of a fundamentally different nature from the relationships which that sentence may bear with, say,

(6) I sometimes token a three-letter noun beginning with a "w."

or even with "I am expressing my disdain for Italians by means of tokening 'wop.'"

Here as before, the result of such a representational stance is important, since the relationships in questions *are* fundamentally different: the relationships between (4) and (5) are meaning-grounded, whereas those between (4) and (6) ensue from presumably inevitable characteristics of speaking—and, in this case, of derogating. That is, the former encode connections derivable from the semantic contribution (in this case, from the expressive element) of "wop," whereas the latter ensue from the allegedly inevitable outcomes of uttering "wop," that is, of instantiating its form.

A relatively familiar terminology in the contemporary literature on slurs may initially obscure this important distinction. I bear part of the responsibility for its promotion: the expressive dimension and the ensuing logic, so I wrote, are sensitive to contexts *of use*, as opposed to whatever parameters end up being appropriate for truth-conditionally relevant outcomes (Predelli 2013, see also Kaplan 1999; Gutzmann 2015). Terminological qualms aside, the point remains: there is eminently little pertaining to the use of an expression in my (and, as far as I can tell, Daniel Gutzmann's) contexts of use, at least as long as "use" is understood as an allusion to the acts of utterance or of tokening.[12]

Thus far, I officially summarized the current take on slurs in section 1, and, in this section, I sketched some general methodological assumptions pertaining to the treatment of meaning in natural-language semantics. Yet, what started with the tone of a brief summary occasionally ended up being unashamedly sympathetic to more than a few substantive theoretical commitments. For instance, I occasionally subscribed to the hypothesis that slurs involve a truth-conditional component, side by side with a derogatory element. More importantly, I also explicitly characterized the representationalist stance described in this section as the result of the correct approach to the derogatory dimension, on a par with the familiar view on the "verities of meaning" at large. These commitments, and probably more besides, unquestionably deserve closer scrutiny. Still, for my purposes here, I can afford to leave these questions as negotiable background. I can do so because my point is not to linger on these relatively well-studied aspects of the meaning of slurs but to *add* to them.

And so, I take on board without further ado (i) the hypothesis that the truth-conditionally relevant part of the semantic contribution of, say, "wop" is a character yielding the property of being Italian, and (ii) the idea that a distinct expressive part of that semantic contribution deals with the speaker's disdain (or something in that vein). Furthermore, I also agree with the notion that (iii) this two-dimensional semantic contribution is explainable according to the representationalist model discussed in this section, that is, independently of the occurrence of tokens of "wop" in particular situations of use. I accept all of this with nonchalance because what interests me in (i)–(iii) is the contrast they provide for my discussion of yet another aspect of an expression's meaning. It is an aspect of meaning which, as I am about to explain, breaks away from the representationalist treatment of semantic contributions and from the accompanying marriage of semantics and logic.

3. TABOO: THE CASE OF COARSENESS

According to the *Oxford English Dictionary*'s main definition, "taboo" refers to "the putting of a person or thing under prohibition or interdict." Derivatively, then, taboo words are expressions addressing said person or thing, as in the prohibition, in certain contexts, to speak of sexual interactions, of bodily functions, or of sacred subjects. In this sense, then, language only *indirectly* interacts with taboo: no word designating a taboo subject may be used because the subject itself should not be brought to the conversational record. Accordingly, from the perspective of this sense of "taboo," co-designating expressions end up being on a par: any designation of x is out of place, simply because what is chastised is discourse about x in the first place. "Thou shalt not take the name of the Lord thy God in vain" admonishes Exodus; if its spirit had been consistent with the considerations from this paragraph, it may well have said: "Thou shalt not take *any* name of the Lord thy God in vain."

The sense of "taboo" that interests me here is different, and only *partially* reflected in what the *Oxford English Dictionary* calls the "linguistic" sense of the term: "in linguistics," so it reads, the word "taboo" pertains to "the total or partial prohibition of the use of certain words, expressions, topics" and is used "with reference to an expression or topic considered offensive." Yet, words and topics may surely come apart. Some of the considerations in the first sections of this chapter already confirm this separation: truth-conditionally indistinguishable expressions may be prohibited or undesirable due to their different registers. And so, mention of sexual interactions or bodily functions may well be appropriate at a doctor's surgery, but the use of coarse expressions designating them probably remains at least out of place, if not downright prohibited.

My use of "taboo" is even more demanding than the "linguistic" sense recorded above. This is so because, in the sense in which I shall use "taboo," taboo may succumb not only to truth-conditionally idle transformations but also to the substitution of expressions that may be assumed to be on a par from the truth-conditional *and* expressive viewpoint alike. The case of taboo names for the divinity may well be apt as an exemplar of what I have in mind, partly as a limiting case of this sort of synonymy: expressively neutral m and n may both be names of God, and may thus be indistinguishable at the referential and expressive levels alike, and yet only one of them may end up being taboo in my sense. These cases are pedagogically apt not only as hypothetical instances of truth-conditional and expressive synonymy, that is, as supposed instances of indistinguishable semantic contributions. Judging from what I hear, they may well also be historically confirmed occurrences. But religious language raises intricate issues, which would lead me perilously close to areas of inquiry about which I have no competence. I thus stick to a safer, albeit not too perfect parallelism having to do with *coarse register*, before I move on to taboo in the case of slurs.

Coarseness is another phenomenon profitably approachable from the two-dimensional viewpoint described in section 1: for instance, "to copulate" and "to fuck" are arguably truth-conditionally indistinguishable, but only the latter is coarse.[13] And so, much of what I wrote regarding the semantic contributions of expressives at large applies here as well, including the by now familiar interaction between the truth-conditional and expressive dimensions. For instance, although

(7) If they fucked all night, they will be late for breakfast.

may not be chastised for being false if the couple in question did not engage in sexual intercourse, it may unconditionally be censored as coarse.

Opting for (7) rather than for its well-mannered alternatives, then, leaves the speaker open to a charge of coarseness. Of course, I did not indulge in a choice of that sort: I displayed (7) as an example, and I did not preposterously make it part of my presentation. And yet, I mentioned it with mild trepidation. I did persevere because, in a linguistic essay about slurs, expressives, and register, *mention* of "fuck" ought to be tolerable. But that is not inevitably the case: a teacher who admonishes her young pupils with "Never say 'fuck'!" had better be prepared for her students' giggles and, perhaps, for some of their parents' objections.

This sort of resistance is not to be expected from any of the standard dimensions of meaning. After all, a sentence such as

(8) "Fuck" contains four letters.

is surely neither false nor coarse: the description of a string's length may or may not hit the target, but hardly qualifies as an instance of coarse register. And yet, as mentioned, there are conversational settings in which utterances of examples such as (8) violate certain social norms: as witnessed by the preferability of substitutes such as "the f-word," those settings prohibit, or at least frown upon the mere mention of the taboo. "Never utter the f-word," a cautious teacher should have intimated, thereby avoiding not only the trap of coarseness but also the mere presentation of that taboo form.[14]

According to common consensus, mention strips an expression of what I have called its "semantic contributions." Surely, the referent of "'Mario'" (i.e., of "Mario" enclosed in quotation marks) is not Mario, the *designatum* of "'fuck'" (i.e., of the result of appending quotes to "fuck") has nothing to do with sexual intercourse, and the character of "'he'" (the quotational expression that mentions "he") is not the function with the contextually salient male as its value. Equally clearly, the status of "'bunny'" is not that of a child-directed expression, the register of "'fuck'" is not coarse, and the expressive status of "'oops'" is neutral. And so, I did not inappropriately shift my register away from that appropriate for an academic essay when I *mentioned* "bunny" or "fuck," and I did not react to any minor mishap when I enclosed "oops" within quotation marks. The expected effects of the teacher's intimation never to say "fuck," namely, the effects of taboo in my sense of the term, must thus escape any regimentation from the viewpoint of *semantic contribution*: in a nutshell, taboo is part of neither truth-conditional meaning nor any aspect of the expressive dimension.

Still, it would be bizarre to insist that, not being a specimen of the truth-conditional or expressive parts of an expression's semantic contribution, its taboo status is not part of its *meaning*. At least, such a conclusion strikes me as out of place from the viewpoint of an intuitive and pre-theoretical, but also theoretically justifiable understanding of "meaning" as the repository of the conventional properties of an expression. After all, the taboo status of "fuck" does not ensue from any noteworthy *natural* property of its form, such as its being phonetically distasteful, its being difficult to pronounce, or anything of that sort. The noteworthy status of "fuck" is not that of a burp; it is, rather, part and parcel of the arbitrary properties that users of "fuck" need to master so as to become competent speakers of the language.[15]

And so, that "fuck" is taboo is an aspect of meaning additional to its truth-conditional profile (that which deals with sexual intercourse) *and* to its non-truth-conditional properties (first and foremost, its coarseness). The terminology that served me well up to now must then be revealed as less than perspicuous: as long as "semantics" is understood as pertaining to the study of meaning, my description of truth-conditional and expressive meaning as exhaustive of an expression's *semantic* contribution is less than ideal. It will nevertheless continue to suffice as a handy moniker, at least if accompanied by a crucial *caveat*: semantics qua study of meaning must concern itself with more than an expression's semantic contribution, since it must also encompass its taboo status.

Or so I have suggested. My introductory discussion of a taboo word, in my sense of "taboo," is admittedly rough, and it is bound to elicit objections that are not of immediate relevance for my aim. And so, I happily abandon "fuck," and I move on to cases that are not only more directly relevant for the case of slurs, but also hopefully provide even more convincing evidence of taboo.

4. SLURS AND TABOO

The case of coarseness provided preliminary evidence that something of interest from the viewpoint of taboo pertains to the *forms* of the expressions in question, rather than to their semantic contributions. For instance, the semantic contributions associated with the four-letter articulation "fuck" have to do with sexual intercourse and with one's allegiance to a coarse conversational register. But the taboo status of "fuck" must be independent of both, since it remains unaffected when that form appears in linguistic settings designed to neutralize them, as in cases of pure mention. In a slogan: taboo, unlike any aspects of an expression's semantic contribution, *scopes out of quotation marks*.

This phenomenon is particularly evident when it comes to *racial* slurs. In my excursus on coarseness in section 3, I could justify my exemplar with only a brief word of apology: in academic essays on non-truth-conditional meaning, a few mentions of "fuck" should not be alarming. And if the prissiest of readers still find something distasteful in them, he or she may legitimately be invited to get over it, and to move her attention to what matters, the point those examples were intended to make.

I do not wish to say that the issue is *utterly* different in the case of racial slurs. Yet, surely, more caution is needed. Following a widespread attitude, when in need of an exemplar of a slur, I chose a tame affair such as "wop." I did so in order to have a few words of excuse at my disposal, if overly sensitive readers wanted to object. For one thing, "wop" is old-fashioned and relatively rarely used. At least as far as I know, its use may well have been accompanied by distasteful discriminatory practices, but none of them may be put on a par with the genocidal oppressions historically perpetrated by users of other exemplars. Last but not least, I stuck to the common tradition in the literature on slurs by choosing an instance that targets a group of which I am a member (more or less, but never mind the details here).[16] And so, all went at least as smoothly with my mentions of "wop" as it hopefully went with my displays of "fuck."

Other instances, though, are a different matter: they, unlike "wop," are not only derogatory but taboo. Accordingly, in the case of the most notorious tabooed slur of recent times, a descriptive moniker has risen to the status of conventional label for the incriminated form: "the n-word" has become a household stand-in for the eight-character quotational term resulting from appending quotation marks to the incriminated form. Partial description of form thus tastefully replaces mention and avoids the mention-resistant effects of taboo. Indeed, even *accidental* occurrences are tokened with trepidation, as witnessed by the notorious 1999 episode involving Washington civil servant David Howard's use of "niggardly," an adverb "probably borrowed from early Scandinavian" (*Oxford English Dictionary*) and etymologically unrelated to slurring.[17]

It is probably no coincidence that tabooed slurs are slurs whose derogatory dimension is associated with extreme forms of prejudice. It is then unsurprising to discover that tabooed forms typically come together with semantic contributions that target historically vilified and abused groups. And so "wop," "Boche," or "limey" may well be poor candidates of unmentionable forms partly because anti-Italian, anti-German, and anti-British derogation has historically not been accompanied by the sort of oppressive practices that have victimized other ethnic groups. Still, historical and political considerations *at best* provide an explanation of *why* certain forms are taboo. But they do not detract from the fact that, for one reason or another, those forms end up being taboo by linguistic convention, and, *at least in principle*, independently of the social intolerability of their denigratory component. And so, slurs that are (or at least may well be) fully synonymous from the truth-conditional *and* expressive viewpoint may nevertheless carry different tabooed status: the n-word is high on the taboo scale, whereas "coon" and "spook" are probably not, even though all of them designate the same ethnic group and target it with comparable prejudice.[18]

Once again, my particular examples may raise a few eyebrows. "Spook," so it may be objected, is not associated with a form of prejudice or disdain comparable with those that accompany the n-word. This objection is of a different nature from the point adumbrated in the previous paragraph: now, the issue is not the (unobjectionable but irrelevant) point that tabooed words tend to be derogatory expressions targeting highly victimized groups—African Americans but not Italians, say. The point of the objection under discussion is rather that, even with a fixed target of derogation, disdain may come in different degrees. Hence, so this objection continues, "spook" and its more tabooed co-extensional counterpart are *not* expressively indistinguishable, since the former is only mildly derogatory whereas the latter is not. The conclusion is that taboo is not an independent facet of meaning, and that it is merely a manifestation of an independently recognized component of semantic contribution: taboo is the equivalent of strong derogation, that is, it is a facet of expressive meaning.

I am willing to concede more than a few parts of this objection, first and foremost those pertaining to the details in my choice of examples. Admittedly, I am neither a habitual user of racial slurs nor an expert in the lexical subtleties of contemporary English. Still, the announced conclusion does not follow even with all of these concessions in place: even if, to my surprise, taboo was inevitably accompanied by an extreme position in the expressive spectrum, its traits would conceptually not be on a par with those of its alleged companion. In all of its manifestations, derogation fails to break free of the neutralizing effects of pure quotation; taboo, as indicated, is not at all diluted by the power of mention.

And so, slurring (and coarse language, some parts of religious discourse, and probably more besides) is more completely understood by enriching the conception of meaning that emerges from the current debate on expressives, register, and all that goes under the heading of "non-truth-conditional meaning." Now, an expression's meaning must exceed its semantic contribution: the taboo dimension conventionally associated with that expression's form comes side by side with its truth-conditional profile (its character, say) *and* its expressive potential, such as its child-directed status, its coarse register, or, in the case most relevant here, its derogatory component.

5. CONCLUSION: THE MEANING OF FORMS

All of the above has remained at an informal and descriptive level: my aim has been that of highlighting taboo as a genuinely idiosyncratic dimension of meaning. As a term of contrast, in section 1 I rehearsed some traits of that which semanticists have always recognized as a core part of an expression's conventional meaning, its truth-conditional contribution, together with those aspects of meaning that have become familiar in the more recent literature on expressives. Both, according to me and to widespread consensus alike, are aptly studied from the representationalist viewpoint summarized in section 2: the parts of meaning included in an expression's semantic contribution display their characteristic properties independently of its form, and a fortiori independently of the tokening process. And yet, as argued in sections 3 and 4, this methodological stance inevitably breaks down when it comes to the study of taboo, that is, when it comes to the parts of meaning that inevitably pertain to the process of articulation.

The analysis of the meaning of forms is in its infancy: I know of no well-developed formal approach to taboo and to other related phenomena, such as the use of *meta-expressions* ("that effing idiot," grawlixes, "the n-word," and the like), the effects achieved by standard devices of quotation, and, more generally, the discursive contributions provided by the mere act of tokening.[19] I leave the study of these phenomena as an intriguing topic for future research.

NOTES

1. The topic has a dignified tradition, probably starting with Gottlob Frege's remarks on tone and coloring (Frege 1892) and continuing with Michael Dummett's commentary in Dummett (1973); see also the collection of essays in Zwicky et al. (1971). For my own views on slurs and related phenomena, see Predelli (2013); for a small sample of the considerable literature spurred by Kaplan's and Potts's works, see the sources cited in Predelli (2013) and in the remainder of this chapter.

2. A partial exception may be Christopher Hom, who, in a few passages in Hom (2008), suggests that slurs are introduced by "defective procedures," and are thus presumably not fully meaningful parts of the language. This suggestion is nevertheless more frequently accompanied by the thesis that "racial epithets are entirely meaningful [but] . . . have null extensions" (Hom 2008, 22; see also Picardi 2006; Hom and May 2018; for my own misgivings on the null-extension view, see Predelli 2013).

3. For unashamedly contentful glosses, see Predelli (2013), and its discussion of the proposals in Williamson (2009); see also approaches to non-truth-conditional meaning in the spirit of the so-called *multiple proposition* tradition, as in Corazza (2005), Neale (1999), Picardi (2006), and Predelli (2005b). Contentful approaches spectacularly come to the foreground in Potts's original approach (Potts 2003), where slurs and expressives are treated side by side with obviously contentful exemplars such as non-restricting relative clauses and nominal appositives.

4. For a sample of the considerable debate on projection, see among many Williamson (2009), Amaral et al. (2007), Anand (2007), Harris and Potts (2009), Kratzer (1999), Kaplan (1999), Potts (2003, 2007), Sauerland (2007), and Simons et al. (2010); regarding the relationships between projection and presupposition, see for instance Potts (2003), Schlenker (2007), and Lasersohn (2007); for an interesting empirical study of the behavior of slurs in attitude reports, see Cepollaro et al. (2019).

5. I am taking on board without further ado the idea that slurs are aptly regimented according to a hybrid format of this sort; see McCready (2010) for a rigorous approach to so-called mixed content, and Predelli (2013) for an informal presentation of my predilections. (Thanks to Andrés Saab for this and other bibliographical pointers).

6. *Modulo* the important caveat mentioned in the previous footnote, namely scepticism about Potts's original bar on mixed contents, see McCready (2010) and, for informal pioneering insights, see Bach (2006) and Williamson (2009).

7. For an extensive discussion of Potts's formalism, see Amaral et al. (2007); for approaches to non-truth-conditional meaning in terms of contexts, see Predelli (2013) and Gutzmann (2015).

8. See in particular Potts's later approach (Potts 2007).

9. See also Kaplan (1989a, 522–523; 546). I have repeatedly stressed my allegiance to Kaplan's methodology in Predelli (2005a, 2013), and in my criticism of so-called token-reflexive approaches to indexicality (Predelli 2006, 2012).

10. "Agent" (rather than "speaker") is borrowed from Kaplan (1989a), and explicitly alludes to the need for a distinction between the relevant contextual parameter and the occurrences of an episode of speaking.

11. See Predelli (2013) in particular its discussion of mere settlement and of witnessing, for further details.

12. For a summary and development of Gutzmann's use-conditional semantics, see Caso (this volume).

13. For a sample of the semantic treatment of register, see Predelli (2013) and the sources cited therein.

14. By the same token, "among several curious by-products of collective, and seemingly unconscious censorship, there is the mysterious appearance of the word donkey. . . . The time-honored accepted synonym, ass, started to fall into disrepute through uncomfortable phonetic proximity to arse" (Hughes 1991, 19; regarding circumlocutions such as "the f-word," "f***," or "I wouldn't give a blank for such a blank blank"; see also Harris 1987; Davis 1989; Allan and Burridge 2006; Zwicky 2003). The prosecutor at the Lenny Bruce trial in the sixties apparently went to great length to avoid mere mention: "I don't think I have to tell you the term, I think that you recall it . . . as a word that started with an 'F' and ended with a 'K' and sounded like 'truck'" (reported in Rawson 1989).

15. When my considerations about taboo are applied to slurs later in this chapter, some of my comments seem consonant with certain ideas in Anderson and Lepore (2013). Three important differences are nevertheless worth noting. (i) In Luvell Anderson's and Ernie Lepore's prohibitionist approach, taboo aims at reflecting many of the aspects that I included as part of a slur's *expressive* meaning; (ii) more generally, much of Anderson and Lepore's polemic is directed against *semantic* analyses of slurs, so that taboo ends up being (inexplicably, in my view) independent from conventional meaning (with a consequent conspicuous absence of any account of the expressive logic engendered by a slur's semantic contribution); (iii) Anderson and Lepore do not stress the articulation based account of taboo that I suggest later in the chapter.

16. Apparently, "wop" was "first applied to young dandified ner'er-do-wells, thugs, or pimps in New York's Little Italy" (Thorne 1990, 569), and I am not from New York. But "wop" will do as a mild derogatory term for Italians at large; see also Dummett's mentions of out-of-fashion "Boche."

17. The incident is reported in the *New York Times*, January 31, 1999.

18. Though see the fictional vicissitudes of Coleman Silk in Philip Roth's *The Human Stain* for the possible effects of uses of "spook" as synonymous with "ghost."

19. Though see Saab (2020) for important considerations regarding the idea that "expressivity is not represented in the Logical Form (LF) of a sentence, but it is deduced at Phonetic Form (PF)."

BIBLIOGRAPHICAL REFERENCES

Allan, Keith, and Kate Burridge. 2006. *Forbidden Words: Taboo and the Censoring of Language*. Cambridge: Cambridge University Press.

Amaral, Patricia, Craige Roberts, and E. Allyn Smith. 2007. "Review of the Logic of Conventional Implicatures by Chris Potts." *Linguistics and Philosophy* 30: 707–749.

Anand, Pranav. 2007. "Re-Expressing Judgment." *Theoretical Linguistics* 33: 199–208.

Anderson, Luvell, and Ernie Lepore. 2013. "Slurring Words." *Nous* 47: 25–48.

Bach, Kent. 2006. "Review of Christopher Potts, *The Logic of Conventional Implicatures*." *Journal of Linguistics* 42: 490–495.

Caso, Ramiro. 2020. "A Bidimensional Account of Slurs." This volume.
Cepollaro, Bianca, Simone Sulpizio, and Claudia Bianchi. 2019. "How Bad Is It to Report a Slur? An Empirical Investigation." *Journal of Pragmatics* 146: 32–42.
Corazza, Eros. 2005. "On Epithets Qua Attributive Anaphors." *Journal of Linguistics* 41: 1–32.
Davis, Hayley. 1989. "What Makes Bad Language Bad?" *Language and Communication* 9: 1–9.
Dowty, David, Robert Wall, and Stanley Peters. 1981. *Introduction to Montague Semantics*. Dordrecht: Springer.
Dummett, Michael. 1973. *Frege: Philosophy of Language*. London: Duckworth.
Frege, Gottlob. 1892. "On Sense and Reference." In *Translations from the Philosophical Writings of Gottlob Frege*, edited by Peter Geach and Max Black, 56–78. Oxford: Basil Blackwell.
Gutzmann, Daniel. 2015. *Use-Conditional Meaning*. Oxford: Oxford University Press.
Harris, Jesse, and Christopher Potts. 2009. "Perspective-Shifting with Appositives and Expressives." *Linguistics and Philosophy* 32: 523–552.
Harris, Roy. 1987. "Mentioning the Unmentionable." *International Journal of Moral and Social Studies* 2: 175–188.
Hom, Christopher. 2008. "The Semantics of Racial Epithets." *Journal of Philosophy* 105: 416–440.
Hom, Christopher, and Robert May. 2018. "Pejoratives As Fiction." In *Bad Words*, edited by David Sosa, 108–131. Oxford: Oxford University Press.
Hughes, Goffrey. 1991. *Swearing: A Social History of Foul Language, Oaths, and Profanity in English*. Oxford: Blackwell.
Kaplan, David. 1989a. "Demonstratives." In *Themes from Kaplan*, edited by Joseph Almog, John Perry, and Howard Wettstein, 481–563. Oxford: Oxford University Press.
Kaplan, David. 1989b. "Afterthoughts." In *Themes from Kaplan*, edited by Joseph Almog, John Perry, and Howard Wettstein, 565–614. Oxford: Oxford University Press.
Kaplan, David. 1999. "What Is Meaning? Explorations in the Theory of Meaning As Use." Manuscript.
Kratzer, Angelika. 1999. "Beyond 'Ouch' and 'Oops': How Descriptive Content and Expressive Meaning Interact." Manuscript.
Lasersohn, Peter. 2007. "Expressives, Perspective and Presupposition." *Theoretical Linguistics* 33: 223–230.
McCready, Elin. 2010. "Varieties of Conventional Implicature." *Semantics and Pragmatics* 3: 1–57.
Neale, Stephen. 1999. "Coloring and Composition." In *Philosophy and Linguistics*, edited by Kumiko Murasugi and Robert Stainton, 35–82. Boulder, CO: Westview Press.
Picardi, Eva. 2006. "Colouring, Multiple Propositions, and Assertoric Content." *Grazer Philosophische Studien* 23: 49–71.
Potts, Christopher. 2005. *The Logic of Conventional Implicature*. Oxford: Oxford University Press.

Potts, Christopher. 2007. "The Expressive Dimension." *Theoretical Linguistics* 33: 165–197.
Predelli, Stefano. 2005a. *Contexts: Meaning, Truth, and the Use of Language*. Oxford: Oxford University Press.
Predelli, Stefano. 2005b. "An Introduction to the Semantics of Message and Attachment." *Croatian Journal of Philosophy* 5: 139–155.
Predelli, Stefano. 2006. "The Problem with Token-Reflexivity." *Synthese* 148: 5–29.
Predelli, Stefano. 2012. "Bare-Boned Demonstratives." *Journal of Philosophical Logic* 41: 547–562.
Predelli, Stefano. 2013. *Meaning Without Truth*. Oxford: Oxford University Press.
Rawson, Hugh. 1989. *Wicked Words*. New York: Crown Trade Paperback.
Saab, Andrés. 2020. "On the Locus of Expressivity: Deriving Parallel Meaning Dimensions from Architectural Considerations." This volume.
Sauerland, Uli. 2007. "Beyond Unpluggability." *Theoretical Linguistics* 33: 231–236.
Schlenker, Philippe. 2007. "Expressive Presuppositions." *Theoretical Linguistics* 33: 237–245.
Simons, Mandy, Judith Tonhauser, David Beaver, and Craige Roberts. 2010. "What Projects and Why." *Proceedings of SALT* 20: 309–327.
Thorne, Tony. 1990. *The Dictionary of Contemporary Slang*. New York: Pantheon Books.
Williamson, Timothy. 2009. "Reference, Inference and the Semantics of Pejoratives." In *The Philosophy of David Kaplan*, edited by Joseph Almog and Paolo Leonardi, 137–158. Oxford: Oxford University Press.
Zwicky, Arnold. 2003. "The Other F Word." *Out* 115: 82–84.
Zwicky, Arnold, Peter Salus, and Robert Binnick. 1971. *Studies Out in Left Field: Defamatory Essays Presented to James D. McCawley*. Edmonton: Linguistic Research Inc.

Chapter 7

Slurs

The Amoralist and the Expression of Hate
Justina Díaz Legaspe

Language is a major source of information about the world and its inhabitants. Most obviously, what people say allows us to gain information not only about the world but also about their beliefs. The way people say what they say, and particularly their use of some words and phrases, also opens an interesting informational window, this time to what they *feel* about the world, how much they value its inhabitants, what their attitudes and emotions are, how they are biased. *Expressive language* comprises then words and phrases that carry with them an expressive dimension, terms whose use allows speakers to exhibit publicly these aspects of their identity that may differ or even clash with what they say about the world. For a long time over the last decades, slurs have been considered as windows to speakers' emotions, attitudes, and prejudices against targeted groups. Thus, while some have considered slurs as semantically expressive, others have associated slur use to conventional implicatures or presuppositions conveying those negative biases. This chapter raises a finger against this conception of slurs. I will propose, instead, that although slurs can be used to express such mental states, these uses should be understood in the wider frame of register and cross-contextual uses of registered words.

1. TYPE-EXPRESSIVISM AND TOKEN-EXPRESSIVISM

"Expressivism" is the name given to a set of different theories sharing some common assumptions. In a broad sense, expressivism is the claim that some words are linguistic devices used to express—as opposed to state—non-cognitive mental states or other miscellaneous elements that range from occurring emotions to attitudes, to biases or allegiance to stereotypes, communitarian perspectives, and even norms. In a narrow sense, expressivism is a systematic semantic approach to some terms or phrases according to which these non-cognitive states of mind, encoded contextual valences, biases, attitudes, and other elements expressed by their use determine their meaning. In other words, the utterance of a sentence that is used to express a non-cognitive mental state, emotion, or attitude—to name a few—does not make it semantically expressive; instead, a term or phrase is considered a semantic expressive when at least one dimension of its meaning is constituted by whatever non-cognitive elements the term is used to express. Thus, an utterance of "Today is Friday" may be used to express happiness or positive expectations about the days to come, but this does not make it an expressive sentence. Instead, utterances of expressive terms or sentences like "Ouch!" or "Lying sucks!," and for advocates of hybrid expressivistic views, uses of moral or aesthetic terms ("good," "beautiful"), either exhaust their meaning in the mental state they are expressing (like "Ouch!") or state a propositional, truth-evaluable semantic content, *and* also a semantically encoded dimension determined by the non-propositional, non-cognitive mental state from the wide pool of options given above that speakers express with their use.

For any given utterance purportedly expressive both in a narrow or a broad sense, there are as many theories about it as there are philosophers of language. Divergences begin with the kind of mental state or non-cognitive element being expressed, but they do not end there. For terms that are expressive in a broad sense, there is a debate as to what mechanism is in place that explains how the utterance manages to express emotions, attitudes, or other non-cognitive mental states. For terms that are semantically expressive, there is a disagreement on the non-expressive dimensions of these terms' meaning; while some of these expressions (like "Ouch!" or "Yikes!") are considered purely expressive, contributing nothing to sentential truth-conditions, others are considered both expressive *and* representational, truth-conditionally contributory with an extra expressive dimension. Given the wide range of theories and debates on these topics, I will not attempt here to provide a detailed account of all of them. Instead, I will use the following terms to refer to generic, simplified versions of the distinction between the narrow and the semantic sense in which terms can be called "expressives":

Expressives in use (or expressives in a broad sense): given a set E of non-propositional, non-cognitive elements including emotions, attitudes, and conative elements, a term or phrase e is considered expressive in use when the utterance of e allows the speaker to express—rather than state—E-elements.

Expressive in type (or expressives in a narrow sense): given a set E of non-propositional, non-cognitive elements including emotions, attitudes, and conative elements, a term or phrase *e* is considered expressive when at least one dimension of its meaning is determined by E-elements.

The reader should keep in mind that E is deliberately vague as to allow for the inclusion of very different elements. In any case, elements in E are susceptible of being expressed on top of being stated; emotions, for example, can be put in words ("I am so pissed right now!"), but contrary to cognitive contents, they can also be expressed, made visible to audiences, without making a truth-conditional assertion (as in yelling "Shit!" in a heated discussion).

A second caveat to keep in mind is that all expressives in type are also expressives in use, but not vice versa. To be clear, all narrow expressives are expressives in use: that is, all narrow expressives are used by speakers to convey emotions, attitudes o, more generally, E-elements. However, not all terms that are used to express are systematically used to express: that is, not all expressives in use are expressives in a narrow sense. There are words and phrases that acquire an expressive force only in some circumstances of use and are therefore only expressive in that particular token. This contrast can be seen clearly in the difference between interjections and other exclamations like "Ouch!" and "Shit!": while the former one is expressive in type, used to express pain in every utterance, the latter can be used as a non-expressive name for feces in some contexts, and as an expression of surprise in others.

According to the deliberately vague definitions provided above, then, type-expressives (expressives in type) are *semantically* expressives: that is, the expressive dimension is part of their standing meaning and not the result of a confluence of contextual factors. Interjections like "Ouch!" or "Yikes!" could be considered as type-expressives. For some,[1] aesthetic, normative, or moral terms also belong to this category of words. In turn, token-expressives are words or phrases that work as expressive devices just in some particular contexts of utterance. Hence, these words do not bear an expressive dimension in virtue of their standing meaning, but in virtue of the way they are used on given occasions. They gain expressive power, provided some contextual factors are in place. Thus, an utterance of "Today is Friday" can be expressive of joy or high expectation for the day to come, with that not being indicative of the existence of an expressive dimension in the meaning of any of the words uttered or in the sentence as a whole; the same sentence, uttered on a different occasion, can fail to express any emotion or E-element.

The distinction between expressives in type and expressives in token purports to track features of typical uses. It does not rely on an exhaustive catalog of how terms have been or could be used. Because speakers use words in heterodox ways all the time, working on an exhaustive catalog encompassing all uses would be a lost cause. With my use of "typical" I do not aim to capture brute statistical patterns of how terms are used. I aim to pinpoint the *function* or job of the term or phrase in the shared tongue, how the term is supposed to be used according to linguistic conventions. Appealing to the main functionality in the idea of "typical" usage makes room for nonliteral uses of type- and token-expressives.

I am aware that the dividing line between type- and token-expressives as sketched above is thin, and the distinction itself is far from being unproblematic. At least for some type-expressive words and phrases, the semantic expressive dimension is acquired over time and can be lost over time, too, in response to social, non-semantic factors. Thus, regular words can be increasingly used to express E-elements, to the point that the E-element crystallizes as a semantic layer of their meaning. Conversely, type-expressives can lose their expressive semantic dimension by way of social pressure, becoming at best token-expressives. Both processes can be observed in the development of words like "gay" or "queer," initially non-expressive adjectives synonymous with "happy" and "bizarre" respectively, which were occasionally used to express disdain or scorn for people outside the norm. Over time, and by means of the frequency of these uses, they moved from the category of token-expressives to the category of type-expressives, as full-fledged contemptuous expressive terms for male homosexuals or homosexuals in general, respectively. Upon being appropriated by the targeted communities, both terms lost their expressive dimension to become referential terms for male homosexuals or members of the LGBTQ community generally.

For words transitioning from one category to the other it may be difficult to determine whether they are type-expressives or token-expressives. Despite this porous delimitation, there is a difference worthy of note between these two categories. On the one hand, at any synchronic slice of time in which a term has an expressive semantic dimension, utterances of this term will be expressive in all contexts of use—as far as the word is used literally. In consequence, their utterance entitles audiences to ascribe the associated E-elements—emotions, attitudes, preferences, or dislikes—to the speaker. On the other hand, token-expressive words are expressively neutral in some contexts of utterance, which means that speakers in those contexts have no intention whatsoever to convey emotions, attitudes, or the corresponding E-element with their uses, and that audiences are neither entitled nor inclined to ascribe those mental states to them. Take "Ouch!" and "Today is Friday" again: at this particular time in which the former is an expressive for pain, any typical utterance of the term constitutes a public exhibition of pain by the speaker, and it entitles audiences to assume the speaker is in pain. More importantly, it does so in all contexts where it is uttered. In contrast, "Today is Friday" may express joy when uttered by an office employee who hates his job, but it does not when uttered by a kindergartener learning the days of the week.

2. EXPRESSING HATE: PEJORATIVES

The difference between type- and token-expressives is even more noticeable among pejoratives. These words, defined as "terms expressing contempt or disapproval,"[2] are common currency in conversations or verbal exchanges where speakers aim to offend, insult, or show derision for other individuals, actions, or situations. Pejoratives are often type-expressives: they are typically used to express or convey negative feelings or attitudes against their target, and their meaning is determined by those feelings or attitudes. Particularly, these are words that cannot be uttered[3] without potentially offending the audience or hurting the target. Note that the distinction between type- and token-expressives is based on (literal) meaning, while the classification of words or phrases as pejoratives depends on the kind of E-elements they purport to express in one way or the other. Hence, type-expressive pejoratives select those words or terms that have an expressive semantic dimension determined by *negative* feelings, emotions, attitudes, biases, or prejudices against people. The distinction is not grammatical: type-expressive pejoratives include a host of different grammatical terms, from adjectives to epithets. The distinction does not divide between particular ways in which the expressive semantic dimension may work, and hence, pejoratives also encompass different types of pejorative mechanisms, from complex expressions built over vulgarities that are now straightforward insults ("*ass*hole," "mother*fucker*") to plain old pejoratives ("idiot," "stupid").

A significant number of pejoratives, though, are token-expressive instead. Unlike type-expressives variants, token-expressive pejoratives can be used as linguistic weapons in some conversational contexts but are typically neutral, non-offensive regular words. Many of these words refer to actions, events, or entities socially endowed with negative features. Take "pig" and "moron," for example, both are terms with neutral literal meanings—"pig" being the common noun used for a certain kind of farm animal, "moron" an outdated technical term for people with mild cognitive disabilities and an IQ between 51 and 70. However, pigs are ill-considered in our society as dirty and sloppy, and disabilities, especially intellectual ones, are often the basis for discrimination in our culture. For this reason, "pig" and "moron" are frequently used to express negative E-emotions: "pig" is often used to condemn bad table manners or excessive eating and "moron" to mock lack of intelligence in intellectually abled people. Token-expressive pejoratives can be nouns and adjectives; some are simple descriptions of groups or traits disfavored in some particular conversational settings but not necessarily always: "antivaxer" and "tree-hugger" are descriptions that are considered insulting among some groups but are perfectly acceptable in others. In any case, it is easy to see that although type-expressive pejoratives cannot be used in regular conversations without triggering offense or startling audiences, token-expressive pejoratives can fit in respectful conversations without a blink, as long as they follow their typical usage.

Register plays a big part in the understanding of pejoratives in both categories and in the distinction between type- and token-expressives in general. "Register" is the name given by sociolinguistics to the phenomenon of language variation determined by conversational context types (among others, Halliday 1973; Halliday and Matthiessen 2004; Hasan 2004; also tackled by philosophers like Predelli 2013; Díaz Legaspe, Stainton, and Liu 2019). In a nutshell, people tend to alter the way they talk—and even the things they talk about—according to social factors, such as social roles occupied in the context of speech, audience types, and relation to them, formality degrees of these relations, and speech media. Thus, even when speakers aim to convey the same idea in different social settings, they tend to adapt the way the information is articulated in correspondence to a complex variety of social features: consider "Katie pooped on her undies today" (appropriate for a child-oriented conversational context), "Kate had a soft bowel movement today" (appropriate for formal or medical conversational contexts) and "Kate shitted all over her panties today" (appropriate for informal conversational contexts). At the bottom of the notion of register lays the idea that, for some words, there is a set of co-referential terms or "sister-words" referring to the same worldly entities, some of which are marked by a register feature and some of which are not. The sociolinguistic phenomenon of registered speech records the fact that speakers will systematically choose some of the words among the set of these sister-words instead of others depending on the role they are playing in the conversational setting where they are located. In the example earlier, "poo," "shit," and "have a bowel movement" are all part of the set of sister-words used to name defecation. The role of the speaker in different circumstances (say, parent in a child-oriented setting, decision-maker or health advocate for a child in a medical setting or friend in an all-adult conversation) determines which of these alternatives is preferred in each case.

Note that the adjustment of behavior to social setting types is not merely a linguistic phenomenon, but it affects behavior in general: we regulate how we move, the way we dress, and how we interact with each other according to the situation we are placed in. Social constraints on behavior are shaped as dress-codes, etiquette rules, standards of procedure, and most commonly, implicit behavior-constraining rules that present as *savoir-faire* for compliant participants. Within this framework of behavioral adjustment to social setting types, some words and phrases end up being *registered*: they become only acceptable in some conversational contexts and are deemed out of place, awkward, or even unacceptable in others. Thus, "poo," "bum," and "tummy" are restricted to child-oriented conversational contexts, "excrement," "anus," and "abdomen" to professional/medical settings, and "shit," "ass," and "pot belly" are vulgarities, used in very informal conversations.

There is something odd about the use of registered terms to express E-elements that is relevant for the above classification of expressives. For example, the use of the infantile "poo" in the context of a conversation between child caretaker and child ("Don't touch that, it's poo!") does not carry with it the expression of any emotion whatsoever; it is simply a referential word for excrement deemed acceptable for children due to non-semantic reasons. However, the use of the same word within an adult conversation ("Did you poo in your pants?") may signal despise and may be used to ridicule the target. Likewise, the formal "madam" that is the preferred term to refer to women in formal contexts may be used in informal conversational contexts to either flatter or put down female interlocutors. Registered words, then, are token-expressives in cross-contextual uses: as "Today is Friday," they can easily be used to express E-elements when used outside their typical conversational contexts.

One potential objection to this idea would be to assign an expressive dimension to registered terms—thereby making them type-expressives in the jargon of this chapter. According to this objection, a word like "poo" carries with it, as part of its meaning, an expressive dimension that allows speakers to express the tender feelings typically directed to children. Thus, the utterance of "Don't touch that, it's poo" by a caretaker is not only a warning about excrement but a way to express loving care, as it is "Oh, I can see you have a booboo." From this perspective, the same tender feeling that is welcomed and expected from caretakers is not well received in adult contexts. Conversely, it could be claimed that the purported expressive dimension of register terms simply changes the kind of E-element expressed depending on the context of utterance, with "poo" and "booboo" expressing derision in adult contexts and loving care in child-oriented conversations.

I do not find this alternative explanation of the expressive power of cross-contextual uses of registered terms plausible. For starters, the idea that registered terms are type-expressives in all contexts does not generalize well to all kinds of registered terms as used in their original conversational context. Infantile words may appear to carry with them an expressive dimension for loving feelings, provided they are used in contexts where children are taken care of in loving ways. But other registered words are used by default in conversational contexts where no obvious E-elements are involved. The preference of physicians for technical words such as "abdomen" instead of "belly," "feces" instead of "shit" or "vomiting" instead of "puking" does not seem to be motivated by the intention to convey respect, distance, or professionalism—although these may be elements constitutive of medical practice. In this context, these words do not seem to be put to the service of expressing, but merely of referring. Even more confusing is the idea that an expressive dimension can be used as a jack of all trades when it comes to E-elements, expressing different emotions, attitudes, or similar in different contexts. Translated to other type-expressive terms, the idea would imply that "Ouch!," say, would express pain in some contexts, delighted surprise in others, hate in a few. With the semantic expressive dimension determined by a particular E-element, this seems pretty much to assign a new meaning to type-expressive terms in each context of utterance. On my perspective, instead, registered terms retain their meanings across all contexts.

However, the objection is based on a couple of good insights worth underscoring. For starters, registered terms associated with particular conversational contexts are typically avoided in other conversational contexts; again, our physician would refrain from using words like "belly" or "shit" and would choose "abdomen" and "feces" instead. Part of this avoidance is related to the fact that the use of these co-referential terms would have a communicational impact in the exchange between both parties in the roles in which they are located at the time. Using the default, context-related expected terms instead ("abdomen" and "belly," or "poo" and "booboo" in infantile contexts) molds the interaction in the expected way. Likewise, the idea that the purported E-element may be well received or expected in some contexts but not in others does not seem to quite fit what happens in cross-contextual uses of registered words but grasps an interesting feature. The utterance of "Did you poo in your pants?" can be used to question a child about his bowel movements in a child-oriented context, and can be used to ridicule a scared adult in an all-adult conversation. But this last use is not due to the fact that the speaker is expressing caring feelings for the recipient, as it would be the explanation on this objection. Instead, it is due to the fact that the recipient is being treated like a child, implicitly compared to a vulnerable, helpless kid, which, on an adult context, signals weakness and immaturity, two traits unwelcome in adults.

Both insights point to the fact that the root of the expressive force of registered words gained in cross-contextual uses lies on the echoes of the original conversational contexts brought by those uses. In our example, the social setting in which a medical interview takes part carries with it a necessary emotional distance between the individual in the role of patient and the individual in the role of doctor and requires doctors to signal professionalism with their behavior (both linguistic and non-linguistic). In child-minding contexts, the opposite is true: the situation requires emotional closeness between those in the role of caretakers and children, and it is based on the root idea that children are helpless and require to be addressed and treated in a way far different from how adults would treat other adults. Carrying elements that make sense in one of these contexts into another imposes a communicational impact based on the echoing of the characteristic traits in the original context in the second context. Thus, a doctor arriving at a friends' gathering still wearing his physician garment will inevitably trigger mockery directed at dispelling the emotional distance echoed by it in this other context ("Here comes Mr. Doctor, please give him some space!"). Likewise, the use of infantile terms in non-infantile contexts automatically conveys the idea that the speaker is a responsible adult taking care of a child. The reason why "belly" is avoided in the physician consult, and the reason why "poo" is used in the friendly mockery in the examples above is that they infantilize the recipient. In turn, the reason why "abdomen" and "feces" are preferred in the medical context is because, like white coats and formal attire, their use marks the role of the individual in the setting. White coats and medical-registered terms do indeed invest the individual with the kind of professional appearance imposed on the role, but they do not *express* E-elements like distance or respect.

Thus, it is on the basis of this echoing of traits belonging in a different context that registered terms gain an expressive power when used cross-contextually. Things get even more interesting when it comes to words registered as *vulgar*. Recall that registered terms belong to sets of sister-words referring to the same worldly entities. "Vulgar terms" are registered terms used in friendly conversation between adults in highly informal contexts. Thus, "fuck" and "shit" (as verbs in the sister-word sets for having sexual intercourse and defecating) are preferred in these conversational settings to other alternatives like "make love" or "defecate," which would sound awkward among friends.[4] While some vulgarities are expressively neutral in their original, informal conversational contexts, others are type-expressive even in them. Words like "fuck" and "shit" in the abovementioned sense belong to the first kind: they are not expressive when used in informal conversations. Instead, in these contexts they are merely referential terms for sexual intercourse or feces fit to the social setting. However, like "booboo" and "madam," these terms cause an expressive impact in cross-contextual uses: in most non-informal conversational contexts, the use of vulgarities signals heightened emotions, both positive and negative, and are often used with the secondary intention of downplaying the formality of the situation. In turn, vulgar words like the C-word—and generally, all vulgar pejoratives or complex pejoratives containing vulgarities, like "asshole" or "motherfucker"—are type-expressive even in typical uses in their original (informal) contexts, and remain so in cross-contextual uses. After all, the pejoratives' main function is to express contempt, hatred, or disdain toward the recipient—or whichever

E-element the reader may prefer, as long as it is negative toward the target. Cross-contextual uses of type-expressive vulgar pejoratives add then an extra layer of offensiveness to the exchange; they are not only offensive in virtue of their meaning but also in virtue of their use constituting a violation of most contexts' rules on registered language. While it is possible to express anger or hate in a way that is appropriate to every conversational context register-wise, appealing to vulgarities in non-informal settings makes the situation escalate quickly. Similarly to cross-contextual uses of non-pejorative vulgarities, vulgar pejoratives also help downplay the formality of the situation, which in the midst of a heated exchange may signal a provocation to get into a physical fight, or may be understood as a veiled threat of physical violence.

Be that as it may, the fact is that there are both type-expressive and token-expressive registered words. Words and phrases registered as vulgar, particularly, belong to both categories and play an important role as pejoratives, undertaking the function of expressing hate or anger.

3. SLURS AND MORAL TERMS

The last decade brought a particular kind of pejoratives to the forum of philosophical discussion. *Slurs* are extremely offensive terms targeting identifiable, often vulnerable groups singled out by ethnicity, religion, nationality, ethnicity, gender, sexual preferences, or disability, among others. Slurs are outstanding pejoratives in virtue of their great virulence: their use manages to be offensive not only for the individual target—if any—but for the entire group, and even for bystanders. Hence, slurs make starring appearances in hate speech, and are majorly used by the bigoted, the xenophobe, the misogynist, the ableist.

The discussion on the source of slurs' extraordinary derogatory force has been long, and the literature on the topic is abundant. For this reason, I will not attempt to go into details here. Instead, I want to focus on the relation between slur usage and expression of negative E-elements within the conceptual frame provided earlier. In this context, we can wonder whether slurs are type- or token-expressives. For many, the answer is obvious enough; all signals seem to point in the direction of type-expressivism. According to the rough definition presented, typical uses of type-expressives are not expressively neutral, but are expressive—and in the case of pejoratives, offensive—in every single use. Slurs are not only generally used to express hatred or contempt against identifiable groups but in some cultures and contexts are also tabooed from conversations to the point of being frowned at even when they appear embedded in indirect reports or quoted for educational purposes (as pointed out by Predelli (2020)). This reaction can be interpreted as indicative of the expressive power these words have in all uses. Hence, expressive-friendly approaches to slur meaning seem to be the most appropriate ones.

I want to contest this idea by comparing the case of slurs with another dispute held over the expressive dimension of another kind of words: moral terms. The question underlying the comparison focus on whether an expressively neutral use of slurs is plausible or even conceivable, for this plausibility would support the idea that slurs are not necessarily type-expressives.

The debate over the neutral use of moral terms is not as structured around the expressive dimension of these terms as it is around their motivational component. The figure of the amoralist[5] emerges in the midst of the discussion between advocates of internalism and externalism about moral judgment. In a cursory sketch, disputants argue over whether linguistic competence with moral terms (and more concretely "thin" moral terms such as "good," "bad," "correct," instead of thick moral terms like "courageous" and "chaste") comes hand in hand with an action-guiding dimension. If it does, a competent utterance of "G-ing is good" (where G is an action available to the speaker as an agent) should be correlated with the willingness to perform G in the proper context and under the right circumstances. For the *moral internalist*, this action-guiding dimension is based on a motivational attitude held by the speaker. An *expressivist* about moral terms could also be satisfied with this picture, by adding to it an extra semantic thesis claiming that the essential semantic function of moral terms is to express the speakers' conative attitudes (Gibbard 1990, 2006).

The figure of the amoralist is designed to challenge this framework: the amoralist is a competent speaker who can make, assent, and understand moral judgments (including first-person moral judgments like "It is morally correct/obligatory/good *for me* to do G") but lacks the motivation to act in accordance with this judgment. It is not a matter of ignorance: the amoralist is aware of the practical significance of moral judgments and knows that classifying an action as good or morally obligatory carries with it a practicality requirement; she even approves when other agents are moved in the appropriate way. Likewise, the amoralist is not akratic; she simply lacks the motivational element connecting her utterance to the appropriate, expected behavior.

The lack of motivation plus the competence in the use of moral terms threatens the internalist perspective, for it seems now possible to be competent in the use of moral terms without holding any motivational or moral attitude. Because of this, the figure of the amoralist is presented and defended by moral externalists,[6] who claim that the presence of such an attitude is not necessary for the competent use of moral judgments. The threat extends to expressivists about moral terms, too, by proving, if sound, that competence with moral terms does not require speakers to hold any particular kind of attitude, and thus those terms do not have a semantic expressive dimension.

So, is the amoralist even plausible? As with any philosophical question, waters divide here. Counterarguments, as expected, aim to cast doubt on the logical, metaphysical, and nomological possibility of that figure. For some, the amoralist's utterance is not actually a genuine moral judgment, and the moral terms in it are enclosed by inverted commas or scare quotes, singling a detached use of the term ("G is 'good'" equals then to "G is what society calls 'good'"). This is important since, according to Hare (1952, 124–26) among others, moral terms have an expressive meaning if used literally, but this aspect is cancellable by using inverted commas. For Smith (1996), sincere amoralists are implausible, leaving the amoralist portrayed as either as someone who is insincere or someone merely pretending to make an utterance. However, these responses are not convincing enough, at least according to Finlay (2004), who claims that many of them seem ad hoc, with no more support than the fact that the amoralist is inconsistent with the internalist/expressivistic perspective. After all, the amoralist seems to be uttering the same sentence uttered by the moral agent.

Interestingly, comparisons between moral terms and slurs are a commonplace in papers involved in this dispute, particularly in those advocating for hybrid approaches to moral terms according to which they comprise both a referential semantic dimension and an E-expressive semantic dimension. And no wonder: for many,[7] slurs combine a referential dimension with an expressive aspect, as do moral terms for (some) advocates of the hybrid approach. The comparison can be taken a little bit further and stretched so as to assess the possibility of detached uses of slurs by means of a replica of the amoralist case. Slur usage is associated with the expression of negative E-elements like hatred or contempt, in the same way moral terms are associated, for some, with the expression of moral approval or recommendation.[8] The motivational element in moral terms can also be compared to the strong association between slur usage and active, unjust discrimination; in the same way we expect someone to do G after an utterance of "G is good," we strongly anticipate discriminatory behavior of different kinds against members of the targeted group from a slur user. The association between motivational elements and the use of these terms supports *internalist* approaches to them. Typically, internalist approaches to the relation between moral terms and motivation claim that moral judgments motivate necessarily: agents making moral judgments have a reason to act in a corresponding way. A parallel internalist approach to slurs would claim, then, that there is a necessary connection between slur usage and discriminatory acts. In contrast, *externalist* approaches claim that motivation to act in a certain way is only contingently related to the use of moral terms or slurs. The relation between non-cognitive mental states or E-elements and the use of these terms can also be necessary or contingent; internalists see a necessary connection between use and E-elements, and expressivists have those E-elements determine part of the meaning of these terms. In the conceptual framework discussed earlier, this assumption matches nicely with the claim that slurs, or moral terms, are type-expressives, that is, terms whose meaning is constituted by E-elements. Correspondingly, claiming that slurs are merely token-expressive implies understanding the relation between emotions or attitudes and slur usage as merely contingent.

Advocates of the plausibility of the amoralist claim that "good" can be used by speakers who are not motivated to act accordingly. Can slurs be used by speakers with no negative attitudes or no relation to discrimination? What is interesting about slurs is that responses to both questions—the one about the plausibility of slur usage with no intention to express an E-element and the one about the plausibility of slur usage with no actual discrimination associated with it—go in different directions. I will consider each response separately below.

4. NON-EXPRESSIVE SLUR USES

We know what an amoralist would look like: a speaker competently using moral terms without the intention to express any conative or motivational mental state regarding what she is saying. What would a detached slur user look like? In order to consider independently both dimensions associated to slur usage—expression of E-elements and discrimination—I think it is wise to split the figure in two. The first resulting figure would be that of a slur user who is aware of the derogatory force of slurs—including their discriminatory effect—but who holds no hate, anger, or contempt (or any other negative non-cognitive mental state or E-element whatsoever) against the target group. Not only does she not entertain these attitudes, but she does not even have the intention to express anything with her use of those terms. On the other hand, our second figure would be that of a slur user who intends to express negative E-elements with her use of slurs, but other than her intention to offend and hurt the individual on the receiving end, she lacks the motivation to actively discriminate the target group in any way, without this lack of motivation being the result either of ignorance or akrasia. Thus, even though this person uses slurs in the same way as the bigot, the racist, and the xenophobe, and is, in this case, using a slur to express a negative mental state (against the recipient individual), her overall treatment of individuals belonging to target groups does not differ from her treatment of individuals belonging to any other group (including her own). Let us consider each figure on its own.

I understand that the common sense reaction to the plausibility of the first figure tends to be that of rejection: for many, the fact that someone consciously chooses to use a slur signals the contempt this person holds against the target group as a whole, to the point of assuming that this emotion is unknown to him or her, bubbling inside without being noticed. Negative emotions and attitudes—or, again, your preferred kind of E-element—are ascribed to slur users even in cases of not straightforward uses: in some cultures and social settings, utterances of embedded uses of slurs (say, in indirect reports) or mentions (say, in educational contexts) are frowned upon as much as straightforward, direct uses. If we guide ourselves by this commonsensical reaction, we should conclude that a non-expressive slur use is entirely implausible. Slur usage is so intimately linked to attitudes of hatred, contempt, or despise against a group that any use, no matter how innocent, should be interpreted as an indicator of the presence of these emotions in the speaker, even if the speaker claims not to have them.

Pace this reaction, I do think that non-expressive slur uses are not only plausible but real. There are many real-life cases where slurs are uttered by speakers who do not intend to express any negative emotion—a fact that is clearly grasped by their audiences. Let's consider some cases:[9]

A. *Forced uses/mentions*: María has been harassed in the street. When she reports the event to the police, she is asked to repeat what she was called. She says: "Spic" or "They called me 'spic.'"
B. *Terms of endearment*: Juan (a cis-male) meets with his dear friend Pedro (gay). He greets him with "Hey, what's up homo?"
C. *Bigoted communitarian usage*: Michael was raised in a strongly anti-Semitic community. Although he himself does not entertain any negative emotion or attitude against Jews, he uses the word "kike" to refer to them in conversations with his peers.

Cases like (A) are misleading since they can be easily construed as mentions or quoted uses, distancing the speaker from the word uttered. However, they are utterances of slurs made by speakers not holding any negative attitude against targeted groups, nor intending to express any negative emotion through those uses. Note, however, that even though it is clear for both speakers and audiences that no negative attitude is being expressed in those cases, there is still a feeling of awkwardness involved. Cases like (B) are very rare in North America, but they are pretty common in Latin America and other countries,[10] where these uses fail to trigger offense in the receptor in most cases. Uses or slurs as terms of endearment, though, can be contested by explaining them as cases where speakers convey closeness to the receptors by means of pragmatic mechanisms in place.[11] Last, cases like (C) point to the fact that, in some social settings—namely, conversations involving the topic of the targeted group or its members carried on by members of bigoted communities—slurs are the default way of referring to them. This fact allows members of the bigoted community to use slurs in an emotionally detached way, neither holding nor expressing negative emotions, but blending anyway into the speakers' community.[12]

Before I add more on the plausibility of the non-expressivistic slur user, let me go back to register and expressives. Recall that, although all registered words or phrases can gain an expressive force in cross-contextual uses, we have two kinds of vulgarities: those like "fuck" and "shit" are only token-expressives and, hence, have a neutral, referential use in informal conversational contexts but gain an expressive momentum in cross-contextual uses. In turn, those like "asshole" are type-expressive even in informal conversational contexts. Advocates of the implausibility of non-expressive slur use seem to construe slurs as type-expressive registered words of the second kind, with no chance for a non-expressive usage unless a pragmatic mechanism is put to work. My rejection of this implausibility is based on my understanding of slurs as token-expressive registered words, more like "fuck" and "shit" than like "asshole."[13] This construal allows me to provide more details concerning the cases of detached uses mentioned earlier.

For example, the reason why users and audiences in cases like (A) may feel uncomfortable or self-conscious about the slur, even though it is clear for all the parties in the conversation that the utterance is not meant to be expressive, lies in the fact that the word itself is vulgar and is being mentioned, right in a formal context. A very similar feeling of awkwardness occurs when a vulgar term is mentioned in formal conversations, which consequently are usually preceded or followed by apologies by the speaker. This does not mean, of course, that slurs are only vulgar terms, for their other traits surpass this one in all situations. But the fact that they are (also) vulgarisms has an impact on audiences aware of the lack of intention to express E-elements on the part of the speaker.

Second, the fact that slurs can be (and actually are) used as terms of endearment reveals some interesting things too: first, cross-contextual uses of vulgarities may have the effect of loosening up rigidities in the conversational setting. In the particular case of vulgar pejoratives used as terms of endearment, they may gain an expressive dimension through pragmatic devices in place even in informal conversational settings, as happens in (B).

Regarding (C), it works as a reminder that for every registered term, there is a conversational context or a social setting where the term is deemed acceptable. Moreover, if the registered term is token-expressive, the term is just the default choice to refer to a given entity. Slurs, considered as registered terms, belong to a very special social setting: they are the default way of referring to targeted groups and their members for speakers in discriminatory communities, that is, groups of speakers whose individual identities and mutual recognition are based, at least partially, in their opposition to another group. Discriminatory communities may contain non-discriminatory individuals; however, even their identity as part of the group comes hand in hand with a perception of "us" that was born from opposition to a "them," a group perceived as radically different even for those who actively aim to treat these "them" equally. Even though the community itself is built around hate and active discrimination, these terms are expressively neutral in them, with the negative attitudes typically associated with their use coming from a different kind of source.[14] In the same way, technical terms used by physicians during consults with patients are not expressive of professionalism or emotional distance, but emotional distance and professionalism are constitutive of the practice involving the roles of physician and patient (more on the notion on *practice* discussed in the following section).

5. NON-DISCRIMINATORY SLUR USES

Non-expressive slur uses are not only plausible but real. They may sound awkward, as it happens with every cross-contextual use of registered words, and the sole sound of the slurs may give us the chills, but it is clear for everybody that, in cases like those abovementioned, there is no expression of a negative attitude. In contrast, I claim that the figure of the non-discriminatory slur user is implausible to the point of being oxymoronic. Again, my reasons to believe this are deeply rooted in my conception of slurs as registered terms and into the social aspects of register.

We know that register is strongly associated with speakers' roles in given social circumstances. These are not just any social circumstances but *practices*, a sociological notion that may require a bit of clarification. As social animals, we spend a large portion of our lives in the company of others. Social life requires the coordination of individual actions, especially when we aim collectively at attaining socially desirable goals. In turn, coordination constraints individuals' range of freedom in exchange for a smoother existence. In our complex social networks, this involves taking part in a myriad of different social settings every day, occupying a different role in each, and adjusting our behavior differently to fit into each. Most of these social settings instantiate *practices*, types of institutionalized social interactions articulated by behavioral constraints, structured by fixed roles with clearly determined obligations and rights that dictate an organized way of interacting to achieve a certain goal. Examples of social practices may be as trivial as behavior in public transportation and as complex as becoming a member of a governmental institution. Each time there is an organized means of achieving a social goal, each time there is a predetermined set of behavioral constraints imposed on us, we are facing a social practice.

Practices emerge as a response to practical problems, as means to achieve socially desirable goods that, up to that point, were not attained, attained unsystematically, or in a systematic way that is no longer satisfactory. They anchor in a seminal idea that serves as a *rationale*; an idea of why things should be done differently. Repetition of behavior adjusted to social constraints leads to institutionalization, and institutionalization, in turn, leads to naturalization: later generations lose sight of the historical trajectory of practices and consider them as the correct/natural ways to achieve the desired goal. The seminal idea that was patent to first-generation participants hides from view too, and it often remains ignored or unacknowledged for late participants.

Importantly, adjusting our behavior to comply with the social constraints of a practice contributes to solidifying it, reproducing it over time and reinforcing the seminal idea it relies on. Accordingly, each compliant action constitutes an implicit endorsement of this seminal idea. Even when this seminal idea is, unbeknownst to participants, acting in compliance with the practice sends out the message that it is okay to act by it. Thus, participants in a practice reinforce the seminal idea that anchors it, even in cases where this idea is not in their minds. Register is just one of the many ways our behaving—linguistically and non-linguistically—that is determined by the social constraints constitutive of practices. Despite being a linguistic feature of our words, using words and phrases marked with certain registers is part of the behavior mandated to participants of a given practice in virtue of being participants. Like any other behavior compliant with the rules determining behavior for participants, the use of registered terms reinforces the practice, as much as any other compliant non-linguistic behavior does. Thus, adjusting our language use to fit the linguistic constraints expected from someone in our role within a practice helps others recognize us as co-participants, but, more importantly for our current concern, it also reproduces, reinforces, and endorses the practice itself. Moreover, at least in most cases, cross-contextual uses of registered terms also reinforce and endorse their original practices. We know that registered words often acquire an expressive dimension in those cross-contextual uses. Although I do not aim to provide an explanation for this phenomenon, I suspect that it is related to the fact that exposure to registered words—like exposure to any gesture or garment characteristic of a given practice, even when they are out of context—leads audiences to evoke stereotypical traits of the original context, I dare to say, automatically. Such a reaction, if there was one, would constitute the very basis of the expressive dimension acquired cross-contextually.

We agree that (most) slurs register as vulgarities. But they also register as "derogatory." Register categories mark words and phrases used by members of a given practice. Social practices, in turn, are singled out by the seminal idea that anchors them, and the social benefit or goal they pursue. In contrast with vulgarities, which find their place in very informal conversational settings within practices tending to generate and maintain communitarian bonds, derogatory terms belong to *discriminatory* practices: that is, social practices aimed at creating or strengthening a communitarian in-group identity by means of opposition and contrast with an out-group. Most generally, discriminatory practices launch from a stereotypical depiction of the perceived out-group,[15] which allows for minimization and even dehumanization of their members. This opens the gates for active, negative discrimination. Register language plays a part in these practices, with slurs being words used to refer to the targeted groups and their members as they are construed in the in-group's ideology. Thus, words and phrases used to talk about the out-group in this kind of discriminatory practice are associated with its seminal ideal and goal, and hence marked as belonging to this specific practice, as derogatory. Interestingly, linguistic behavior compliant with these discriminatory practices involves the use of these terms even in cases where conversations are not meant to ratify the negative attitudes of speakers against the target group. Thus, in-practice uses of slurs are not necessarily expressive.[16] As mentioned, expressively neutral uses of registered terms are common phenomena; for example, the use of infantile words in child-oriented conversational contexts not always signals care and tenderness, and medical terms used by physicians in conversation with patients are not expressive of emotional distance. However, even in the case of these expressively neutral in-group uses, slur usage reproduces the discriminatory practice and reinforces its seminal idea: the constitution of a strong sense of communitarian identity and internal bonds based on the detrimental conception and mistreatment of a group of people as undeserving the basics of human respect. As mentioned earlier, this reinforcement is not exclusive of slur usage but of register usage; for example, the use of infantile terms always reinforces the idea that children should not be exposed to "adult" words, either registered (like "shit") or non-registered (like "penis"). Instead, words registered as infantile are used instead (like "poo" or "pipi"), reinforcing the seminal idea of children being radically different from adults. Of note, the assumption of this radical difference that is constitutive of child-oriented practices also impacts the non-linguistic behavior of caretakers, who, for example, allow children to act in ways that would be inappropriate for adults.

In the case of slurs, though, things get much worse, for hand in hand with the reinforcement of discriminatory ideas comes the implicit endorsement of damaging discriminatory actions that may have been pursued by the original users of these terms in the past or even until today. Note, also, that an implicit endorsement of discriminatory practices is different from having clear attitudes of contempt toward an individual and/or a group, which underscores the fact that slur usage is not necessarily expressive, but it is always discriminatory, even in the mouth of speakers clearly not bigoted, xenophobe, misogynist, or similar. Moreover, the use of slurs slips into the conversation a perception of the targets in tune with the negative ways in which they were perceived by the discriminatory group, locating them in the oppressed role.[17] This nefarious endorsement is a direct consequence of slur usage in the original, discriminatory context, but it is equally a direct consequence of slur usage in cross-contextual uses.

If things are so, slur usage is not only an objectionable choice of words (Bolinger 2017). Both in cross-contextual and in contextual uses where they are mere default referential tools (as in (C) above), slur usage is still part of a bigger scheme where it counts as a discriminatory (linguistic) action, not only in a trivial sense—whereas discrimination amounts to differential treatment (Eidelson 2015)—but in a full-fledged, negative way. Thus, although all speakers in (A), (B), and (C) may be exempted from the ascription of expressive intentions or negative attitudes, they are responsible for using words with such a heavy load. Although they are not expressive users of slurs, their uses of them constitute discriminatory acts to various degrees (less in the case of (A) for the utterance was forced, more in the case of (B) and mostly in the case of (C)).

Note that the immediate relation between slur usage and discrimination accounts for the commonsensical reaction that seemed to oppose the plausibility of non-expressive slur uses. The visceral feeling we get when exposed to slur usage is mistakenly interpreted as coming from the ascription to the speaker of emotions or attitudes against the target group that we find objectionable, to say the least. However, my claim is that this reaction comes instead from the evocation of discriminatory practices triggered by derogatory words, or better, from understanding the use of those words as an act of discrimination. We react to the act of discrimination, and not to the purported emotions we think the word is conveying. Thus, non-expressive slur users should not be accused of harboring unconscious negative emotions or attitudes against targeted groups, for a careful revision of what is going on in the conversation would quickly disprove this assumption. But they can be accused in all rights of acting like undercover racists, xenophobes, or misogynists, for, after all, the sole use of those words constitutes discrimination, whether they like it or not. Slur usage reproduces and reinforces the minimization, stereotyping, and dehumanization of others carried on within discriminatory practices. Coming back to our comparison with the amoralist figure, we can now see that in the same way in which it is difficult to conceive of a competent speaker who uses moral terms correctly but is not committed to the expected courses of action ensuing from it, it is difficult not to expect discriminatory behavior from a slur user. Mainly, using slurs already constitutes discriminatory behavior, because it is indicative of a distinction made between "them" and "us" that could escalate to more concrete, less linguistic discriminatory actions.

6. CONCLUSION

Slurs, therefore, are not, as one may feel inclined to think, type-expressive words, like "asshole" or "jerk." It is not their semantic or pragmatic function to express negative emotions or attitudes against targeted groups—even though *they can be used* to express these negative emotions or attitudes. If anything, they are token-expressive words, more like "fuck" or "shit": they may acquire on occasions an expressive dimension, but for the most part, they are referential terms only appropriate within a given practice. Slurs are not the only words that work in this way: token-expressive registered words are expressively neutral in their original conversational contexts and gain expressive power cross-contextually. Registered words, like any behavior adjusted to comply with the social constraints associated with a practice, reproduce, reinforce, and endorse that practice. In the case of words registered as *derogatory*, like slurs, that practice of origin is discriminatory. Slurs are the terms used to refer to out-groups in complex practices of in-group identity constitution that result in unjust, unequal, and disrespectful treatment of members of the out-group.

These aspects of slurs and slur usage come to sight when illuminated by the comparison with the figure of the amoralist. The plausibility of the amoralist, a fully competent speaker who uses moral terms without committing herself to the associated actions, is highly contended in debates on hybrid approaches to moral terms. Similarly, the sole idea of a non-expressive slur user seems implausible on the basis of the gut reaction we get when exposed to slur usage, which we ascribe to the rejection of the emotions and attitudes typically associated with their use. However, I have claimed that there is nothing wrong with the figure of non-expressive slur uses, except for the awkwardness of the words used out of context. In contrast, it is the figure of the non-discriminatory slur user that is implausible, for, due to the role of slurs in discriminatory practices, all uses of slurs constitute discriminatory acts. Slurs are, then, non-expressive terms, but that does not prevent us from holding an internalist approach to the relation between slur usage and discrimination, even stronger than moral internalism: slur use constitutes an act of discrimination.

ACKNOWLEDGMENTS

The ideas in this work are the result of the rich discussions held in two reading groups on slurs and on moral terms: the Philosophy of Language group (BA-LingPhil) in the Argentinean Society of Philosophical Analysis (SADAF, Buenos Aires) and the reading group on Philosophy of Language in the Philosophy Department at the University of Western Ontario. I am thankful to each of the participants: Eleonora Orlando, Andrés Saab, Ramiro Caso, Nicolás Lo Guercio, and Alfonso Losada (among others), and Rob Stainton, Chang Liu, Jiangtian Li, and Dylan Hurry (among others). I am particularly thankful for the comments and corrections to this version of the chapter made by Eleonora Orlando and Andrés Saab, who did their best to help me state the ideas more clearly; it goes without saying, remaining obscurities are on me and not the reflection of their editorial work. Due to the nature of the topic, I mentioned slurs and pejoratives throughout this chapter. I apologize for it: it is not my intention to offend anyone, and I do not subscribe to any of the ideas or feelings associated with the use of these terms.

NOTES

1. Marques (2016), Barker (2000), Copp (2001), Finlay (2005), Schroeder (2014).
2. Source: Oxford Dictionary.
3. Again, this impossibility restricts to typical uses.
4. Neutral—as in non-registered—terms within a sister-words set are always allowed in any conversational context. It is just registered terms that are not easily accepted for the reason discussed in this work.
5. A nice presentation of this debate can be found in Finlay (2004).
6. See Putnam (1981, 209), Railton (1986, 168–70), Brink (1989, 37–80), Smith (1996, 72).
7. With notorious exceptions like Hom (2008, 2010, 2012) and Hom and May (2013, 2018). See also Camp (2013) and Losada (2020).
8. Slurs are also paired with the moral terms discussed by advocates of hybrid approaches to moral terms insofar as both slurs and moral terms have—according to hybrid approaches—a descriptive or representational dimension on top of an expressive dimension. In this regard, see Orlando and Saab (2020a) for a construction of slurs as complex concepts constituted in part by thick ones.
9. For a more extended consideration of detached uses of slurs, see Díaz Legaspe and Stainton (2019).
10. See Technau (2018) on German detached uses of slurs.

11. It could be said that the use of slurs as terms of endearment go against the *Maxim of Manner,* thus conveying a second message, something along the lines of "I am so sure you know I like you I can even insult you and you will assume I don't mean it."

12. See Camp (2013) for a similar idea.

13. See Díaz Legaspe, Li and Stainton (2019) and Díaz Legaspe (2019). We claim that slurs are registered as [+derogatory] and [+slang], are always [-polite] and [-formal], and in most cases they are also [+vulgar].

14. In many cases, these neutral terms used by discriminatory communities become marked as slurs once they are rejected by members of the targeted group, based on their right to choose how to be called. The constant conversion of initially neutral terms to refer to African American people by white people to slurs is a good example of this phenomenon.

15. For stereotypes, see Pickering (2001) and Orlando and Saab (2019, 2020a,b).

16. Neutral in-practice uses of registered terms do not cease to be "registered," that is, being words or phrases of choice in particular practices. Hence, non-expressive, neutral uses of slurs by participants of a discriminatory practice are still registered as "derogatory."

17. See Poppa-Wyatt and Wyatt (2017) for an enlightening account of how uses of slur impact on the perception of the targets in conversational dynamics.

BIBLIOGRAPHICAL REFERENCES

Barker, Stephen J. 2000. "Is Value a Component of Conventional Implicature?" *Analysis* 60(267): 268–79.

Bolinger, Renee. 2017. "The Pragmatics of Slurs." *Noûs* 51(3): 439–62.

Brink, David. 1989. *Moral Realism and the Foundations of Ethics*. Cambridge: Cambridge University Press.

Camp, Elizabeth. 2013. "Slurring Perspectives." *Analytic Philosophy* 54(3): 330–49.

Copp, David. 2001. "Realist-Expressivism: A Neglected Option for Moral Realism." *Social Philosophy and Policy* 18(2): 1–43.

Díaz Legaspe, Justina. Forthcoming. "What Is a Slur?" *Philosophical Studies.*

Díaz Legaspe, Justina, Chang Liu, and Robert Stainton. 2020. "Slurs and Register: A Case Study in Meaning Pluralism." *Mind and Language* 35(2): 156–82.

Díaz Legaspe, Justina, and Robert Stainton. 2019. "Emociones, ofensa y registro sociolingüístico: el caso de los 'usos distantes' de los términos discriminatorios." *Crítica. Revista Hispanoamericana de Filosofía* 51(153) (in press).

Eidelson, Benjamin. 2015. *Discrimination and Disrespect*. Oxford: Oxford University Press.

Finlay, Stephen. 2004. "The Conversational Practicality of Value Judgment." *The Journal of Ethics* 8(3): 205–23.

Finlay, Stephen. 2005. "Value and Implicature." *Philosophers' Imprint* 5(4): 1–20.

Gibbard, Allan. 1990. *Wise Choices, Apt Feelings*. Cambridge: Harvard University Press.

Gibbard, Allan. 2006. "Moral Feelings and Moral Concepts." *Oxford Studies in Metaethics* 1: 195–215.
Halliday, Michael A. K. 1973. *Explorations in the Functions of Language.* London: Edward Arnold.
Halliday, Michael A. K., and Christian M. I. M. Matthiessen. 2004. *An Introduction to Functional Grammar.* London: Arnold.
Hare, Richard M. 1952. *The Language of Morals.* Oxford: Clarendon Press.
Hasan, Ruqaiya. 2004. "Analyzing Discursive Variation." In *Systemic Functional Linguistics and Critical Discourse Analysis: Studies in Social Change*, edited by Lynne Young and Claire Harrison, 15–52. London and New York: Continuum.
Hom, Christopher. 2008. "The Semantics of Racial Epithets." *Journal of Philosophy* 105(8): 416–40.
Hom, Christopher. 2010. "Pejoratives." *Philosophy Compass* 15(2): 164–85.
Hom, Christopher. 2012. "A Puzzle About Pejoratives." *Philosophical Studies* 159(3): 383–405.
Hom, Christopher, and Robert May. 2013. "Moral and Semantic Innocence." *Analytic Philosophy* 54(3): 293–313.
Hom, Christopher, and Robert May. 2018. "Pejoratives As Fiction." In *Bad Words*, edited by David Sosa, 108–31. Oxford: Oxford University Press.
Losada, Alfonso. 2020. "*Sudaca*: Slurs and Typifying." This volume.
Marques, Teresa. 2016. "Aesthetic Predicates: A Hybrid Dispositional Account." *Inquiry* 59(6): 723–51.
Orlando, Eleonora, and Andrés Saab. 2019. "Términos peyorativos de grupo, estereotipos y actos de habla." *Crítica. Revista Hipanoamericana de Filosofía* 51(153): 31–58.
Orlando, Eleonora, and Andrés Saab. 2020a. "Slurs, Stereotypes and Insults." *Acta Analytica*. https://doi.org/10.1007/s12136-020-00424-2.
Orlando, Eleonora, and Andrés Saab. 2020b. "A Stereotype Semantics for Syntactically Ambiguous Slurs." *Analytic Philosophy* 61(2): 101–129.
Pickering, Michael. 2001. *Stereotyping: The Politics of Representation.* New York: Palgrave.
Poppa-Wyatt, Mihaela, and Jeremy L. Wyatt. 2017. "Slurs, Roles and Power." *Philosophical Studies* 175(11): 2879–906.
Predelli, Stefano. 2013. *Meaning Without Truth.* Oxford: Oxford University Press.
Predelli, Stefano. 2020. "Taboo: The Case of Slurs." This volume.
Putnam, Hilary. 1981. *Reason, Truth and History.* Cambridge: Cambridge University Press.
Railton, Peter. 1986. "Moral Realism." *The Philosophical Review* 95: 168–70.
Schroeder, Mark. 2014. "Truth in Hybrid Semantics." In *Having It Both Ways: Hybrid Theories and Modern Metaethics*, edited by Guy Fletcher and Michael Ridge, 257–309. Oxford: Oxford University Press.
Smith, Michael. 1996. "Internalism's Wheel." In *Truth in Ethics*, edited by Brad Hooker, 69–94. Oxford: Blackwell Publishers.
Technau, Björk. 2018. "Going Beyond Hate Speech: The Pragmatics of Ethnic Slur Terms." *Lodz Papers in Pragmatics* 14(1): 25–43.

Chapter 8

On the Moral Import of Using Slurs

Eleonora Orlando

In this chapter I examine the thesis that there is a theoretically interesting relation between the semantic account of slurs, namely, expressions such as "spic," "nigger," "faggot," "dyke," "kike," "whore," and so on, and the adoption of a morally correct stance on issues such as racism, sexism, and homophobia. As is well known, those expressions are prima facie associated with the speaker's conveyance of contemptuous feelings for the members of a certain group of people identified in terms of their origin ("spic"), ethnicity ("nigger"), sexual orientation ("faggot," "dyke"), religion ("kike"), gender ("whore"), and so on.[1] Recently, Hom and May (2013) have claimed that adopting a morally correct stance on such crucial issues requires supporting a certain account of the meaning of slurs, namely, one that has been classified in the Introduction to this book as Lexical Monism, on which they are conceived of as general terms expressing empty concepts. From their perspective, only by depriving slurs of extensions is it possible to come up with a semantic view that accords with the commonsensical moral belief that nobody should be despised because of qualities concerning her origin, ethnicity, sexual orientation, religion, gender, and similar aspects. Moreover, this implies a position on the moral import of slur use: those uses denying the ascription of the corresponding property to an individual, like "Victor is not a kike," or those interpreted as manifesting the empty character of slurwords, such as "There are no spics" and "No lesbians are dykes," are to be considered morally correct ones. So, Hom and May's position encompasses both a proposal about what it takes for a semantic account of slurs to be morally correct and a thesis, following the proposed account, about what kinds of slur uses are morally correct.

My purpose in this chapter is twofold: first, I will analyze and criticize their position; second, I will draw the main guidelines for an alternative semantic account. From my perspective, on the one hand, the relation between the account of the meaning of slurs and the adoption of a morally correct stance on bigotry of different kinds does not have the restriction set forth by Hom and May: the kind of moral correctness at stake is compatible with an alternative, dualistic semantic account like the one hereby defended. On the other hand, their semantic account has implications concerning the moral import of slur use that I will reject: in contrast with Hom and May, uses like the above-mentioned ones will turn out to be morally incorrect in some way.

The chapter has the following structure. In section 1, I summarize Hom and May's position and reconstruct their main argument, identified as "the master argument." In section 2, I explain what I consider to be the main flaws affecting it. Section 3 contains the guidelines for an alternative, dualistic account in which slur-words are semantically associated with stereotypes that constitute their expressive meaning dimension. In section 4, and against the background of the previous proposal, a different conception of the moral import of using slur-words is brought to the fore. Section 5 briefly summarizes the main ideas defended in the chapter.

1. A MONISTIC ACCOUNT OF SLURS

Hom and May (2013), as well as Hom (2008, 2010, 2012), have proposed a monistic account of slurs according to which slurs have only one meaning dimension that is contributed to the truth-conditions of the sentences in which they occur, namely, a representational or truth-conditional meaning dimension. Hom and May's monistic account is Fregean, since they claim that a slur, like any other expression, has a *dual truth-conditional meaning*: it expresses a *sense* and denotes a *referent*. As usual with general terms, its sense can be identified with the general concept that is *expressed* by the term, whereas its referent can be understood in terms of the property that it *denotes*.[2] Now, this is where slurs stopped being similar to other general terms like, say, "horse."

On the one hand, a slur expresses a complex concept: as an example, "spic" expresses the concept PERSON WITH A LATIN AMERICAN ORIGIN WHO *OUGHT TO* BE THE TARGET OF NEGATIVE MORAL EVALUATION FOR THAT REASON.[3,4] As just emphasized, it is not purely factual but includes a *normative* component. In contrast, its so-called neutral counterpart, "Latin American," expresses the concept PERSON WITH A LATIN AMERICAN ORIGIN, which does not include any normative component but is purely factual. More specifically, they think that a slur expresses a complex concept constituted by the second-level functional concept PEJ ('pejorative') combined with the concept expressed by the slur neutral counterpart: PEJ(X), equivalent to

PERSON X WHO OUGHT TO BE THE TARGET OF NEGATIVE MORAL EVALUATION BECAUSE OF BEING X, where X is to be replaced for a general concept expressing the possession of a certain origin, ethnicity, sexual orientation, religion, gender, and so on. Since the concept expressed by a slur involves an obligation to hold a certain attitude or behave in a certain way (indicated by the deontic operator in the specification given before), it can be considered to be a kind of ethical concept. Their idea seems to be that the concept that is at the heart of a slur involves an objective moral obligation *for the bigot*, namely, from the standpoint of the bigoted ideology she subscribes to.

On the other hand, they point out that, as opposed to most general terms, there is no set of objects possessing the property denoted by it, namely, in the case at hand, there are no people with a Latin American origin who ought to be the target of negative moral evaluation for that very reason, and hence the term applies to nobody o, more precisely, its extension is empty or null. This is the Null Extensionality Thesis for slurs (from now on, NET), namely, slurs do not apply to anybody.

NET follows from the nature of the concept expressed by a slur, plus the Fregean thesis that sense determines reference and, of course, the way things are, which crucially includes some commonsensical moral beliefs, such as the moral belief that nobody ought to be despised because of qualities like her origin. In a nutshell, the inference to NET involves adopting the commonsensical moral perspective according to which nobody ought to be despised because of her origin and similar qualities. In contrast, if an alternative moral perspective were held, such as the one that is characteristic of a bigoted ideology, slurs would turn out to apply to certain people. This prompts Hom and May (2018) to compare slurs with fictional terms: if the actual world were the world of the fiction, fictional terms, such as "hobbit," "unicorn," and so on, would also apply to real individuals "in the world of the fiction." Bigoted ideology is, therefore, like mythology and fiction.

On the basis of these considerations, they claim that there is a tight connection between the meaning of slurs and a commitment to our commonsensical moral beliefs: more specifically, a semantic account of slurs subscribing to NET (like theirs) clearly vindicates those beliefs and is thus morally correct or, in their choice of words, innocent. In contrast, all those semantic accounts that take slurs to apply to certain people (namely, not to have an empty or null extension) seem to contradict those beliefs, and are then akin to the bigot's moral perspective, and hence morally incorrect or corrupt. A way of interpreting that tight connection is by means of the following argument (from now on, referred to as the "master argument"):

(i) Intuitively, a slur does not have the same meaning as its neutral counterpart: whereas the former can be taken to express a normative concept, along the lines of PERSON X WHO OUGHT TO BE THE TARGET OF NEGATIVE MORAL EVALUATION FOR BEING X, the latter expresses a purely factual concept X, where X stands for a personal quality such as having a certain origin, ethnicity, sexual orientation, religion, gender, and so on.

(ii) It is a commonsensical moral belief that nobody ought to be the target of negative moral evaluation for having a certain origin, ethnicity, sexual orientation, religion, gender, and so on.

(iii) Understanding a slur and holding the commonsensical moral belief mentioned in (ii) implies knowing that it applies to nobody, namely, its extension is empty or null.

Then,

(iv) A morally innocent semantic account of slurs must include NET.

2. TWO CRITICISMS

In subsection 2.1, I will argue that the argument can be objected on the grounds of the rejection of premise (i): the intuition that a slur and its neutral counterpart have different meanings is not enough to establish that the former expresses an objective normative concept as suggested. Ascribing that kind of meaning to slurs involves a commitment to what I would call "Normative Realism about Slurs," which is a controversial ontological commitment. In contrast, by avoiding Normative Realism about Slurs, a monistic account could be considered innocent without subscribing to NET. In subsection 2.2, I will argue that the inclusion of NET is not sufficient for a semantic account to be innocent and suggest the need for a radically different (namely, dualistic) account.

2.1. Why Being a Normative Realist about Slurs?

Hom and May's previously reconstructed argument involves an implicit assumption that can be objected, namely, a commitment to Normative Realism about Slurs. I take this position to be a peculiar instance of Normative Realism: to give a rough characterization, the thesis that there are objective normative concepts (like the thin ethical concepts RIGHT and WRONG) correlated with objective normative properties (moral rightness and moral wrongness, respectively). In the case at stake, the presupposed thesis is that a slur expresses an objective normative concept (in the example, PERSON WITH A LATIN AMERICAN ORIGIN WHO OUGHT TO BE THE

TARGET OF NEGATIVE MORAL EVALUATION FOR THAT REASON) and denotes an objective normative property (the complex property of being Latin American and the target of moral evaluation for that reason). That objective property can be considered to be the source of a moral obligation (in the example, the obligation to have a disparaging attitude toward Latin Americans), which only holds from the bigot's perspective.

Two clarifications are in order. First, the objective normative concept expressed by a slur is a *thick ethical* concept. It is thick because, as shown before, it encompasses both a normative and a factual component. It is ethical because, as explained, it involves an obligation to hold a certain attitude toward certain people.[5]

Second, the property denoted by a slur is taken to ground a moral obligation; it is clear, though, that the obligation only holds from a certain perspective, namely, the perspective of the corresponding bigoted ideology. So, the corresponding concept can be construed as a *perspectival* thick ethical concept, namely, one that belongs in a set of moral beliefs and norms constituting *the bigot's moral perspective* that is part of her characteristic ideology.[6] More specifically, perspectival concepts can be conceived in terms of concepts that determine perspectival thoughts (in the sense of Recanati 2007, ultimately based on Lewis 1979). In a nutshell, a perspectival thought is one that is true at a center that is not represented in the thought in question; in other words, the conceptual representation of the center is not a constituent of the thought. For instance, an I-thought, also called "*de se* thought," like I AM COLD is true *at me* but the concept of myself is not part of it. Likewise, Hom and May may be interpreted as implying that the thought expressed by

(1) María is a spic.

is true *at a certain moral perspective* that is not part of the thought expressed by the sentence, namely, the bigot's perspective. Of course, that perspective is to be rejected on the grounds of our basic and commonsensical moral beliefs and norms, which allows for the privileged perspective from which (1) comes out false.

I have several worries about this position. First, one may think that using a sentence that expresses a thought deploying a concept of the kind suggested is already a violation of moral innocence, even if the concept at stake is considered not to be exemplified by anyone.[7] As it will be developed in the next subsection, moral corruption can be thought to be a question not of holding some slur sentences true but of using those sentences to begin with, independently of their truth-value. The main problem can be thought to be the expression of thoughts deploying bigoted concepts like the one that is associated with "spic" according to Hom and May: why would anyone possess and deploy the concept PERSON WITH A LATIN AMERICAN ORIGIN WHO OUGHT TO BE THE TARGET OF NEGATIVE MORAL EVALUATION FOR THAT REASON? Why would anyone partake in the bigot's ethical concepts structuring her bigoted beliefs and norms? Another way of making this point is claiming that Hom and May's conception of moral innocence in terms of supporting the commonsensical belief mentioned in (ii) is too narrow: on a wider conception of moral innocence, one could be morally corrupt by taking part in what may count as a discriminatory linguistic practice deploying concepts like the one discussed earlier.[8]

Second, there might be reasons to avoid ascribing the bigot an ethical concept, featuring in a set of moral beliefs and norms that is part of her ideology. Some bigots do not subscribe to a particular ideology: they just have negative emotions (basically, contempt) concerning certain people—their attitude seems to be not the product of an allegiance to a certain ideology but something more basic and less structured, grounded on an active endorsement of prejudices. In other cases, they do subscribe to an ideology, but there is no reason to think that it must include a set of specific moral beliefs and norms.

Third, the commitment to objective ethical concepts is unnecessary since bigoted attitudes can be conceptually represented in a way that makes the respective bigoted perspectives explicit, namely, by means of subjective concepts that do not involve moral obligations. Accordingly, "spic" would express a psychological/anthropological fact about some people, for instance, some bigots' attitude toward Latin Americans—rather than the moral obligation to despise a person for being Latin American that is supposed to hold from a, certainly very controversial, ideological and moral standpoint. The suggestion is that Hom and May should substitute the concept PERSON WITH A LATIN AMERICAN ORIGIN WHO OUGHT TO BE THE TARGET OF NEGATIVE MORAL EVALUATION FOR THAT REASON with the concept PERSON WITH A LATIN AMERICAN ORIGIN WHO IS SUBJECTIVELY CONSIDERED BY SOME BIGOTS TO BE THE TARGET OF NEGATIVE MORAL EVALUATION FOR THAT REASON; in other words, that they substitute an objective ethical concept with a subjective concept that may be considered to be ethical in a broad sense (since it contains an embedded normative concept, that is, CONSIDERED TO BE *THE TARGET OF NEGATIVE MORAL EVALUATION*) but is not objective, since it is not correlated with an objective moral property.[9] In a nutshell, I suggest that Hom and May should give up Normative Realism about Slurs.

Taking this suggestion on board would imply that the position should keep some distance from its original Fregean spirit, in the sense that the concept in question would not be something the speakers need to be aware of (at least, not entirely). In other words, as opposed to what is fairly typical of Fregean conceptions of semantic competence, the proposed account would allow for the competent speaker to not fully grasp the concept semantically associated with a slur. This can be seen as putting forward a distinction between the *concept* semantically associated with a slur and the *conception* of the target group that is part of a bigot's psychological profile: concepts and conceptions are independent of each other, as shown by the fact that it is possible to be competent with a slur without sharing the bigoted conception of the target group that is tightly associated with it. Back to the example, even if what accounts for a speaker's competence with "spic" would be her possessing the abovementioned subjective *concept*, a bigot would still have the belief that Latin Americans are objectively despicable for being Latin Americans, stemming from her characteristic bigoted *conception* of that group—something in which the non-bigot does not partake.[10]

Now, once the idea of an objective concept is set aside, moral innocence can be construed in terms different from the ones proposed by Hom and May: more specifically, there is no longer any motivation to associate the commitment to moral innocence with the thesis that slurs are empty terms. Being ontologically committed to objectively despicable groups of people on bigoted grounds is, of course, being morally corrupt, but something that is not a consequence of the bigot's, or, for that matter, any other person's, use of slurs. If a slur is taken to express a subjective concept of the abovementioned kind, PERSON WITH A LATIN AMERICAN ORIGIN WHO IS SUBJECTIVELY CONSIDERED BY SOME BIGOTS TO BE THE TARGET OF NEGATIVE MORAL EVALUATION FOR THAT REASON, there is no moral consideration preventing us from taking it to be exemplified by some people—since, to go on with the example, there are in fact Latin Americans who are subjectively considered by some bigots to be the target of negative moral evaluation.

On this assumption, the theory would no longer accord with the alleged intuitive truth of

(2) There are no spics.
(3) No Latin American is a spic.

which would come out false, namely, respectively equivalent to

(4) There are no people with a Latin American origin who are subjectively considered by some bigots to be objectively the target of negative moral evaluation for that very reason
(5) No Latin American is a person who is subjectively considered by some bigots to be objectively the target of negative moral evaluation for being Latin American.[11]

However, I see no reason for Hom and May to stop considering them to be morally innocent.

Be that as it may, the important point that I want to emphasize is that, once Normative Realism about Slurs is given up, moral innocence need not be defined in terms of denying the instantiation of objective properties correlated with the objective ethical concepts expressed by slurs, since slurs will not be taken to express objective ethical concepts to begin with. For Normative Anti-Realism about Slurs, being morally innocent is not a question of not being ontologically committed to objectively despicable groups of people but a question of not endorsing the bigot's attitude, be it cognitive or purely affective, toward groups of people descriptively identified in terms of their origin and similar qualities.[12]

To end this subsection, it may be worth clarifying the following point: I have been arguing not against Normative Realism in general but against Normative Realism about Slurs. A moral realist could perfectly subscribe to the version of Hom and May's account I have just proposed, in which slurs are taken to express a kind of subjective ethical concepts that can serve to represent the bigoted attitudes underlying their use.

2.2. Moral Corruption and Non-Displaceability

Hom and May's argument has an important consequence concerning the use of slurs: in particular, it implies that slurs have some morally innocent uses, that is, those involving no ascription of the corresponding negative objective moral property. They encompass uses of the negative quantified sentences that make their emptiness or vacuity explicit, like the abovementioned (2) and (3), and of those denying the ascription to a particular person of the corresponding property, such as the negation of (1).

(6) María is not a spic.

All of them turn out to be not only true but also morally innocent. To focus on (6), its uses turn out as both true and morally innocent on account of the fact that it is equivalent to

(7) María is not a person with a Latin American origin who ought to be the target of negative moral evaluation for that very reason.

A clarification is in order. On Fregean grounds, (6) and (7) have the same truth-value but they do not seem to be expressing the same thought: they seem to be a pair of sentences containing two co-referential general terms expressing different senses, namely, "spic" and "person with a Latin

American origin who ought to be the target of negative moral evaluation for that very reason." These terms involve two different bigoted ways of referring to the uninstantiated property of being a person with a Latin American origin who ought to be the target of negative moral evaluation for that very reason. They are not synonyms by Fregean criteria: a competent speaker may have different epistemic attitudes toward (6) and (7)—she may accept one but reject the other, for instance.

Be that as it may, as pointed out before, one may think that the expression of a thought deploying a bigoted concept, independently of the truth-value it determines, already involves a certain degree of moral corruption. In other words, using a sentence like (6), in as far as it expresses a thought that deploys a bigoted concept, allows us to take the speaker not to be (at least, completely) morally innocent.

Moreover, I think that this is exactly what grounds a feature of slurs that has been repeatedly emphasized by many authors (Potts 2005; Schlenker 2007; McCready 2010; Predelli 2013, among others): their *non-displaceability* or failure to embed under the scope of the usual truth-conditional operators. As is well known, there seems to be an offensive component to slurs that projects out of the scope or "scopes out" of sentential operators like negation, conditionals, propositional attitude verbs, modals, and so on, namely, those affecting the truth-conditions of the sentences in which they appear. In other words, even when slurs occur under the scope of such operators, they still keep the offensive component that is characteristic of standard assertive sentential contexts. Accordingly, someone uttering (6) is usually interpreted as endorsing some kind of negative attitude against Latin Americans, in spite of the explicit presence of a negation operator. The only way of keeping the speaker distant from the slur's offensive component seems to be interpreting those sentences in metalinguistic terms, namely, as involving an open quotation, where a term is not used but scare quoted, as in

(8) Here comes "Sally"!

said by John to Peter, while noticing that Tally is approaching, and it is common ground between them that Peter systematically confuses "Tally" with "Sally." Likewise, (6) can be interpreted in terms of

(9) María is not a "spic."

where the slur-word is not used but scare quoted, and the sentence can be complemented as in

(10) María is not a "spic," she is Latin American.[13,14]

As is known, Hom and May (2013) admit that uses of sentences like (2), (3), and (6), though interpreted as non-derogatory, can be offensive, which is understood as a purely pragmatic effect: those uses trigger the conversational implicature that the slurs involved are not empty (as opposed to what is indeed the case according to them, namely, the fact that they are empty). From my perspective, this relies on a controversial conception of the distinction between derogatory character and offensiveness: if offensiveness is regular and systematic, in what sense can it be detached from derogatory character? Why is that regular and systematic negative component, whatever it is called, a pragmatic effect rather than a conventional factor? Moreover, if it is a pragmatic effect, it must be possible to cancel it, presumably by making it explicit that there are no people to whom the slur applies. But how is this mechanism supposed to work in cases like (2), which can be interpreted as the explicit cancellation of the supposed non-emptiness or non-vacuity implicature ("There are spics.") but involves, that fact notwithstanding, as much offensiveness as the other kind of examples?[15]

In sum, the well-established projectability data allow us to draw an important consequence: any use of a slur can be taken to involve *a certain degree* of moral corruption. If that is so, Hom and May's commitment to NET does not seem to guarantee the moral innocence of uses of sentences of the likes of (2), (3), and (6). Therefore, NET is neither necessary nor sufficient for a theory's moral innocence.

On the basis of the considerations advanced in subsections 2.1 and 2.2, I will propose an alternative account with the following features: (i) given that moral innocence does not require a theoretical commitment to NET, the account will be an instance of Normative Anti-Realism about Slurs, namely, it will not take slurs to express objective thick ethical concepts as their representational meanings, and (ii) given the phenomenon of scoping out, it will be an instance of a dualistic approach, namely, it will recognize an independent, expressive dimension of meaning, along with the representational one. From this perspective, moral innocence will be perfectly compatible with the thesis that slurs apply to real people, whose existence is independent of the fact that they have been unfortunately associated with culturally determined negative stereotypes.

3. AN ALTERNATIVE

3.1. Some Preliminaries

Unlike Hom and May's account, the alternative proposal I offer belongs in the approach inspired by Kaplan (1999), according to which certain expressions, including some pejoratives, require a dualistic semantics, committed to the existence of two meaning dimensions: a representational or truth-conditional meaning, making a contribution to the truth-conditions of the sentences in which they occur, and an expressive or use-conditional meaning, making a contribution to their expressive correctness-conditions.[16] The last one is understood in terms of the set of contexts in which sentences containing slurs can be considered to be (independently of being true or false) expressively correct or incorrect. How are those two different meaning dimensions constituted?

On the one hand, as far as the representational meaning is concerned, this kind of accounts presupposes the Identity Thesis, according to which the representational meaning of a slur is identical to the representational meaning of its neutral counterpart. In terms of the previous example, "spic" has a representational meaning constituted by the property of having a Latin American origin (on an intensionalist framework) or the set of people with a Latin American origin (on an extensionalist one), which is contributed to the truth-conditions of the sentences in which it occurs. In this regard, "spic" is identical to the expressively neutral "Latin American," whose representational meaning is also constituted by that property or that set. Accordingly, all instances of (1), repeated below, and (11).

(1) María is a spic.
(11) María is Latin American.

will have the same truth-condition, namely,

(12) "María is a spic" is true = "María is Latin American" is true iff (the world is such that) María has a Latin American origin.

On the other hand, unlike their neutral counterparts, slurs are not purely representational or expressively neutral terms. As for the expressive meaning, this is exactly the point in which dualistic accounts differ: my proposal is based on the notion of stereotype, namely, it will be a culturally determined stereotype associated with the group determining the extension of the slur that plays a key role in selecting the set of contexts where its use in a sentence will turn out to be expressively correct.[17,18] Although this will become clearer below, roughly, the expressive correctness-condition of an instance of (1) will be understood as follows:

(13) "María is a spic" is expressively correct iff it is uttered in those contexts in which a cultural stereotype associated with Latin Americans, epitomized in the "spic" semantic stereotype, is in force.

Naturally, the two sets of conditions need not coincide: there might be world-conditions in which a sentence comes true that do not belong to contexts in which it is expressively correct to use it. On account of (12) and (13), (1) turns out true if the world contains the fact that María is Latin American and expressively correct if the context in which it is used contains a culturally determined stereotype about Latin Americans—therefore, on the one hand, if the world contained that fact but the sentence were used in a context in which Latin Americans were not stereotyped, it would be true but expressively incorrect; on the other hand, if the world did not contain that fact but the sentence were used in a context in which there was a culturally determined stereotype about Latin Americans, the sentence would be false but expressively correct.

So, in contrast with what is involved in premise (i) of the master argument, the intuitive meaning difference between a slur and its neutral counterpart is grounded on the fact that the slur has an expressive meaning dimension whereas its neutral counterpart is purely representational or expressively neutral.

3.2. A Stereotype Semantics for the Expressive Dimension

As is well known, there are cultural stereotypes associated with different groups of people, such as Latin Americans, African Americans, homosexuals, lesbians, prostitutes, women, the working class, and so on. Some of them are the same across different communities, whereas some others vary according to the community at stake. Most of them can considerably change across time; some disappear and new ones are born. Cultural stereotypes are sets of schematic, simple-minded, oversimplified, and mostly false beliefs involving a prejudicial view of the corresponding target groups. They are founded on discriminatory attitudes and practices that are deeply entrenched in a community. Now, given that among those attitudes and practices, the symbolic ones are prominent, slurs can be conventionally linked to those stereotypes. It is then possible to derive, from the cultural stereotypes associated with some groups, semantic stereotypes for the corresponding slur-words, more specifically, constitutive of their expressive meaning dimension.[19]

A semantic stereotype is a stereotypical or prototypical concept, namely, a special kind of concept. Two are its main theoretical sources. On the one hand, Wittgenstein's (1953) reflections on meaning, according to which a natural language term is to be defined in terms of an open list of characteristics, none of which is a necessary or sufficient condition for the application of the term. On the other hand, the semantic theory put forward by Putnam (1970, 1975) makes use of a similar notion to explain the meaning of natural kind terms: a natural kind term has a dual meaning constituted basically by a stereotype and an extension. The stereotype is a set of typical or paradigmatic characteristics, providing a conventional, not necessarily accurate, general, approximate, and simple-minded idea of something, that is, the members (exemplars or samples) of the natural kind constituting the extension of the corresponding term.

The notion of stereotype can be put to work to account for the expressive meaning dimension of slurs. Accordingly, the "spic" stereotype may be specified as follows:

"spic" = ILLEGAL, WITH A SPANISH ACCENT, POOR, FAMILY ORIENTED, DEFIANT, UNTRUSTWORTHY, RESPONSIBLE, HARD WORKER, GOOD DANCER, PRONE TO LAZINESS, and so on.

A slur stereotype is then a complex concept, constituted by an open list of more basic ones; some of them are central (ILLEGAL, WITH A SPANISH ACCENT, POOR, FAMILY ORIENTED) whereas some others may be more peripheral (GOOD DANCER). Each one represents a feature of the original cultural stereotype associated with the target group—notice, though, that the relation is not bi-univocal, since there may be different ways of conceptually representing a certain stereotypical feature. Notice as well that some stereotypes may encompass two concepts that are contradictory with each other, such as HARD WORKER and PRONE TO LAZINESS. This is not surprising, since stereotypes are based on prejudices, which cannot be counted among the rational beliefs.

Slurs' stereotypes differ from natural kind terms' ones in two important respects: they typically include normative concepts and encode a negative global value. As already mentioned, normative concepts can be purely normative (like MORALLY CORRECT) or thick (like COURAGEOUS). A thick concept is a mixed one, namely, it combines a factual and a normative component; as a consequence of being mixed, it is usually taken to encode a global (positive or negative) value, called "valence."[20] Back to the "spic" stereotype, it clearly involves those different kinds of concepts: on the one hand, WITH A SPANISH ACCENT is a factual concept; on the other hand, ILLEGAL and UNTRUSTWORTHY are thick ethical concepts with a negative valence, and RESPONSIBLE is a thick ethical concept with a positive one.[21]

Moreover, the stereotype as a whole has its own negative valence, due to the underlying prejudicial belief, which is part of the corresponding cultural stereotype that the people belonging in the target group are significantly different from the rest of the community, and the consequent need to set them apart and take them symbolically under control. The stereotype valence is not thus determined by (the valences of) its constitutive concepts but by the prejudicial belief that the target group must be subordinated, on grounds of the existence of well-entrenched discriminatory attitudes—the suspicion, rejection, and even fear generated by what is perceived as different. That is why each concept of the semantic stereotype, even the purely factual ones (such as, in our previous example, WITH A SPANISH ACCENT) turns out to be regarded as a trace or indicator of the subordinate status in question.

The negative valence of a slur stereotype can be considered to be a generic offensive component that is independent of any individual attitude. It means that a competent speaker *will tend to have a derogatory intention* leading her to evaluate the members of the target group according to that valence, namely, in a negative way. This accords with another feature characteristically ascribed to slurs, namely, their offensive or derogatory autonomy: in Hom's terms, "the derogatory force for any epithet is independent of the attitudes of any of its particular speakers" (2008, 426). On this proposal, it is the negative valence encoded in the slur stereotype that determines its offensiveness, that is, the fact that its use (be it derogatory or not, as will be explained in section 4) warrants by default (a certain degree of) offense of the people they target and their potential hearers—notice that this does not imply that those people will actually feel offended but that they will have reasons to feel offended (to a certain degree).[22]

3.3. Some Precisions (and Another Criticism of Hom and May)

The proposal is then to construe the expressive meaning dimension of a slur in terms of a culturally determined normative stereotype with a negative valence. Two semantic aspects are worth being pointed out. First, unlike Fregean senses and traditional intensions, stereotypes do not determine extensions. Accordingly, the fact that a concept such as ILLEGAL is included in the "spic" stereotype does not mean that it is true, let alone an analytic truth, that all the individuals in the "spic" extension have the feature at stake, namely, that all Latin Americans are illegal. Moreover, someone may have none of the features represented in the "spic" stereotype and be Latin American (some Latin Americans are legal, do not have a Spanish accent, are rich, not family oriented, trustworthy, etc.) or, conversely, someone may have all those features and not be Latin American (she can be from the Philippines, for instance).[23]

Second, knowledge of the stereotype is linked to competence: to be competent with a slur, the speaker must grasp at least some concepts of the corresponding open list, together with the stereotype's negative valence. Notice, though, that in as far as the list of concepts is open, every speaker might grasp a different subset of concepts—though, as a matter of fact, most will tend to agree on some of the central concepts. Be that as it may, apprehending the entire stereotype is not a requirement for competence: depending on the centrality of the concepts being apprehended, it might be possible to establish different degrees of competence. As an example, a speaker who, in relation to "spic," only grasped FAMILY ORIENTED and GOOD DANCER might be said to be *less competent* with the word than another one who grasped the most central concepts.[24] So, competence with a slur implies being able to (regularly) associate the word with *a subset of stereotypical concepts* and *a negative valence*.[25]

Now, it is important to notice that, according to this account, as much as it happens with natural kind terms, a speaker who is competent with a certain slur might be ignorant or mistaken about its extension. In terms of the previous example, a speaker who competently uses "spic" in connection with people who are illegal, have a Spanish accent, are poor, family oriented, untrustworthy, and so on might not know exactly which property it represents, hence, she might mistakenly believe that, for instance, "spic" applies to Colombians and Mexicans but not to Peruvians. In contrast, in the case of its neutral counterpart, "Latin American," a competent speaker must know that it applies to people of a Latin American origin—neither ignorance nor mistake is allowed. Accordingly, slurs seem to semantically behave like natural kind terms, whereas their neutral counterparts can be assimilated to semantically descriptive terms. On the one hand, slurs are causally grounded on a certain prejudicially discriminated group of people, whose real and underlying nature may be ignored by a competent speaker; moreover, they are subsequently transmitted in terms of the associated prejudices, namely, for most competent speakers, slurs are learned by mastering (not a descriptive concept that is true of the corresponding extension but) the respective associated stereotype. On the other hand, their neutral counterparts are both descriptively introduced and transmitted: their competent use requires mastering a true description of the corresponding extension—in the example, "people having a Latin-American origin."[26]

Therefore, from my perspective, Hom and May's account gets the epistemology of meaning wrong. Premise (iii) of their master argument states that understanding a slur and holding the abovementioned commonsensical moral belief implies knowing that slurs are empty or have null extensions. But this cannot be taken for granted since it is plausible to think that slurs are semantically on a par with natural kind terms: competence with them would then be compatible with ignorance and error about their respective extensions. If that were so, contrarily to premise (iii), a speaker could be competent with a slur, hold the commonsensical moral belief that nobody ought to be the target of negative moral evaluation by virtue of her origin and similar qualities, and, yet, not know or be confused about the slur's extension—a fortiori, if slurs were empty, she may ignore it altogether. Accordingly, if premise (iii) follows from Hom and May's semantic account, in particular, if it follows from their conception of the kind of concept that is semantically associated with a slur, it is possible to reject it by means of the following *Modus Tollens*:

(i) If the concept semantically associated with a slur is the ethical concept PERSON X WHO OUGHT TO BE THE TARGET OF NEGATIVE MORAL EVALUATION FOR THAT REASON, where X stands for a personal quality such as having a certain origin, ethnicity, sexual orientation, religion, gender, and so on, then understanding a slur, plus holding the commonsensical moral belief that nobody ought to be the target of negative moral evaluation by virtue of her origin and similar qualities, implies knowing that the slur is empty.

(ii) Understanding a slur plus holding that commonsensical moral belief does not imply knowing that it is empty (for the reasons suggested earlier).[27]

(iii) Then, the concept semantically associated with a slur, if there is any, is not the ethical concept PERSON X WHO OUGHT TO BE THE TARGET OF NEGATIVE MORAL EVALUATION FOR THAT REASON, where X stands for a personal quality such as having a certain origin, ethnicity, sexual orientation, religion, gender, and so on.

4. PRAGMATIC AND MORAL ASPECTS

4.1. The Different Kinds of Uses

Any use of a slur involves prima facie an endorsement of the cultural stereotype epitomized in its semantic stereotype or, in other words, taking on board the attitudes and practices of discrimination concerning the target group at stake—with the only exception of appropriated or reclaimed uses, as explained below. But, there are different kinds of uses, which can be roughly classified into two main groups, which I will call, with a neologism, *insultive* and *non-insultive* ones.

The original and most paradigmatic uses involve an *active endorsement of the corresponding stereotype*, characterized by the presence of a negative emotional attitude on the speaker's part that might be called a "*derogatory intention*," namely, the intention to express, by means of using a certain sentence, an emotion of contempt/derogation for the group at stake. Accordingly, on top of the classificatory or predicative intention that is characteristic of the use of any general term, these uses involve a derogatory intention on the speaker's part, namely, an intention to use the slur as a means to express contempt for a certain group.[28] They are acts of insulting someone, namely, a kind of speech act or illocutionary force that can be characterized as *insultive*. In as far as they are performed with the intention to express an emotion, they are a sub-kind of expressive speech acts.[29]

More specifically, insulting is a complex speech act that is implemented by a more basic one, namely, an assertion, a question, an order, and so on, involving a slur or another pejorative expression—or even an expressively neutral one.[30] Back to the previous example, a paradigmatic use of (1), once again, repeated below,

(1)   María is a spic.

can be interpreted as an insult that is implemented by an assertion: the speaker is both *asserting* that María is a spic and *insulting her* by using a slur, in as far as she not only classifies María in a group of people associated with a negative stereotype (namely, she has a classificatory intention), but she also expresses contempt/derogation for that group (i.e., she has a derogatory intention, which includes the belief that the people in that group have certain stereotypical characteristics with a negative valence, together with a negative evaluation and some affective or sentimental component). As for the uses of (6), its negation, they are also *insultive*, though the insult is not directed toward María but toward Latin Americans—unless, of course, they are interpreted in metalinguistic terms, as in (10).

It is worth pointing out that I take an insult to be a kind of speech act because it is achieved by means of a Gricean mechanism (Grice 1975), which can be taken to distinguish a genuine illocutionary force from a perlocutionary effect. Notice that, as much as it is sufficient for someone to get warned that she recognizes the speaker's intention to warn her, it is also sufficient for someone to get insulted that she recognizes the speaker's intention to insult her (the hearer's recognition of the speaker's intention to generate in her a certain mental state is a reason for that state to take place).[31]

As is well known, not all uses of slurs involve the presence of a derogatory intention on the speaker's part; in my terms, some uses are *non-insultive*.[32] Some members of a linguistic community do not intend to express contempt for the groups of people they use slurs for; insofar, their endorsement of the corresponding stereotypes can be considered to be passive, determined by inherited prejudices they do not personally subscribe to. One may think that this is similar to inheriting knowledge by taking part in a linguistic community that includes experts in different fields, what Putnam (1970) called "The Linguistic Division of Labor": even if one does not individually know anything about the molecular structure of carbon dioxide, one can be taken to inherit or borrow that piece of chemical knowledge from the experts who are part of the linguistic community. Unfortunately, by means of the same mechanism, one can inherit or borrow prejudices, which thus accompany or underlie some *non-insultive* uses of slurs. These, which can have all the usual kinds of illocutionary force, can be exemplified by instances of the following sentences, made with a classificatory intention but with no concomitant derogatory intention:

(14)   You, my friend, are my favorite spic!

Notice that uses of the previous (2) and (3), repeated as follows,

(2)   There are no spics.
(3)   No Latin American is a spic.

turn out to be *non-insultive* as well, since the speaker cannot be ascribed a derogatory intention toward Latin Americans, even if, of course, she is still endorsing the corresponding stereotype. Notice, incidentally, that on the above-suggested metalinguistic interpretation of these sentences, they would also turn out to be *non-insultive*—moreover, if the insulation determined by quotation is considered to be not partial but total, the metalinguistic reading could be taken to be deprived not only of a derogatory intention but also of a derogatory component whatsoever, since there would be no endorsement of the associated stereotype.

Likewise, when members of the target groups apply the slurs to themselves, in so-called appropriated, in-group, or reclaimed uses, not only is there no derogatory intention involved but also no real or genuine endorsement of a prejudicial view. Consider a use of the following sentence by an African American kid talking to another African American kid:

(15)   You are my nigga!

Without trying to account for their full complexity, appropriated uses seem to be those in which the speaker intends to classify the addressee, or a third person, into a certain group of people but clearly does not intend to express contempt for the group at stake. One possibility is ascribing the speaker a special kind of endorsement of the slur stereotype, through which she manages to reverse its negative valence by adopting a new political and, fundamentally, moral perspective on the target group. In other words, on these occasions, the endorsement of the stereotype may be interpreted as involving an intention to reassess its global value from a different perspective—as is clear, it need not be a conscious intention. As a consequence, the valences of the constituent thick concepts end up being reversed as well: for instance, in the case of "spic," a positive global value may be ascribed to ILLEGAL and DEFIANT, while WITH A SPANISH

ACCENT and FAMILY ORIENTED might be deprived of all negative overtones; besides, some negative concepts may be altogether dropped off, such as PRONE TO LAZINESS. Alternatively, it may be thought that the speaker is not really endorsing the corresponding stereotype: she merely pretends to be endorsing it, to make it explicit for everybody in the linguistic community that a certain group of people has been unfairly discriminated and stigmatized.[33]

4.2. A Brief Excursus on Bigotry and Fiction

The previous distinctions concerning use have consequences that affect the plausibility of Hom and May's (2018) analogy between slurs and fictional terms. As mentioned, they claim that slurs are similar to fictional terms in the sense that, in as much as the endorsement of a bigoted ideology makes one believe that there are people who are objectively despicable by virtue of their origin or similar qualities (namely, the people slurs are applied to by the bigot), the immersion in a fictional narrative makes one believe that there are people and other entities with the features ascribed to them in the context of a fictional narrative (namely, the objects fictional terms are applied to by authors and readers). I think both extremes of the analogy involve some problems.

To begin with, what could be agreed to is that only in the case of so-called *insultive* uses the endorsement of the bigoted ideology amounts to (something similar to) the belief that there are people who are objectively despicable by virtue of their origin or similar properties—in fact, the belief in play might be, as suggested, that a certain group of people has certain stereotypical characteristics with a negative global value but not necessarily the belief that they are *objectively* despicable. As explained earlier, there are other uses in which the speaker has a more passive role: she seems to merely inherit social prejudices by taking part in certain linguistic practices.

Secondly, the other extreme of the comparison involves the use of fictional terms while being immersed in a fictional narrative. Even if this is not completely clear, Hom and May seem to allude to what are called "fictive" or "textual" uses of fictional terms, namely, those concerning the very sentences constitutive of a fictional narrative, both in the original act, performed by its author, of creating it and in the subsequent acts, performed by her and many other people, of reading, reciting, memorizing, or replicating it in some way, as an instance of

(16)   For the time will soon come when hobbits will shape the fortunes of all. (extracted from *The Lord of the Rings*)

produced by a reader of Tolkien's novel. However, even if restricted to fictive uses, the claim does not hold. As is known, many fictionalists, paradigmatically represented by Walton (1990), have suggested that fictive uses can only be fictionally true, namely, they can be considered true only in the framework of a pretense or "a game of make-believe." Moreover, some fictionalists, such as Currie (1990) and García-Carpintero (2007), have attributed to fictive uses a dedicated illocutionary force, the fiction-making force: according to this view, they are performed with the intention of making the occasional reader *imagine* herself to be imagining (or *de se* imagine) the content expressed by means of his recognition of that very intention. Without intending to get the specific details of those views, the point I want to emphasize is that the main kind of propositional attitude ascribed to the person who is immersed in a fictional narrative is not belief but *imagination:* that is the central capacity that she is taken to exercise in both creating and consuming fiction. Therefore, whereas in subscribing to a bigoted ideology, one *might believe* that there are people who are X and objectively despicable for being X, in fictively using fictional terms one does not believe but *imagine* that, for example, hobbits become very important—this is what *The Lord of the Rings* prescribes a reader to do. Consequently, complying with this prescription does not presuppose or require that one must believe that there are objects to which the corresponding fictional terms apply, namely, that those terms are not empty. In terms of the example, imagining that hobbits become very important is compatible with believing that there are no hobbits—it is not even necessary to think that this belief is suspended or canceled while one is reading, or somehow, replicating *The Lord of the Rings.*

4.3. On the Connection between Expressive Correctness and Moral Innocence

As already emphasized, Hom and May's commitment to Normative Realism about Slurs leads them to tightly relate the notions of truth and moral innocence, on the one hand, and falsity and moral corruption, on the other hand. As seen before, for them, (2) and (3), repeated below for the sake of clarity,

(2) There are no spics.
(3) No Latin American is a spic.

are both *true* and *morally innocent*, whereas (17),

(17) All Latin Americans are spics.

is *false* and *morally corrupt*. In contrast, by adopting an approach like the one defended here, committed to a dualistic version of Normative Anti-Realism about Slurs, the notions in each pair come apart: (2) and (3) turn out *false* and *prejudicial* and hence somehow *morally corrupt*, whereas (17) comes as *true* but also *prejudicial* and hence somehow *morally corrupt*. It may be worth taking into account that this version of Normative Anti-Realism about Slurs is then different from the one suggested as a replacement for Hom and May's original account: rather than subjective ethical concepts working as the Fregean senses of purely representational meanings, it involves stereotypes playing the role of expressive meanings. In this framework, the separation between truth and moral innocence is thus grounded on the dualistic character of the account: truth and falsity are properties related to the representational contribution of the slur, whereas moral innocence and corruption are associated with its expressive one.

However, being *expressively* correct does not make a sentence *morally* correct: the set of contexts in which it is expressively correct clearly does not coincide with the set of contexts in which it is morally correct. Given the previous considerations, I would say that the contexts at stake are those in which there is a culturally determined stereotype but its valence has been reversed to positive by a process of reappropriation or reclamation by the members of the target group. Accordingly, the only uses of a sentence containing a slur that are innocent from a moral point of view turn out to be the appropriated ones; all the rest are morally corrupt. However, not all of them are equally so: those uses in which the speaker has a derogatory intention are more corrupt than those in which she does not. In other terms, the set of contexts in which the culturally determined stereotype is actively endorsed determines a higher degree of moral corruption than those in which the culturally determined stereotype is passively endorsed.

Therefore, embracing a dualistic semantic account allows for Normative Anti-Realism about Slurs, according to which moral innocence depends not on the speaker's ontological commitment to objective normative facts, like in Hom and May's proposal, but on the speaker's attitude toward the socially entrenched discriminatory practices that back up the stereotypes associated with slurs: (unless it is an appropriated or reclaimed use) when using a slur she is somehow endorsing the underlying prejudices, and so she is somehow morally corrupt. But she can do it actively or passively, which allows for *different degrees of moral corruption*. Moral innocence is thus a question not of rejecting a certain ontological commitment but of taking a decision regarding our linguistic heritage.

5. CONCLUSION

Hom and May claim that agreeing to a semantic account implicating that slurs express empty concepts (NET) is necessary to adopt a morally innocent stance toward delicate moral issues concerning unfair discrimination of the kind involved by racism, sexism, and homophobia. This implies a position on the moral import of slur use: those uses that make that implication explicit, in accordance with commonsensical moral views, are, among others, morally innocent ones. So, Hom and May's position encompasses both a ponderation of the moral status of a semantic account of slurs and a position on the moral import of slur use according to such an account (section 1). In this chapter I have argued that agreeing to a semantic account that takes slurs to be empty terms is not necessary for moral innocence, unless one also agrees to Normative Realism about Slurs; but that is a controversial position, mainly, because it involves a commitment to objective ethical concepts. Moreover, I have argued that agreeing to a semantic account that takes slurs to be empty terms is also not sufficient for moral innocence: it implies that slurs have some morally innocent uses, such as those that serve to make their emptiness explicit or deny the ascription of the corresponding normative property to an individual; but, on account of the phenomenon of non-displaceability, those uses can be construed as involving a certain degree of moral corruption (section 2). Then, I have offered an alternative semantic account that presupposes a dualistic version of Normative Anti-Realism about Slurs (section 3). Against this new background, a new conception of the moral import of slur use has emerged, according to which no use is completely innocent from a moral point of view. As mentioned, both in making purely classificatory uses of slurs and in insulting with them, a certain degree of moral corruption is determined by the endorsement of a prejudicial stereotype (section 4). Two main corollaries have been drawn. First, the morality issue has been moved from the level of the theory's ontological commitment to the level of slur use. Second, moral innocence and moral corruption are not an all or nothing question but a matter of degree. As I have argued, the degree of moral corruption involved in a particular use of a slur-word ranges from those cases in which the speaker is perfectly aware of her endorsement of a cultural stereotype associated with it to those in which her endorsement is a by-product of her involvement in the linguistic practices of her community.

ACKNOWLEDGMENTS

This chapter has been written in the framework of a research project given by the University of Buenos Aires (UBACyT 20020170100649BA, Res. 1041/2018) and another one granted by the National Agency for Scientific and Technological Promotion (PICT 2016-0438). I want to specially thank Andrés Saab, since most of the ideas contained in this chapter have been discussed with him and took their final form as a product of those discussions. Moreover, special thanks go to Eduardo García Ramírez and Nicolás Lo Guercio, whose detailed written comments have enabled me to substantially improve it. I also want to thank the other members of the BA-LingPhil group for their insightful comments to previous versions of this work—Eduarda Calado, Ramiro Caso, Sofia Checchi, Federico Jaimes, Laura Skerk, and Matías Verdecchia.

NOTES

1. All the slur-words that appear in this chapter are mentioned and not used, for the sake of theoretical analysis. Anyway, I apologize in advance if anyone feels offended by the mere mention of those words.

2. As is clear, this is not a strict application of the theory proposed by Frege (1892). As is known, for Frege, a general term, namely, a functional expression, expresses a sense, conceived of not as a mental representation but as an abstract entity, and denotes the kind of unsaturated entity he calls a "concept" (roughly, a property); besides, it possesses an extension, what Frege calls "*Vertverlauf*" (range of values), which is different from the usual notion of class. Hom and May's proposal is thus Fregean in spirit but not strictly Frege's.

3. I follow the convention of using capital letters to designate concepts and thoughts.

4. A similar idea can be found in Hom's (2008) proposal, according to which the concept expressed by a slur includes a reference to some stereotypical features of the people belonging in the target group: "For example, the epithet 'chink' expresses a complex, socially constructed property like: *ought to be* subject to higher college admissions standards, and *ought to be* subject to exclusion from advancement to managerial positions, and . . . because of being slanty-eyed, and devious, and good-at-laundering, and . . . all because of being Chinese." (Hom 2008, 431; the emphasis on the normative components is mine.)

5. Typical examples of thick concepts are the ethical COURAGEOUS, CHASTE, and CRUEL, and the aesthetic BALANCED, DYNAMIC, and SOMBRE.

6. It is worth pointing out that this is an interpretation of Hom and May's position—not anything that they have explicitly said in their articles.

7. In Hom and May's Fregean framework, thoughts are to be interpreted as Fregean or conceptual propositions.

8. I thank Nicolás Lo Guercio for pressing me to add this important clarification.

9. The proposed distinction between objective and subjective concepts is similar to the distinction between objective and subjective constraints for non-defective uses of slurs made by Predelli (2010).

10. I owe this clarification to a very insightful comment made by Eduardo García Ramírez.

11. This presupposes that terms expressing thick concepts can occur in purely factual statements, as in "There are no brutal people in this tribe" and "No XIX.th. Century literary heroine is chaste," which could be part of an anthropological and a literary essay, respectively.

12. This seems to be similar to the point Jeshion (forthcoming) is making toward the end of her paper, in claiming that "what divides racist from nonracist is not their beliefs about which individuals exist in the world but rather their attitudes toward those individuals that both most assuredly realize exist."

13. See Cepollaro and Thommen (2019) for a detailed argument, based on three tests, in favor of the thesis that the negation involved in sentences like (6) is metalinguistic (rather than propositional) negation.

14. It should be noticed, though, that according to views like the prohibitionist approach defended by Anderson and Lepore (2013a,b), the mere mention of slur-words can be considered to be derogatory or offensive. See also Predelli's considerations on taboo (this volume).

15. For a related criticism (to the effect that uses of sentences like (2) do not trigger the non-vacuity implicature to begin with), see Cepollaro and Thommen (2019).

16. See, for instance, the proposals advanced by Predelli (2013) and Gutzmann (2015).

17. Other dualistic proposals have conceived of the expressive dimension in different terms: a conventional implicature (Potts 2003, 2005; Williamson 2009; McCready 2010; Whiting 2013), an expressive index (Potts 2007), a rule of use (Jeshion 2013b), a set of register features (Díaz Legaspe, Liu and Stainton 2020). My proposal can be considered to be a variant of the use-conditional approach developed by Predelli (2013) and Gutzmann (2015). In fact, it may be thought that the bias of a slur, in Predelli's sense, is determined by the set of contexts in which its corresponding cultural stereotype is in force.

18. The section summarizes the view that is presented with more detail in Orlando and Saab (2020a,b).

19. I agree with Nunberg (2018) that slurs can be considered to be prejudicials, that is, expressions whose use involves the endorsement of a prejudicial view about certain groups of people. But, unlike him, I take those prejudicial views to give rise to stereotypes that are conventionally associated with those expressions.

20. The metaethical debate on thick concepts has opposed cognitivists (McDowell 1981; Kirchin 2017, among others) and non-cognitivists (such as Gibbard 1992; Blackburn 1992). The former tend to take the two components to be non-separable, deeply intertwined (although there are exceptions), whereas the latter take them to be independent and identify the normative component with an encoded evaluative attitude. In this chapter I remain neutral between these options, since nothing of what is said here hinges on that.

21. There are thick concepts whose valences are underspecified but can be specified as positive or negative in different contexts (Väyrynen 2011; MacNally and Stojanovic 2017). In the example, DEFIANT may be considered a thick concept with an underspecified valence.

22. For reasons of space, I will not examine the concept of offense, which probably involves a kind of moral emotion. For some interesting distinctions around this concept, see Bolinger (2017).

23. Therefore, this proposal is not open to the kind of criticism that has been targeted at Hom and May's account (see, for instance, Jeshion 2013a; Technau 2016). As has been argued, grasping the "spic" stereotype does not imply believing that all, most, normal or even some Latin Americans have any of the abovementioned features. Moreover, grasping each one of the concepts featuring in the stereotype is not an individually necessary condition for the correct application of the term. So, a sentence like "All spics are illegal" not only is not analytically true but also plainly false.

24. This is the phenomenon that Burge (1979) has called "partial understanding."

25. This allows for conceiving of semantic competence as a kind of know-how or ability.

26. For the semantic and meta-semantic differences between natural kind terms and descriptive terms, see Kripke (1980).

27. As pointed out to me by E. García Ramírez, what follows from the conjunction of our linguistic competence and our commonsensical moral beliefs is not that slurs have null extensions but that there is no moral justification to use them and, hence, that they apply to no one justifiably.

28. Being contempt/derogation a complex emotional attitude, my hypothesis is that it has at least three different components: (i) a cognitive one, namely, the belief that the members of the target group have certain stereotypical, mostly negative features, (ii) an evaluative one, that is, a negative global evaluation of the group as a whole (i.e., the active endorsement of the stereotype's negative valence), and (iii) an affective one, namely, some negative feelings for all the people in the group.

29. For a classical taxonomy of speech acts, see Searle (1969).

30. *Insultive* speech acts can be performed by using not only slurs but also other kinds of pejoratives:

(i) Keep silent, you stupid woman!

It is also possible to perform an *insultive* speech act by using a purely factual sentence, such as

(ii) I don't think that Latin American will be invited to the party.

with a concomitant contemptuous gesture or tone. As is known, certain prosodic elements (like voice pitch, pitch variation, intonation contour, duration of prosodic units and the manner of stress realization, etc.) usually indicate contempt/derogation (Sendlmeier, Steffen and Bartels 2016).

31. The idea of distinguishing between illocutionary and perlocutionary acts by considering that the former involve a Gricean mechanism while the latter do not is based on Strawson (1964), who opposes the illocutionary act of warning to the perlocutionary act of impressing someone, among other examples.

32. See Cepollaro and Zeman (2020) for a survey of the main varieties of the so-called non-derogatory uses, which they take to encompass reported speech, pedagogical scenarios, fiction, quotation, and reclamation.

33. Notice, incidentally, that, for Hom and May, any use of (15) would come out as both false and morally corrupt, on account of its being semantically equivalent to a

sentence along the lines of "You are my African American person who is objectively despicable for being African American."

BIBLIOGRAPHICAL REFERENCES

Anderson, Luvell, and Ernest Lepore. 2013a. "Slurring Words." *Nous* 47: 25–48.
Anderson, Luvell, and Ernest Lepore. 2013b. "What Did You Call Me? Slurs As Prohibited Words." *Analytic Philosophy* 54: 350–363.
Blackburn, Simon. 1992. "Morality and Thick Concepts: Through Thick and Thin." *Proceedings of the Aristotelian Society*, Supplementary vol. 66: 285–299.
Bolinger Jorgensen, Renée. 2017. "The Pragmatics of Slurs." *Noûs* 50(3): 439–462.
Burge, Tyler. 1979. "Individualism and the Mental." *Midwest Studies in Philosophy* 4: 73–121.
Camp, Elizabeth. 2013. "Slurring Perspectives." *Analytic Philosophy* 54(3): 330–349.
Cepollaro, Bianca. 2015. "In Defense of a Presuppositional Account of Slurs." *Language Sciences* 52: 36–45.
Cepollaro, Bianca, and Dan Zeman. 2020. "Editors' Introduction." *Grazer Philosophische Studien* 97 (Special Issue *The Challenges from Non-Derogatgory Uses of Slurs*): 1–10.
Cepollaro, Bianca, and Tristan Thommen. 2019. "What's Wrong with Truth-Conditional Accounts of Slurs." *Linguistics and Philosophy*. https://doi.org/10.1007/s10988-018-9249-8.
Currie, Gregory. 1990. *The Nature of Fiction*. Cambridge: Cambridge University Press.
Díaz Legaspe, Justina, Chang Liu, and Robert Stainton. 2020. "Slurs and Register: A Case Study in Meaning Pluralism." *Mind and Language* 35(2): 156–182.
Frege, Gottlob. 1892. "On Sinn and Bedeutung." In *The Frege Reader*, edited by M. Beaney, 151–171. Oxford: Blackwell.
García-Carpintero, Manuel. 2007. "Fiction-Making As an Illocutionary Act." *Journal of Aesthetics and Art Criticism* 65: 203–216.
Gibbard, Alan. 1992. "Morality and Thick Concepts: Thick Concepts and Warrant for Feelings." *Proceedings of the Aristotelian Society*, Supplementary vol. 66: 267–283.
Grice, H. Paul. 1975. "Logic and Conversation." In *Syntax and Semantics* 3, edited by P. Cole and J. Morgan, 22–40. Cambridge: Academic Press.
Gutzmann, Daniel. 2015. *Use-Conditional Meaning: Studies in Multidimensional Semantics*. Oxford: Oxford University Press.
Hom, Christopher. 2008. "The Semantics of Racial Epithets." *The Journal of Philosophy* 105: 416–440.
Hom, Christopher. 2010. "Pejoratives." *Philosophy Compass* 5(2): 164–185.
Hom, Christopher. 2012. "A Puzzle About Pejoratives." *Philosophical Studies* 159(3): 383–405.
Hom, Christopher, and Robert May. 2013. "Moral and Semantic Innocence." *Analytic Philosophy* 54(3): 293–313.

Hom, Christopher, and Robert May. 2018. "Pejoratives As Fiction." In *Bad Words: Philosophical Perspectives on Slurs*, edited by David Sosa, 108–131. Oxford: Oxford University Press.

Jeshion, Robin. 2013a. "Slurs and Stereotypes." *Analytic Philosophy* 54: 314–325.

Jeshion, Robin. 2013b. "Expressivism and the Offensiveness of Slurs." *Philosophical Perspectives* 27: 231–259.

Jeshion, Robin. Forthcoming. "Embracing Corruption: A Response to Hom and May." *Analytic Philosophy*, Special Volume on Pejoratives, edited by David Sosa.

Kaplan, David. 1999. "The Meaning of 'Ouch' and 'Oops': Explorations in the Theory of Meaning As Use." Manuscript.

Kirchin, Simon. 2017. *Thick Evaluation*. Oxford: Oxford University Press.

Kripke, Saul. 1980. *Naming and Necessity*. Cambridge: Harvard University Press.

Lewis, David. 1979. "Attitudes *De Dicto* and *De Se*." *Philosophical Review* 88: 513–543. Also in D. Lewis. *Philosophical Papers*, vol. 1. Oxford: Oxford University Press.

McCready, Elin. 2010. "Varieties of Conventional Implicature." *Semantics and Pragmatics* 3(8): 1–57.

McDowell, John. 1981. "Non-Cognitivism and Rule-Following." In *Wittgenstein: To Follow a Rule*, edited by Stephen Holtzman and Christopher Leich, 141–162. London: Routledge and Kegan Paul.

MacNally, Louise, and Isidora Stojanovic. 2017. "Aesthetic Adjectives." In *Semantics of Aesthetic Judgments*, edited by James Young, 17–37. Oxford: Oxford University Press.

Nunberg, Geoffrey. 2018. "The Social Life of Slurs." In *New Work on Speech Acts*, edited by D. Fogal, D. Harris, and M. Moss, 237–295. Oxford: Oxford University Press.

Orlando, Eleonora, and Andrés Saab. 2020a. "Slurs, Stereotypes and Insults." *Acta Analytica*. https://doi.org/10.1007/s12136-020-00424-2.

Orlando, Eleonora, and Andrés Saab. 2020b. "A Stereotype Semantics for Syntactically Ambiguous Slurs." *Analytic Philosophy* 61(2): 101–129.

Potts, Christopher. 2003. "Expressive Content As Conventional Implicature." In *Proceedings of the North East Linguistic Society* 33, edited by Makoto Kadowaki and Shigeto Kawahara, 303–322. Amherst, Mass.: GLSA.

Potts, Christopher. 2005. *The Logic of Conventional Implicatures*. Oxford: Oxford University Press.

Predelli, Stefano. 2010. "From the Expressive to the Derogatory: On the Semantic Role for Non-Truth-Conditional Meaning." In *New Waves in Philosophy of Language*, edited by Sarah Sawyer, 164–185. New York: Palgrave Macmillan.

Predelli, Stefano. 2013. *Meaning Without Truth*. Oxford: Oxford University Press.

Predelli, Stefano. 2020. "Taboo: The Case of Slurs." This volume.

Putnam, Hilary. 1970. "Is Semantics Possible?" Reprinted in *Mind, Language and Reality. Philosophical Papers*, vol. 2. Cambridge: Cambridge University Press, 1975.

Putnam, Hilary. 1975. "The Meaning of 'Meaning'." Reprinted in *Mind, Language and Reality. Philosophical Papers*, vol. 2. Cambridge: Cambridge University Press, 1975.

Recanati, Francois. 2007. *Perspectival Thought*. Oxford: Oxford University Press.

Schlenker, Paul. 2007. "Expressive Presuppositions." *Theoretical Linguistics* 33(2): 237–245.

Searle, John. 1969. *Speech Acts: An Essay in the Philosophy of Language*. Cambridge: Cambridge University Press.

Sendlmeier, W., Steffen, I., and Bartels, A. 2016. "Pejorative Prosody." In *Pejoration*, edited by Rita Finkbeiner, Jörg Meibauer, and Heike Wiese, 21–40. Amsterdam-Philadelphia: John Benjamins Publishing Company.

Strawson, Peter. 1964. "Intention and Convention in Speech Acts." *The Philosophical Review* 73(4): 439–460.

Technau, Bjorn. 2016. "The Meaning and Use of Slurs: An Account Based on Empirical Data." In *Pejoration*, edited by Rita Finkbeiner, Jörg Meibauer, and Heike Wiese, 187–218. Amsterdam-Philadelphia: John Benjamins Publishing Company.

Väyrynen, Pekka. 2011. "Thick Concepts and Variability." *Philosophers' Imprint* 11(1): 1–17.

Walton, Kendall. 1990. *Mimesis As Make-Believe: On the Foundations of the Representational Arts*. Cambridge: Harvard University Press.

Whiting, David. 2013. "It's Not What You Said, It's the Way You Said It: Slurs and Conventional Implicature." *Analytic Philosophy* 54(3): 364–377.

Williamson, Timothy. 2009. "Reference, Inference, and the Semantics of Pejoratives." In *The Philosophy of David Kaplan*, edited by J. Almog and P. Leonardi, 137–158. Oxford: Oxford University Press.

Wittgenstein, Ludwig. 1953. *Philosophical Investigations*. The German text, with an English translation by Gertrude Elizabeth Anscombe, Peter Hacker, and Joachim Schulte, revised 14th edition by P. M. S. Hacker and Joachim Schulte. Oxford: Blackwell, 2009.

Chapter 9

Sudaca

Slurs and Typifying

Alfonso Losada

Slurs are predicates that allegedly apply to individuals in virtue of (at least) their belonging to a certain group determined by ethnicity, nationality, religious or political views, or sexual orientation, among others. Paradigmatic uses of slurs have the force of an insult as they are typically used to express a negative attitude toward the individuals belonging in that group. In this sense, it is held that these terms are derogatory and may thus cause offense—not only to the people in the target group but also to third parties. Examples of slurs are "faggot," "nigger," "kike," and the likes.[1]

In this chapter, I will focus on the semantics of slurs, where "semantics" means the study of what is conventionally expressed through the use of the terms of a language, and which, in turn, determines the contributions those terms make to the truth or satisfaction conditions of the complex expressions in which they figure. Therefore, I will mainly leave aside the pragmatic aspects of derogation and offense, as well as the deep reasons behind the insulting character of these expressions.

It seems that using slurs is wrong. A number of views hold that this *wrongness* is due either to the pragmatic effects that such a use would have or to non-truth-conditional aspects of meaning. The minority of views holds that it is in the truth-conditional content of slurs. My account will be part of this minority, as I will argue that slurs are, from a non-discriminatory perspective, empty terms, namely, terms with a null extension. Unlike other minority views (such as those presented in Hom 2008; Hom and May 2013), I will hold that the semantic wrongness of slurs is ultimately related not to moral reasons but to the mistaken typifying nature of the concepts that they express. This way of understanding the semantics of slurs will allow me to explain the fact that for some people slurs are not proper means of representing the world or, more specifically, human beings. The position implies that there are no faggots, that Jews are not kikes, and so on.

In section 1, I focus on the difference between slurs and their neutral counterparts, and I present a case of disagreement among speakers in which both kinds of terms are involved. In section 2, I put forward the abovementioned semantic proposal, and show that it provides the right framework to account for the previous disagreement. Section 3 is devoted to further semantic issues, such as analyzing other examples and replying to possible objections. In section 4, I examine the similarities and differences between my account and other descriptively loaded semantic accounts of slurs.

1. SLURS AND DISAGREEMENT

There is a prima facie difference between, say, the terms "homosexual man" and "faggot." Although they can be both used to say something similar about a given individual's sexual orientation, their uses present some differences. Saying that John is a homosexual, with a neutral voice tone and with no disparaging gestures, simply expresses the fact that John feels sexual attraction toward other men. In the absence of any other clues or contextual setting, this does not indicate or imply any attitude on behalf of the speaker regarding John or his sexual orientation. But if someone says "John is a faggot," an extra element appears: roughly, there is a negative attitude being expressed by the speaker. This is so because the term "faggot" is part of a perspective on sexuality: it is a way of referring to men with a *deviant* sexual orientation—deviant from the point of view of those who hold a heteronormative discourse. As the term "homosexual" lacks this evaluative charge, it is considered the *neutral counterpart* of the slur. Similar stories can be told for pairs such as "dyke" and "homosexual woman," "kike" and "Jew," "nigger" and "African American," and so on.

The picture of slurs presented so far is, of course, a very basic and simplified one. For it ignores *friendly* uses of the terms, that is, those made by speakers who do not hold a negative attitude toward the target group—and who can even belong themselves to that group, as in the cases of appropriation. For the most part of this chapter, I will restrict my analysis to *primary*, *core* uses of slurs, that is, those involving a negative attitude. Other uses and their relation to primary ones will be briefly considered toward the end. But until then, whenever I use the word "slur," only primary uses will be under consideration.

A basic point of discussion regarding slurs and their neutral counterparts is whether there is a semantic difference between the two kinds of expressions. The most widely held position is that slurs and their neutral counterparts do not differ semantically—at least, in the abovementioned sense of semantics as concerned with truth or satisfaction conditions.² From this perspective, slurs and their neutral counterparts are believed to make the same contribution to the truth-conditions of the sentences containing them. In other words, slurs and their neutral counterparts have the same extension; and that is why this is known as the Identity Thesis: the extension of a slur is identical to the extension of its neutral counterpart. The forthcoming proposal will deny the Identity Thesis.³

As a starting point, I will present an imaginary conversation. But a quick notice before that. I will ground my analysis on examples belonging to Spanish. Since slurs are highly socially dependent terms, it is not always easy to understand examples belonging to foreign languages. Hence, I will use examples I feel fully competent with. I hope the indications provided will help the non-Spanish speaker understand the gist of the examples, and that she can find examples from her own language that play analogous roles. In my imaginary conversation I will make use of the Spanish slur *"sudaca."* The term *"sudaca"* originated in Spain between the late 1970s and the early 1980s, and it is now recognized by the Real Academia Española as a derogatory colloquial expression used to talk about South American people.⁴ In order to simplify the exposition, I will ask the reader to make as if the term *"sudaca"* were part of English, with the same meaning it has in Spanish.

So, imagine the following scenario: after organizing the *First Meeting of South American Philosophers in the UK* in London, Mary is exhausted and very disappointed at the behavior of the participants—for they showed up late, were not really prepared for their talks, did not pay real attention to the speakers, and so on. Once home, as she is talking to her husband John, she breaks down and screams: "I went out of my way organizing this meeting and all I got is a bunch of *sudacas*!" To which John replies: "Well, what did you expect? If it's a *South American* philosophers meeting, of course it's going to be full of *sudacas.*" Mary, in turn, says: "Why? Not all South Americans are *sudacas.* Some of them are and some of them are not." And John says: "Yes! All South Americans are *sudacas.*" Their daughter Lucy is overhearing the conversation, and at some point she feels the need to intervene by saying: "You guys, what are you talking about? There are no *sudacas.*" It is then possible to isolate the following sentences, held by John, Mary, and Lucy, respectively:

(1) All South Americans are *sudacas.*
(2) Some South Americans are *sudacas*—namely, by means of a conversational implicature, not all South Americans are *sudacas.*
(3) There are no *sudacas.*

Prima facie, there seems to be a disagreement among the three speakers. The disagreement is related to the extension of the term *"sudaca,"* and its coincidence or not with the extension of "South American (person)." If one were to hold the Identity Thesis, this intuition could not be taken at face value. In fact, given that all the speakers must be taken to agree that there are South Americans, the only acceptable content would be the one expressed by (1)—since uttering (2) would amount to conveying, by means of a conversational implicature, that not all South Americans are South Americans, and uttering (3) would amount to saying that there are no South Americans. Is there any alternative for the Identity Thesis's supporter? I think she does have some alternatives, and to them I now turn.

A first option would be considering that the speakers are attaching different meanings to the term "*sudaca.*" So, suppose, for example, that Mary is understanding "*sudaca*" as "South American person with dark hair," John as "South American person" and Lucy as "South American person who can breathe under water." Were this the case, then, of course, we would not have a disagreement but a misunderstanding. But let us assume that all the speakers in the conversation agree on the meaning of the term. Which meaning this is will be the topic of the next section; for the time being, I will continue to take the Identity Thesis for granted.

On the assumption that the meaning of "*sudaca*" is common to all the participants, a second strategy would be claiming that their utterances involve a metalinguistic use of the term. So, for example, one could read Mary's claim as stating that not all South Americans deserve to be called "*sudacas*" or Lucy's claim as stating that one should not use the word "*sudaca.*" Now, this may be a plausible explanation for those conversational contexts involving some particular voice intonation and face gestures indicating the presence of metalinguistic intentions. But it cannot be ruled out in principle that there can be contexts in which the speakers use the term in a standard manner, that is, with the intention to express a property in order to describe the world, and not to say something about the use of a term. If the possibility of these contexts exists, the challenge remains: how do we account for the cases in which the speakers are not having a verbal disagreement or misunderstanding one another *and* in which they are using the term in the standard manner?[5] In sum, the disagreement initially presented still awaits an explanation. In what follows, I will provide and defend an account of the meaning of slurs according to which these terms have a complex semantic nature.

2. MEANING AND EXTENSIONS

2.1. The Semantic Proposal

According to my understanding of slurs, as of many other people's, these are words used to purport to refer to a given group that can, in fact, be referred to by a different, neutral expression. However, I believe that it is not merely in virtue of some individuals having a particular property that they are taken to fall under the extension of a slur but also in virtue of their being considered to belong to a *type of being*, that is, an alleged way of thinking, feeling, and behaving in the world.

To cash out this idea, I propose to analyze slurs as having a complex semantic value. On the one hand, there is the property expressed by the so-called neutral counterpart of the slur: *the property of being a South American person* for *"sudaca," the property of being a homosexual man* for "faggot," *a Jewish person* for "kike," and so on. The representation of this first element will be called the "neutral condition" or "condition" for short. On the other hand, there is a bundle of properties ascribed to the members of the corresponding group from the racist, homophobic, xenophobic (and so on) perspective. I will call the mental representation of this second element a "conceptualization." Conceptualizations can be read as analogous to what Putnam labeled "stereotypes": a standardized and schematic description of features of the members of the corresponding kind that are considered to be typical or "normal" (Putnam 1975, 147).[6] Conceptualizations also provide a list of features that are thought to be typical of the target group. But, unlike Putnam's stereotypes, as we will see, conceptualizations and the typifying element they involve will be truth-conditionally relevant in my theory.

In articulating my account I appeal to conceptual semantics (Fodor 1975, 1998; Davis 2003). In that framework, the semantic value of expressions is identified with conceptual entities; in the case of predicates, in particular, it is identified with general concepts—playing a role analogous to the one played by properties in a referential semantics. So, for example, the value of the predicate "lawyer" is the concept (LAWYER) and the value of "John is a lawyer" is (LAWYER [JOHN]), which amounts to the truth-conditions that the referent of the concept JOHN falls under the extension of the concept LAWYER.[7] According to my understanding of slurs, these predicates express complex concepts that can be represented by an ordered pair. For any slur *s*, its semantics value will have the following components:

"*s*": [<CONDITION>, <CONCEPTUALIZATION>][8]

Suppose that the conceptualization attached to South Americans involves the thoughts that they are unrefined, irresponsible, and untrustworthy. The semantics of *"sudaca"* will then be:

"*sudaca*": [<SOUTH AMERICAN PERSON>, <UNREFINED, IRRESPONSIBLE, UNTRUSTWORTHY>]

However, I believe this is still not a fully satisfactory characterization of the meaning of *"sudaca."* In order to see why, let's consider the following example. Imagine a woman named "Susana" who was born in Brazil. At a very young age, say two months old, she is adopted by a Turkish family and is raised in Turkey, under every common aspect of the culture of that country. As Susana grows up, she happens to develop a personality that encompasses the characteristics of the conceptualization of *"sudaca"*: she is unrefined, irresponsible, and untrustworthy. Although Susana behaves like a *sudaca*, I hesitate to agree that the term *"sudaca"* could be correctly applied to her (from a discriminatory perspective, I mean). Even though she fulfills both the condition (she is South American by birth) and the conceptualization, something seems to be missing. I believe there should be some sort of link between the two components in order for the concept to be correctly applied. I will propose then that a third element should be included when it comes to the semantic characterization of slurs. The exact nature of this element is, I believe, varying. In this case, it seems to be a *consequential* link: given that x is South American, x will be unrefined, irresponsible, and untrustworthy. If this were so, the full semantic characterization of *"sudaca"* would be:

"sudaca": [<SOUTH AMERICAN PERSON>, *therefore* <UNREFINED, IRRESPONSIBLE, UNTRUSTWORTHY>]

It is important to note that the element linking both aspects of the concept does so in what I will call a "typifying manner": it is not based on facts about the individuals that are allegedly referred to via the slur but on a prejudicial view of them. In the case of *"sudaca,"* it is used with the intention to refer to South American people based not on the proven fact that exposure to a given culture will generate such and such traits but in virtue of a prejudicial view of South Americans. So, in general, we can represent the semantic structure of a slur s as follows, where "typ-link" denotes this third element under discussion ("typ" being an abbreviation for "typifying"):

"s": [<CONDITION>, typ-link, <CONCEPTUALIZATION>]

This is the basic picture of the account that I would like to put forward for slurs. In section 3, I will come back to it in order to try to clarify it. But before that, let's go back to our initial disagreement and see how it can be explained with the elements of the present proposal.

2.2. Back to Disagreement

Remember that, in the disagreement presented above, three sentences had been identified, each of them held by a different member of the family, John, Mary, and Lucy, respectively:

(1) All South Americans are *sudacas*.
(2) Some South Americans are *sudacas* (and some of them are not).
(3) There are no *sudacas*.

As I claimed earlier, I am assuming that these three statements involve standard, non-metalinguistic uses of the term and that all the members of the family attach the same meaning to it. Given the account just sketched, this can be represented by a complex concept constituted by a condition and a conceptualization, and the corresponding link between them.

It is quite straightforward to see what goes on with Mary and John: Mary seems to believe that not all South Americans are to be considered in the typifying manner involved by the meaning of "*sudaca*"; John, on the contrary, believes that all of them do present the properties represented in the conceptualization. According to him, every South American person is a *typical* South American person, on the one hand. Mary, on the other hand, believes the link can be broken, at least in some cases. So, one could understand this disagreement as depending on the scope given to the typifying: should one accept *total typifying* or only *partial typifying*?

Attributing to Lucy a belief that would allow for an explanation of her claim can amount to two different things. First, she might believe, along with her parents, that "*sudaca*" is a *valid* descriptive term, that is, a term that can be properly used to describe some individuals. On this reading, she just believes that no individual falls in fact under the concept expressed by that predicate—although there could have been in the past individuals who did and there might be in the future others who will. On a second reading, Lucy believes that "*sudaca*" is an ill-conceived term, that is, one with no chance of having an extension because of the requirements it imposes on individuals to fall under it. In this scenario, Lucy has a *non-typifying* stance. This second alternative is, of course, more interesting, as it displays an attitude of complete opposition to the legitimacy of the slur. That attitude represents the correct stance for those of us who do not believe that slurs can properly describe or classify human beings, given that they are terms born from an incorrect way of conceptualizing the world, namely, one encompassing a perspective according to which human beings can be typified over in virtue of features such as their religion, sexuality, ethnicity, origins, and the like, ultimately to denigrate or disdain them.

From this perspective, slurs simply cannot have an extension, for the application requirements they imposed are wrong by principle in a conceptual sense of the word: they are *representationally* wrong. Thinking through stereotypes can surely be useful in many cases. So, for example, if I think of grizzly bears as dangerous, that representation can probably save my life in the presence of one of them. If I think of water as thirst-quenching, I will surely benefit from my way of thinking. But nowadays it is greatly accepted that typifying over humans beings with respect to their behavior, personalities, or qualities on the basis of the abovementioned conditions of religion, sexuality, ethnicity, origins, and the like is a plain mistake, for it is based on unwarranted generalizations, and precludes actual knowledge of others. In a world that is gradually more and more open to the diverse and the unique, this typifying way of thinking puts up barriers for social interaction. And that is, first of all, a conceptual flaw, an improper way of representing the world. In my view, the representational wrongness of slurs is thus previous and independent of their moral wrongness.

I will elaborate on this final thought in section 4. To sum up this section, the disagreement among Mary, John, and Lucy can be explained by considering that (a) the three of them are using the word "*sudaca*" in a straightforward, non-metalinguistic manner, (b) they all attach the same meaning to it, namely, the one specified above, and (c) the differences among them arise from their attitudes regarding the scope of the typifying element involved in the concept expressed by "*sudaca*," which I labeled *total, partial,* and *non-typifying*, respectively. The last one is the correct stance to adopt for those of us who do not think that typifying over human beings in the abovementioned way is representationally legitimate.

3. FURTHER SEMANTIC ISSUES

In this section, I will elaborate on the semantic analysis of slurs that I have just offered by considering some other examples and replying to possible objections. These examples belong to Argentinean Spanish but can hopefully offer some clues for an understanding of slurs belonging to different languages.

3.1. Other Examples

Based on what has been argued so far, a slur's meaning can be represented in the following manner:

"*s*": [<CONDITION> typ-link <CONCEPTUALIZATION>]

As explained before, the meaning can be taken to be constituted by the combination of a concept representing a neutral property, which serves to identify a given group, and a bundle of other concepts, derived from a stereotyped view regarding the members of that group; the link between the two elements reflects the scope of that prejudicial classification or typifying. This link, as most probably is the case with the example examined so far, can have a causal nature. Another example points out in the same direction, namely, the word "*puto,*" the Spanish version of "faggot," namely, a slur directed toward homosexual men. In this case, the slur can be analyzed as follows:

"*puto*": [<HOMOSEXUAL MAN> *therefore* <COWARD, SENSITIVE, COMPLICATED>]

Without claiming to be offering a deep conception of the homophobic view that sustains the typifying discourse behind the uses of "*puto,*" the relation between the two elements could be thought to stem from the alleged fact that, in virtue of feeling sexually attracted to other men, homosexual men tend to adopt the role of females and this, in turn, explains their having certain traits that are characteristic of (in turn, stereotyped) women. Again, this is only a hint of a possible explanation of what the homophobe could have in mind when linking a sexual condition to a set of properties allegedly characteristic of those who exemplify it.

Now, I believe that not every slur's typifying link will be explainable in the same way. Consider the slur "*facho,*" derived from "*fascista,*" the Spanish equivalent of "fascist," which is aimed at people with right-wing political views—in my terms, the condition of the slur's meaning. Calling someone a "*facho*" seems to involve a depiction of that person as authoritarian, violent, and very little disposed to accept divergent opinions on many fields. These properties would then be represented in the conceptualization of "*facho.*" But I would hesitate to see a causal relation between the condition and the conceptualization here. It seems to me that in this case the conceptualization is *giving grounds* for the condition, and not the other way around, in the sense of aiming at understanding the human nature behind the adherence to a given position in the political spectrum. Perhaps a "because" link would be more appropriate in this case:

"*facho*": [<INDIVIDUAL WITH RIGHT-WING POLITICAL VIEWS> *because* <AUTHORITARIAN, VIOLENT, VERY LITTLE DISPOSED TO ACCEPT DIVERGENT OPINIONS >]

Other examples may present different ways of understanding the typifying link. The aim of this section has been presenting a couple of tentative examples of this difference. Perhaps one could stop the semantic analysis at the general idea of a typifying link, and leave to other fields of inquiry the specification of its exact nature in different cases.[9]

3.2. Contradictions

A common argument against the idea that descriptive elements such as those involved in the conceptualization are semantically encoded in a slur relates to the assumed fact that, while an utterance of (4) leads to a contradiction, an utterance of (5) does not:

(4) Juan es puto y no es homosexual.
    Juan is *puto* and not is homosexual
    "Juan is *puto* and he is not homosexual."
(5) Juan es puto y no es sensible.
    Juan is *puto* and not is sensitive
    "Juan is *puto* and he is not sensitive."

However, if both being homosexual and being sensitive (or their conceptual representations, in my theory) are part of the meaning of "*puto*," this difference cannot be accounted for (see Nunberg 2018 for a criticism along these lines).[10]

There are two things to be replied to this objection, depending on what one might have in mind regarding an utterance of (5). This sentence can be uttered in a context in which the components of the conceptualization are under discussion. So, for example, imagine a scenario in which Mario thinks that being sensitive is constitutive of being *puto*; Carlos, who does not agree, then utters (5) with the hope of convincing Mario that he is wrong. Mario might then accept that being sensitive is not constitutive of being *puto*; or he can stick to his position, denying that Juan, who is *puto*, is not sensitive. What we have in this scenario is a *negotiation* of the concepts that should be included in the conceptualization of "*puto*." For Mario, (5) is not acceptable. For Carlos, it is. Until this debate is settled, one cannot rule out the possibility of (5) being contradictory.

This leads us to my second point concerning this objection: whether (5) is contradictory or not can be a subject of debate. Suppose Mario has the right theory of what being *puto* amounts to. If so, (5) is, in fact, a contradiction. Of course, it may not *sound* like a contradiction for those who do not use the word "*puto*" from the homophobic perspective. But what I am proposing is that the core uses of slurs involve typifying perspectives, in which prejudicial generalizations over the ways of being of the members of the target group are at stake. Thus, sentences such as (5) may give rise to contradictions, all appearances notwithstanding.[11]

3.3. Semantic Competence and Knowledge

The semantic account of slurs proposed so far incorporates descriptive components into their meanings. These components are distributed between the condition and the conceptualization. The question that may arise at this point is one related to semantic knowledge and competence. We assume that competent speakers know the meaning of the expressions of the language they speak, that these meanings are shared among them, and that it is in virtue of this knowledge of shared meanings that they communicate with one another. Thus, if the meaning of an expression contains descriptive elements, speakers should know and share them. However, the objection is raised, on the assumption that the meaning of a slur is constituted as suggested in the present account, it is very likely that there are speakers who do not know it, and, even if they had access to something like it, it is doubtful that it would be the same for all of them. In sum, one might object, it is not easy to arrive at a shared, standard conceptualization that could be considered part of the meaning of a slur. And, even if one could get to it, many speakers could not know it while still being competent in the use of the corresponding slur.[12]

In order to reply to this objection, let's concede the main point: conceptualizations are not entirely defined sets of concepts; on the contrary, conceptualizations are diffuse bundles of concepts, varying across time and among speakers. Since conceptualizations play a role in the meaning of a slur, only those features ascribed to the target group that are presumed to be shared among speakers should be kept. There is, however, space for negotiation: speakers who take a typifying stance toward a certain group can get into an argument regarding the features that should belong to the *typical* depiction of that group. As long as there is a common ground among speakers regarding the traits of the typified group, communication can be successful. As differences among them give rise to misunderstanding or difficulties in communication, a space of negotiation opens up. In sum, I am willing to accept that slurs express *fuzzy* concepts, that is, concepts that do not carve up the world in a precise manner; this should be no surprise, given the lack of objectivity on which they are based. The conceptualization is therefore composed of a bundle of more or less shared concepts, namely those representing the properties thought to be possessed by the individuals belonging in the target group from the perspective of those who hold a typifying view of them.

Now, moving on to the other aspect of the objection, what happens to those speakers who do not have a defined conceptualization of the corresponding group? They seem, though, to be perfectly capable of using the slur and communicating with other speakers by means of it. Thus, competence and knowledge come apart, contrary to what we assumed. I believe we are here in the presence of an analogue to what is known as *deference to experts*, namely, the idea that ordinary speakers need not know the application conditions or requirements for all the terms they use, as long as these conditions are known by the experts of the corresponding field—to which ordinary speakers defer. Semantic competence can thus be compatible with ignorance of full meaning.[13] A speaker may competently use an expression by identifying herself as part of a community in which there are experts.

Experts, in this case, will be those who not only have a typifying view of the individuals of the target group (be it partial or total typifying) but also have the corresponding conceptualization *in mind*. Independently of the scope an ordinary speaker agrees to give to the typifying link, she may not have a full grasp of the meaning of *"sudaca"* because she may not know which concepts are included in the conceptualization that is associated with the term. For all those speakers who are not aware of the corresponding conceptualization, whether they have a partial, total, or non-typifying attitude, their uses will ultimately rely on those who have explicit knowledge of the corresponding conceptualization.

3.4. A Simpler Account?

A final possible objection to the view can be summed up in the following question: why not simplify the picture and consider the meaning of a slur to be equivalent to the meaning of "typical *C*," where *C* stands for the neutral counterpart of the slur? So, for example, *"sudaca"* would mean "typical South American person." On the one hand, one could then run the same explanation of the disagreement in terms of a total typifying position, a partial typifying position and a non-typifying position, which would give the term divergent extensions. On the other hand, by assuming this account, one would not get into trouble concerning the properties represented in the conceptualization or the relation between the condition and the conceptualization.

Although this alternative could work, I believe the more robust account presented here is to be preferred. To illustrate why, I will briefly discuss two other tentative phenomena regarding the use of slurs in Argentinean Spanish. First, consider the fact that different slurs may be used to purport to refer to different subgroups of individuals belonging in the extension of the same neutral counterpart. So, for example, with respect to homosexual men, Argentinean Spanish contains the slurs *"puto," "marica,"* and *"loca"* (and perhaps others). But it doesn't seem to be the same to call a homosexual man by any of these terms, as the aptness of the following stands:

(6) Juan es *puto* pero no es una loca.
 Juan is *puto* but not is a loca
 "Juan is *puto* but he is not a *loca*."
(7) No todos los putos son maricas.
 not all the *putos* are maricas
 "Not every *puto* is a *marica*."
(8) Yo seré puto pero no soy un marica.
 I will.be *puto* but not am a marica
 "I may be *puto*, but I'm not a *marica*."

The fact that these sentences are not contradictory leads to the thought that, although the terms *"puto," "loca,"* and *"marica"* imply typifying homosexual men, their meaning must exceed that fact. Therefore, I would propose a *different conceptualization* must be involved in each case. Leaving aside the precise nature of the typifying link which does not concern us right now, and according to my intuitions stemming from common uses of those terms, the following characterizations can be provided:

"puto": [<HOMOSEXUAL MAN> *typ-link* <COWARD, SENSITIVE, COMPLICATED>]
"marica": [<HOMOSEXUAL MAN> *typ-link* <COWARD, SENSITIVE, COMPLICATED, EFFEMINATE, SUSCEPTIBLE>]
"loca": [<HOMOSEXUAL MAN> *typ-link* <GREATLY EFFEMINATE, HYSTRIONIC>]

When expressing thoughts by using the abovementioned sentences, speakers seem to have these distinctions in mind and, I believe, they express them in a direct way: the different terms are tools for expressing different ways of representing homosexual men in a conventional manner. That is why I propose to consider them as part of the meanings of the corresponding slurs.

A second possible phenomenon to be considered is that slurs seem to be gradable terms. So, for example, we might compare these two sentences:

(9) Juan es más *puto* que Pedro.
    Juan is more *puto* that Pedro
    "Juan is more *puto* than Pedro."
(10) Juan es más homosexual que Pedro.
    Juan is more homosexual that Pedro
    "Juan is more homosexual than Pedro."

While it seems that (9) can be used to express a thought in a straightforward manner (i.e., the thought that Juan has the characteristics of a *puto* in a higher degree than Pedro), (10) can be used to express a thought in an indirect way, by resorting to a conversational implicature or other kinds of derived content. I believe this hints again toward the idea that slurs involve some sort of descriptive meaning, amenable to admit degrees.

In sum, if this tentative piece of evidence holds, I believe the more robust picture of the meaning of slurs is explanatorily more powerful than the simpler one considered at the beginning of this section. However, the two alleged phenomena just considered deserve more discussion. For reasons of space, I will leave it, though, for another occasion.

4. OTHER DESCRIPTIVELY LOADED ACCOUNTS OF SLURS

In this final section, I will compare the account proposed in this chapter with two other accounts that present some similarities with it. First, I will focus on Croom's descriptive account and argue that its alleged advantages are not intractable in my framework. Second, I will consider Hom and May's semantically innocent account and review the major differences between that account and mine.

4.1. Descriptive Elements and Conversational Contexts

In his 2011 paper, Adam Croom has provided a semantic account of slurs that makes use of descriptive components. Croom's general idea is that the user of a slur "intends to express (i) her endorsement of a (usually *negative*) *attitude* (ii) towards the *descriptive properties* possessed by the target of their utterance" (Croom 2011, 353). The descriptive properties at stake are the ones typically associated with the target group (resembling those constitutive of a stereotype, as we have seen). Croom uses "nigger" as an example, for which he proposes the following descriptive elements as its constituents:

P1. African American
P2. Prone to laziness
P3. Subservient
P4. Commonly the recipient of poor treatment
P5. Athletic
P6. Emotionally shallow
P7. Simple-minded
P8. Sexually licentious

Now, Croom is actually using a family-resemblance framework (Rosch and Mervis 1975) and applying it to a theory of slurs. According to that framework, it is not necessary for an item to possess all the properties associated with a slur in order for it to belong in the category expressed by the slur (in this previous example, the category *nigger*). Some properties will be higher ranked because they are considered more prototypical, but in different conversational settings different properties can be made salient, and only those will be considered.

Croom then argues that his account is better suited to explain a couple of phenomena: first, the fact that speakers may use a slur in order to describe a target that does not possess the highest ranked property (in his example, calling someone a "nigger" even though he or she is not African American in order to describe him or her as possessing properties P2–P8). And second, it allows to account for in-group or appropriated uses, in which, given enough common ground among the speakers, the speaker may employ the slur in order to predicate some of the properties of the list (P1 and P4 in his example) but not all of them, and especially not the negative attitude toward the target; in these cases, Croom claims, it is very hard to accept that the word does not refer or that is has an empty extension.[14]

I will restrict myself to the phenomena presented by Croom, and will not consider his theory as a whole. As mentioned, the theory presented in this chapter also makes use of prototypical properties in providing a semantics for slurs, but it does so in a different way. I have distinguished a nuclear property, the *condition,* and a set of properties determining the *conceptualization.* While the components of the second element can be negotiated and its limits are vague, the target of the slur cannot fail to possess the nuclear property. So, how to account for the first phenomenon presented above? I believe Croom's point reaches into a gray area that can be doubted to belong in the semantic domain. To me at least, there is a sense of indirectness to such uses. One can maintain, I believe, that literal, direct uses of slurs are targeted at members of the relevant group and that uses directed at individuals who do not present the highest ranked property or, as I would put it, do not fall under the condition, are only successful inasmuch as the participants in the conversation are collaborative enough to accommodate this fact and reinterpret the speaker's intended message.[15]

Let us now consider the other case that Croom presents, namely, that of in-group or appropriation cases. First, note that a number of things can be going on in cases of appropriation: in-group speakers may still have in mind a set of properties close enough to that of the prototype but reevaluate them, or they may keep some but not others, add new ones, or perhaps even forget about stereotypes and just use the word as a friendly identity-marking device. So, for example, South Americans could appropriate the word "*sudaca*" and drop the feature of being untrustworthy and add the features of being fun and warm; Argentinean Spanish speakers can appropriate the word "*puto*" and reevaluate the associated features, for example by considering that being a coward is a good thing in opposition to the stereotypical brave *macho*-figure socially imposed to males. Or they may devoid the word from all its typifying elements and just consider it a friendly, informal word to denote homosexual men, in analogy with the "eye doctor"-"ophthalmologist" pair—but of course with a political burden to it.

Now, in some of these scenarios, if the variation is not accepted by the bigot, racist, or homophobe as a legitimate use of the term, is it not the case that a change in meaning has occurred? If John and Mary, in our example, are convinced that the term "*sudaca*" expresses the concept indicated above and someone claims that it does not, for *sudacas* are trustworthy and also fun and warm, one could claim that there is a dispute over the meaning of the term. In other scenarios, such as those in which a re-evaluation of the features that figure in the meaning of the term takes place, it seems that, as the term loses the negative evaluation that it had in the mouth of the bigots, it is no longer a slur. And then a new discussion emerges: are words that express a typifying concept with a positive evaluation legitimate terms to use? For some of the individuals who belong to the target group these friendly, in-group uses could be inappropriate and could also lack an extension, as typifying can be considered wrong even when it's done with no harmful intention. For example, feminist women can reject in-group uses of "bitch," even if a complete re-assessment of the (initially sexist) features indicating what being a *bitch* amounts to has taken place; for the word can still be seen as a typifying device, and an opposition to typifying over humans beings in virtue of their gender has been at the top of the list of the feminist movement. Finally, in the case of uses of a (once) slur with no descriptive intention beyond that of signaling a property with a friendly or informal attitude, it is mostly clear that a meaning shift has occurred, at least from the point of view of any theory of slurs as descriptively loaded terms.

In sum, I believe that Croom raises some interesting phenomena to discuss. Some of them are amenable to treatment within my approach as well. As for others, it seems either that there has been a change of meaning or that we are not in the presence of a slur anymore. Therefore, I believe that those phenomena do not pose a threat to my theory. A major difference between Croom and I is that I believe that slurs, when literally used, are empty terms. If you look at the many uses of those words, Null-Extensionality may be a harsh stance to defend. But if you look at *core uses* of them, I still believe it is the right one. In the next section, I will review the theory posited by Christopher Hom and Robert May, who share this way of looking at things. Since they are usually the target of criticism of theorists who deny the extensional vacuity of slurs, I will try to differentiate my position from theirs so as to show that that criticism doesn't apply to my theory.

4.2. Null-Extensionality and Its Grounds

Christopher Hom and Robert May are perhaps the most well-known and debated defenders of the Null-Extensionality Thesis, that is, the claim that core, primary uses of slurs do not have (and cannot have) an extension or, in other words, that slurs are empty terms. The theory presented by these authors basically consists in analyzing a slur directed toward group g as expressing the concept that for any individual x who belongs to g, "x ought to be the target of negative moral evaluation because of being [g]" (Hom and May 2013, 298). So, for example, the meaning of "kike" would be "ought to be the target of negative moral evaluation for being Jewish." Null-Extensionality follows from this meaning and some basic moral facts: "If one knows certain *a priori* facts such as that being of a race or religion is not morally evaluable, then knowing the meaning of a pejorative is sufficient to know that the concept it expresses is not instantiated" (Hom and May 2013, 297).[16]

It is convenient to start by emphasizing the fundamental difference between Hom and May's account and mine. As I mentioned at the end of section 3, I believe that slurs are words that express misguided representations of the world or, more specifically, human beings. But the reason for this, contrary to what Hom and May claim, is not related to the derogatory aspect of slurs. In my view, the flaw comes from a representational error in the sense of an erroneous *way of conceptualizing* the world: as I said before, thinking through stereotypes can be useful in some respects, but thinking about humans through *types of being* is just representationally wrong. In short, Hom and May locate the problem in the morally incorrect derogatory content they ascribe to slurs (given some basic moral facts); I find it in the typifying nature of the concepts expressed by means of them (given some more or less basic representational constraints).

Now, moving on to the objection to their theory, it goes as follows: if the derogatory element were part of the content expressed via the slur, it should be put on hold or even denied in certain contexts such as negation, conditionals, and attitude reports. However, the derogatory aspect of slurs seems to persist even in those contexts, as the following examples show:

(11) John is not a faggot.
(12) If my daughter were a dyke, I would still love her.
(13) Mary believes that Mario is a *sudaca*.

In each of these cases, a derogatory attitude seems to be involved in uttering the sentence containing the slur. But if their content is paraphrased in terms of *ought to be the target of negative moral evaluation because of being a homosexual man/homosexual woman/South American*, the derogatory force will vanish away, contrary to intuition.

Regardless of what Hom and May (2013, 309) reply to this objection, I would simply like to point out that it cannot be replicated against my account. This is so because, in my view, the derogatory attitude that typically accompanies the use of slurs is not part of what is semantically expressed by them. My understanding of the semantics of slurs may be compatible with different ideas regarding their derogatory aspect, but it is certainly not an aspect of their truth-conditional meaning: derogation is not part of the content expressed in using slurs.[17] Thus, it is neither denied nor embedded in the antecedent of a conditional or in a psychological verb in sentences such as (11)–(13).

Of course, given that I claim that the meaning of a slur does encompass typifying, and that such typifying involves a list of features that are most likely evaluated in a negative way, there is a close relation between its (truth-conditional) meaning and derogation: unsurprisingly, typifying over human beings has been accompanied by an attitude of disdain. Even if one takes the non-typifying stance and thus holds the Null-Extensionality concerning slurs, there is still a sense in which the use of slurs is derogatory. This is probably why speakers committed to the adoption of a non-typifying stance are reluctant to use these expressions at all. Derogation is not something that you choose to do; it is something that the word does for you.

The distinction between typifying and derogation has interesting effects. Note that while the first pair of sentences below is infelicitous, the second one seems fine, at least from the non-typifying stance:

(14) a. #John is not a faggot, and I do not hold a derogatory attitude toward homosexual men.
b. #Mary believes that John is a faggot, and I do not hold a derogatory attitude toward homosexual men.
(15) a. John is not a faggot, and I do not hold a typifying stance toward homosexual men.
b. Mary believes that John is a faggot, and I do not hold a typifying stance toward homosexual men.

As is clear, the derogatory attitude and the typifying stance behave in different ways: the former scopes out of the context of negation and attitude report, making (14a) and (14b) infelicitous. The latter does not. In the case of (15a), the speaker is perfectly capable of adopting a non-typifying stance, which explains her denial of the first clause of the sentence; in the case of (15b), her stance need not be that of the person whose belief is being reported: Mary may adopt a total or partial typifying stance, but the speaker need not. Still, in both cases, the derogatory aspect still arises.

In conclusion, given that, in contrast with Hom and May's theory, my account takes the meaning of a slur to codify a conceptual structure rather than a moral attitude, it is not subject to the same kind of criticism that has been presented many times against them.

5. CONCLUSION

In this chapter, I have proposed and defended an account of slurs according to which their truth-conditional meaning has a complex nature. Through this account, I have provided an explanation of a possible disagreement involving slurs and their neutral counterparts. And, most importantly to me, I have also explained why slurs, in their core uses, have no extension for some of us: they express concepts that are ill-conceived representations of the world, as they stem from a prejudicial view of human beings, what I have characterized as "typifying." This sets my theory apart both from those who hold the Identity Thesis and from those who hold the Null-Extensionality Thesis but on moral grounds. I believe this way of looking at things has the virtue of denying the discriminatory perspective of its aptness at the representational level. And this fits with the fact that some of us do not want to agree that there are kikes, faggots, or *sudacas*; we do not want to give those terms an extension and then run a pragmatic account of why it is inappropriate to use those words. We want to claim that slurs, in their core uses, are wrong at the semantic, truth-conditional level.

ACKNOWLEDGMENTS

I would like to express my deepest gratitude to the editors, Eleonora Orlando and Andrés Saab, for their trust and support throughout the making of this chapter. Their insightful comments have helped me immensely to get my thoughts across. Special thanks to the audience at the *V Workshop on Issues in Contemporary Semantics and Ontology*, held in Buenos Aires, in 2019, where previous versions of these ideas were presented. Thanks also to my colleagues, Ramiro Caso, Nicolás Lo Guercio, and Tomás Castagnino, for their discussion and advice. Finally, to all of those who fight against prejudice and for openness to diversity on any field of inquiry and beyond.

NOTES

1. Needless to say, I am not here *using* these terms. I am only *mentioning* them in order to give a semantic account that will help us understand their representational nature (which, I will argue, is misguided).

2. But see, for example, Predelli (2013) for a different approach, according to which semantics involves non-truth-conditional meaning as well.

3. There are many upholders of the Identity Thesis; just to mention a couple of them, see Jeshion (2013) and Predelli (2013). For criticisms and defenses of the thesis, see Sennet and Copp (2015), DiFranco (2015), and Caso and Lo Guercio (2016). Some authors who also reject it, such as Croom (2011, 2015), Hom (2008), and Hom and May (2013), will be discussed in the final section of the chapter.

4. See the entry for *"sudaca"* in the *Diccionario de la Lengua Española* at https://dle.rae.es.

5. A third alternative could consist in defending some sort of relativistic account for slurs along the lines proposed for a variety of terms such as "tasty," "funny,"

"comfortable," and so on, in domains such as ethics, epistemic modals, future contingents, logical validity, among others. Following the terminology coined by John MacFarlane (2014), the general idea of such accounts is that the truth value of the content expressed by some sentences may depend on a perspective represented by a parameter of a context of assessment: a taste standard, a moral system, and so on. In a sense, my proposal will involve a perspectival aspect. For now, I would just like to point out that, in any case, if the Identity Thesis were to hold, resorting to a relativistic account of slurs would seem implausible on its own, since that thesis does not allow for the possibility of divergent truth values according to different perspectives: for any individual x, if x is South American, then x is *sudaca*. Therefore, all South Americans are *sudacas*, no matter who is assessing the content expressed.

6. For a non-truth-conditional application of stereotypes to a theory of slurs, see Orlando and Saab (2020). As we will see in the final section, Croom (2011) also makes use of these prototypical descriptions in his account of slurs.

7. As is common, I use uppercase to denote concepts. This is a way of representing the elements of the account, but the theory does not depend on it. An analogous account can be given in terms of properties as the semantic values of predicates.

8. In this framework, a conceptualization can be understood in terms of the content of a mental file (Recanati 2012).

9. I agree with Croom (2015), who claims that a look at social studies can be very beneficial for semantics, especially in the case of slurs. The aim of this chapter is to present a general proposal for the semantics of slurs. The precise content of its elements will surely depend on what studies on social fields can tell us. But I believe the proposal can stand before filling in the blanks.

10. I will be working under the assumption that (4) is contradictory.

11. Nunberg's objection also considers the informative character of sentences such as "*Putos* are sensitive": if *being sensitive* were semantically codified in the meaning of "*puto*," it is hard to explain why this sentence can be informative. This is related to the topic of the next section, in which contexts of making explicit and negotiating the elements of the conceptualization are considered; these processes may easily explain the abovementioned informative character of that kind of sentences.

12. This objection follows the familiar lines drawn by Kripke (1980).

13. This, of course, is related to Putnam's division of linguistic labor (Putnam 1975).

14. Croom's discussion is directed toward Hom's theory, which will be the subject of the next section, but the criticism would apply to my theory as well.

15. As the reader probably knows, I am paraphrasing Grice's words from his (1975)'s paper.

16. A similar but more complicated account is provided by Hom in his (2008), where the meaning of slurs is read as: "ought to be subject to these discriminatory practices because of having these negative properties, all because of being [neutral-counterpart term]" (Hom 2008, 431). Although this account makes use of a stereotypical description of the target group, the reason that Hom posits for thinking that slurs are empty terms is pretty much the same as in his and May's (2013) paper quoted earlier: that no one ought to be subject to discriminatory practices because of his/her ethnicity, gender, sexuality, origin or descent, and so on (see Hom 2008, 437).

17. See the Introduction to this book for a summary of these positions.

BIBLIOGRAPHICAL REFERENCES

Caso, Ramiro, and Nicolás Lo Guercio. 2016. "What Bigots Do Say: A Reply to DiFranco." *Thought: A Journal of Philosophy* 5(4): 265–274.
Croom, Adam M. 2011. "Slurs." *Language Sciences* 33: 343–58.
Croom, Adam M. 2015. "Slurs and Stereotypes for Italian Americans: A Context-Sensitive Account of Derogation and Appropriation." *Journal of Pragmatics* 81: 36–51.
Davis, Wayne A. 2003. *Meaning, Expression, and Thought*. Cambridge: Cambridge University Press.
DiFranco, Ralph. 2015. "Do Racists Speak Truly? On the Truth-Conditional Content of Slurs." *Thought: A Journal of Philosophy* 4(1): 28–37.
Fodor, Jerry. 1975. *The Language of Thought*. New York: Crowell.
Fodor, Jerry. 1998. *Concepts: Where Cognitive Science Went Wrong*. Oxford: Clarendon Press.
Grice, H. Paul. 1975. "Logic and Conversation." In *Syntax and Semantics* 3, Speech Acts, edited by Peter Cole and Jerry L. Morgan, 41–58. New York: Academic Press.
Hom, Christopher. 2008. "The Semantics of Racial Epithets." *The Journal of Philosophy* 105(8): 416–440.
Hom, Christopher, and Robert May. 2013. "Moral and Semantic Innocence." *Analytic Philosophy* 54(3): 293–313.
Jeshion, Robin. 2013. "Expressivism and the Offensiveness of Slurs." *Philosophical Perspectives* 27: 231–259.
Kripke, Saul A. 1980. *Naming and Necessity*. Cambridge, MA: Harvard University Press.
MacFarlane, John. 2014. *Assessment Sensitivity: Relative Truth and Its Applications*. Oxford: Oxford University Press.
Nunberg, Geoff. 2018. "The Social Life of Slurs." In *New Work on Speech Acts*, edited by Daniel Fogal, Daniel Harris, and Matt Moss, 237–295. Oxford: Oxford University Press.
Orlando, Eleonora, and Andrés Saab. 2020. "Slurs, Stereotypes and Insults." *Acta Analytica*. https://doi.org/10.1007/s12136-020-00424-2.
Predelli, Stefano. 2013. *Meaning Without Truth*. Oxford: Oxford University Press.
Putnam, Hillary. 1975. "The Meaning of 'Meaning'." *Minnesota Studies in the Philosophy of Science* 7: 131–193.
Recanati, François. 2012. *Mental Files*. Oxford: Oxford University Press.
Rosch, Eleanor, and Carolyn B. Mervis. 1975. "Family Resemblances: Studies in the Internal Structure of Categories." *Cognitive Psychology* 7: 573–605.
Sennet, Adam, and David Copp. 2015. "What Kind of Mistake Is It to Use a Slur?" *Philosophical Studies* 172(4): 1079–1104.

Index

Page references for figures are italicized

Anderson, Luvell, 12n3, 41n10, 45–47, 56, 132n15, 182n14
Ashwell, Lauren, 41n10, 62n2

bias, 5, 10, 23, 26–30, 33, 35–39, 41n9, 96–97, 99–100, 106–7, 109–11, 112n4, 113nn20, 23, 135–36, 138, 182n17; biased expressions, 99–100, 105, 110; biased meaning, 105; biased words, 9, 39; theory of, 10, 95, 111
bidimensional logic, 68
bidimensional semantics, 9, 69, 71, 91
Bolinger, Renee Jörgensen, 8, 12n6, 41n12, 45, 63n7, 153, 183n22

Camp, Elisabeth, 5, 57, 155nn7, 12
Cepollaro, Bianca, 7, 46, 63nn8, 15–16, 131n4, 182nn13, 15, 17, 183n32
Chomsky, Noam, 21–22, 24
conventional implicature, 6, 9, 19, 33, 35, 37, 46, 48, 51–54, 63n18, 119, 135, 182n17
conversational implicature, 7, 46, 168, 189–90, 199
Croom, Adam M., 7, 13, 200–202, 205n3, 206nn6, 9, 14

disagreement, 188–90, 192–94, 198, 204
Döring, Sophia, 104, 113nn19, 22
dualism, 1, 4–6, *8*, 9, 12n8; expressivist dualism, 6, *8*, 12n8; propositional dualism, 6, *8*

ellipsis, 9, 20–21, 25, 28–32, 34, 36–37, 39, 41n6, 41n12; NP-ellipsis, 28–29, 32–33, 36, 41n9; TP-ellipsis, 27, 29, 33; VP-ellipsis, 26
Embick, David, 21–22
expressives, 3, 10, 12nn4, 6–8, 17, 20, 35, 39, 69–70, 95–97, 100, 103–9, 111nn1–2, 112nn6–7, 113n20, 117, 122, 126, 130, 131n3, 136–37, 141, 149; token-expressives, 12n4, 137–41, 144, 149; type-expressives, 137–41, 144–46
expressivity, 2, 7–*8*, 12n4, 17–22, 29, 32, 35–37, 39, 41n12, 118

fiction, 161, 177–78, 183n32; fictional terms, 161, 177–78
Frege, Gottlob, 1–2, 12n3, 18, 130n1, 160–61, 164, 166–67, 172, 179, 181nn2, 7
Fregean. *See* Frege, Gottlob

Geurts, Bart, 101, 111n2, 112n15, 114n27
Grice, Paul, 7–8, 19, 49, 175, 183n31, 206n15
Gricean. *See* Grice, Paul
Gutzmann, Daniel, 5, 9, 12n8, 19, 46, 63n18, 67–71, 74, 81–82, 86, 87, 91, 104, 111n1, 112n5, 113nn19, 21, 114n28, 124, 131nn7, 12, 182nn16–17

Hom, Christopher, 6, 11, 41n10, 46, 52, 56, 62nn2–3, 63nn15, 18, 68, 131n2, 155n7, 159–66, 168, 172–74, 177–81, 181nn2, 4, 6–7, 183nn23, 33, 187, 200, 202–5, 205n3, 206nn14, 16
hyper-projectability, 4, 9. *See also* non-displaceability

identity thesis, 4, 11, 35, 41n10, 68, 169, 189–200, 205n3, 206n5
illocutionary act, 9, 47, 96, 106, 111, 183n31; illocutionary force, 47, 49–50, 57–58, 106, 113n21, 175–76, 178

Jeshion, Robin, 5–6, 12n8, 41n10, 60, 182nn12, 17, 183n23, 205n3

Kaplan, David, 2–3, 18–19, 40n5, 69–71, 92n8, 96–97, 111n1, 112n5, 113n18, 118, 122, 124, 130n1, 131nn4, 9–10, 168
Kirk-Giannini, Cameron Dominico, 57, 60, 67
Kratzer, Angelika, 50–51, 63n18, 72, 81, 104, 111n1, 114n27, 131n4

Langton, Rae, 46–48, 56–57, 63n5
Lepore, Ernest, 12n3, 18, 41n10, 45, 132n15, 182n14
Lewis, David Kellog, 46–47, 163

Macià, Josep, 7, 46, 63n16
MacKinnon, Catherine Alice, 47

Matsuda, Mari, 47
May, Robert, 6, 11, 25, 46, 52, 56, 63nn15, 18, 68, 131n2, 155n7, 159–66, 168, 172–74, 177–81, 181nn2, 6–7, 183nn23, 33, 187, 200, 202–5, 205n3, 206n16
McCready, Elin, 3, 5–6, 9, 12n8, 17, 19, 35, 37, 41nn10–11, 46, 48, 52–55, 58, 71, 131nn5–6, 182n17
McGowan, Mary Kate, 47–48, 57
meaning, 3, 6–7, 10–11, 17–19, 21, 23–25, 35, 37–39, 46, 48, 52–54, 56, 60–61, 70–71, 95–97, 99–101, 104–7, 109–10, 112nn5–6, 8, 117–18, 120–24, 127, 129–30, 132n15, 136–39, 141–44, 146, 159–62, 169–70, 173, 189–91, 193–99, 201–4, 206nn10, 16; dimension of, 53–54, 61, 68, 71, 73, 104–5, 117, 120, 123, 126, 130, 136, 168; expressive meaning, 4–6, 12nn4, 9, 13n9, 20, 24, 103–4, 106–7, 111n1, 127, 129, 132n15, 146, 160, 169–71; meaning dimension, 3–4, 9, 17, *19*, 35, 39, 46, 55; non-truth-conditional meaning, 96, 103, 110, 114n28, 128, 131nn3, 7, 187, 205n2; truth-conditional meaning (TC-meaning), 13n9, 17, 69, 73–74, 122, 127, 160, 203–4; use-conditional meaning (UC-meaning), 69–79, 82, 90–91, 105, 169
monism, 1, 7–8; expressivist monism, 8, 12n9; lexical monism, 6–8, 11, 159; pragmatic monism, *8*; presuppositional monism, 7–*8*
moral corruption, 11, 163, 166–68, 178–80
moral innocence, 11, 163–66, 168, 178–80
moral terms, 2, 10, 137, 144–47, 153–55n8; thick moral terms, 145; thin moral terms, 3, 145. *See also* normative concept, thick (ethical) concept

neutral counterpart, 4, 35, 38, 41n10, 62n2, 68, 92n2, 97, 103, 113n19, 119, 160–62, 169–70, 173, 188–89, 191, 198, 205

non-displaceability, 4, 10, 103, 106–7, 109, 120, 166–67, 180

normative concept, 162–64; thick (ethical) concept, 155n8, 163, 168, 171, 176, 181n5, 182nn11, 20–21; thin ethical concept, 162. *See also* moral terms

Nunberg, Geoffrey, 7, 41n12, 45, 63n8, 182n19, 196, 206n11

pejoratives, 3–4, 64n21, 112n16, 139–40, 143–44, 149, 169, 183n30, 203; pejorative term, 19

perlocutionary act, 183n31, 47; perlocutionary effect, 47, 62, 175

Popa-Wyatt, Mihaela, 12n8

Portner, Paul, 9, 48–51, 63nn9, 11, 13, 71, 73, 75

Potts, Christopher, 3, 5–6, 9, 12nn6, 8, 17, 19–20, 37–38, 46, 53, 71, 73, 75, 81, 95, 103, 106–7, 109, 111nn1–2, 113nn20, 24, 114n28, 118–19, 130n1, 131nn3–4, 6–8, 167, 182n17

pragmatics, 8, 50, 56, 112n5; dynamic pragmatics, 48, 52, 60

Predelli, Stefano, 3, 5, 10, 12, 18–19, 23, 35, 41n10, 46, 95–97, 100, 102, 107, 109, 111, 112nn5–6, 9–12, 14, 16–17, 113–14, 114nn20, 26, 124, 130n1–3, 5, 7, 9, 11, 13, 140, 144, 167, 181n9, 182nn14, 16, 17, 205n2–3

Recanati. François, 112nn5, 8, 163, 206n8

register, 5, 9, 12n4, 17, 23, 25–26, 28, 30, 34, 37–39, 41n13, 113n20, 122, 125–28, 130–31n13, 135, 140, 149–52; registered terms, 141–43, 149–52, 155n4, 156n16, 182n17;

registered words, 141–42, 144, 149–51, 154

Roberts, Craige, 49, 63n12, 113n24

Schlenker, Philippe, 7, 41nn11–12, 46, 63n16, 81, 90, 92nn3, 8, 109, 114n27, 131n4, 167, 182n17

scoping out, 68, 77, 80, 168

semantics, 1–2, 8–9, 18–19, 45, 49–50, 55–56, 64n22, 69, 72, 77, 80, 83, 87, 89, 112n5, 121–22, 124, 127, 187, 189, 191, 201, 205n2, 206n9; dualistic semantics, 3, 169; intensional semantics, 87; multidimensional, 122; of slurs, 8, 89, 120, 187, 203, 206n9; stereotype semantics, 170; stylistic semantics, 18, 20, 24, 36, 39; truth-conditional semantics, 122; use-conditional semantics, 131n12

slur, 1, 3–11n1, 12n4, 6, 8–9, 18–19, 21, 24, 34–40n1, 41n10, 13, 45–48, 50–62, 62nn1–2, 4, 6–7, 63nn15, 20, 64n22, 67–72, 75, 77–78, 80–82, 86–92, 92nn2, 4, 111n1, 112n16, 117–24, 126–30, 130nn1–5, 132n15, 135, 144–55, 155nn8–11, 13, 156nn14, 16–17, 159–63, 165–81, 181nn1, 4, 9, 182nn17, 19, 183n27, 30, 187–205, 205n5, 206nn6, 9, 16; normative realism about, 162, 164, 166, 178, 180; slur-word, 1, 4–5, 7, 9, 11, 159–60, 167, 170, 180

Spanish, 3–4, 22, 28, 30–31, 36, 189, 194–95; Argentinian Spanish, 17, 19, 26, 28, 198, 201; Rioplatense Spanish, 67–68, 80–81, 83, 86, 90–92n4

speech act, 30, 48–49, 51, 57–58, 61, 63n12, 82, 175, 183nn29–30

Stainton, Robert, 5, 140, 155nn9, 13, 182n17

Stalnaker, Robert, 48

stereotype, 5, 10–11, 35, 38, 46, 135, 156n15, 160, 168–77, 179–80, 182nn17, 19, 183nn23, 28, 191, 193–95, 200–201, 203, 206n6; cultural stereotype, 10, 169–71, 174, 180, 182n17; semantic stereotype, 169–70, 172, 174. *See also* semantics, stereotype semantics

syntax, 9, 19–22, 32–34, 37, 80

taboo, 9–10, 117, 120, 125–30, 132n15

vehicle change, 25, 30, 40n4; bias vehicle change, 27–33

Whiting, David, 5, 41n10, 182n17
Williamson, Timothy, 5, 131nn3–4, 6, 182n17
Wittgenstein, Ludwig, 170

About the Contributors

Ramiro Caso ("A Bidimensional Account of Slurs") has a PhD in Philosophy from the University of Buenos Aires. He specializes in philosophy of language. Currently he is an assistant researcher at the IIF-SADAF-CONICET and has a teaching position at the Philosophy Department of the University of Buenos Aires. He is currently working on contextualist and relativist theories of meaning, in particular with respect to epistemic and deontic modality and on hyperintensional theories of content. He is also interested in fictionalism, the semantics and ontology of fictional terms, the semantics of aesthetic predicates, and the metaphysics and epistemology of chance.

Justina Díaz Legaspe ("Slurs: The Amoralist and the Expression of Hate") obtained her PhD in Philosophy in 2011 from the University of Buenos Aires. She specializes in philosophy of language. She is an associate researcher at the IIF-SADAF-CONICET and an associate professor at the Philosophy Department of the National University at La Plata (Argentina). She is interested in semantic contextualism, taste predicates, the semantic/pragmatic boundary, and in the past few years, she has worked on a register-based approach to slurs.

Nicolás Lo Guercio ("The Discursive Dimension of Slurs") obtained both his undergraduate degree and his PhD in Philosophy from the University of Buenos Aires. Currently, he has a postdoctoral fellowship from the ANPCyT. He specializes in philosophy of language and epistemology. Within philosophy of language, he has worked on contextualism and relativism about truth, the semantic/pragmatic divide, and fictional names; currently, he is interested in the semantics and pragmatics of proper names and non-truth-conditional meaning, especially, the semantics of slurs. Within epistemology, his main interest is in the epistemology of disagreement, higher-order evidence, and epistemic *akrasia*. He has taught several courses and seminars at the National University of Quilmes, the University of Buenos Aires, and the University Torcuato Di Tella (Argentina).

Alfonso Losada ("*Sudaca*": Slurs and Typifying") got his MA degree from the University of Buenos Aires. His main interests lie in the area of the philosophy of language: the semantic-pragmatic divide, relative truth and disagreement, and two-dimensional semantics. He has published in several international journals, and taken part in readings such as *Significados en contexto y verdad relativa. Ensayos sobre semántica y pragmática* (Título, 2015) and *A medio siglo de Formas lógicas, realidad y significado. Homenaje a Thomas Moro Simpson* (Eudeba, 2016). He has been granted PhD fellowships from the University of Buenos Aires and the CONICET. He is currently working on his PhD dissertation.

Carlos Márquez ("Expressives and the Theory of Bias") is currently a postdoctoral fellow at the University of São Paulo/FFLCH on a FAPESP scholarship. He received his PhD in Philosophy from the National University of Colombia (2015). He spent one year as a postdoctoral research fellow at the Philosophy Department of PUC-Rio (2016–2017) on a *CNPq* junior postdoctoral scholarship. His areas of expertise are philosophy of language, philosophy of mind, and logic, focusing on theories of meaning, theories of content, and formal semantics. He is currently working on situated and dynamic cognition, more specifically on objective representation, object perception, spatial cognition, cognitive maps, dynamic thoughts, singular reference, indexicality, and semantic flexibility.

Eleonora Orlando ("On the Moral Import of Using Slurs") got her MA degree from the University of Maryland and her PhD from the University of Buenos Aires. She is currently an associate professor at the Philosophy Department of the University of Buenos Aires and an independent researcher at the IIF-SADAF-CONICET. She specializes in different topics in the philosophy of language, more specifically, general term rigidity, the semantics of fictional terms, the contextualist and relativist debates, and the relation between semantics and ontology. Recently, she has also focused on the semantic analysis of aesthetic judgments and its relation to aesthetic experience. Her publications include *Concepciones de la referencia* (Eudeba, 1999), *Significados en contexto y verdad relativa. Ensayos sobre semántica y pragmática* (Título, 2015), and a variety of essays on general terms, fictional names, contextualism, and relativism. She has been the president of the Argentinian Society for Philosophical Analysis (SADAF, 2015–2017) and the Latin-American Association of Analytic Philosophy (ALFAn, 2010–2012). She is currently the editor in chief of SADAF's editorial seal.

Stefano Predelli ("Taboo: The Case of Slurs") completed his doctoral studies at UCLA in 1991, with a dissertation on indexicals supervised by David Kaplan. He then moved to Norway, where he taught for a few years at the University of Oslo. He is currently a full professor at the University of Nottingham. His publications include *Contexts: Meaning, Truth, and the Use of Language* (Oxford University Press, 2005), *Meaning without Truth* (Oxford University Press, 2013), and *Proper Names: A Millian Account* (Oxford University Press, 2017).

Andrés Saab ("On the Locus of Expressivity: Deriving Parallel Meaning Dimensions from Architectural Considerations") studied literature and linguistics at the University of Buenos Aires and at the National University of Comahue (Argentina). In 2009, he defended his PhD dissertation on the theory of ellipsis. Currently, he is an associate researcher at the Argentine National Scientific and Technical Research Council (CONICET), having the Argentinian Society for Philosophical Analysis (IIF-SADAF-CONICET) as official work-place, and an associate professor at the University of Buenos Aires. His main research topics are ellipsis, copy theory of movement, null subjects, and, more broadly, the syntax-interface connection. His research has been published by international journals and books (among others, *Linguistic Inquiry*, *The Oxford Handbook of Ellipsis*, *Natural Language and Linguistic Theory*, *Lingua*, *Probus*, *Studia Linguistica*, *Analytic Philosophy*, and *Acta Analytica*). He is also the coauthor of *Dimensiones del Significado. Una Introducción a la semántica formal* (SADAF) and the coeditor of the volume *Romance Language and Linguistic Theory 2010* (John Benjamins).

Ludovic Soutif ("Expressives and the Theory of Bias") is currently an associate professor at the Philosophy Department of the Pontifical Catholic University of Rio de Janeiro and *CNPq Research Productivity Grantee* (Brazil). He received his PhD in Philosophy (2005) from the University of Paris I-Panthéon-Sorbonne and spent two years as a postdoctoral research fellow at the University of São Paulo on a FAPESP scholarship. He is the author of *Wittgenstein et le problème de l'espace visuel* (Vrin, 2011), *Qu'est-ce qu'une pensée singulière?* (Vrin, in press) and papers published in international journals in English, French, and Portuguese. His current research focuses on topics in philosophy of language (singular reference, expressive meaning, cognitive dynamics) and mind (singular/de re thought, mental imagery, spatial experience), and on the history of analytic philosophy.

www.ingramcontent.com/pod-product-compliance
Lightning Source LLC
Chambersburg PA
CBHW020118010526
44115CB00008B/879